This is the testimony

and all that I have learned . . .

It has been more than thirty years since the events I am about to describe. They involve a world—a demimonde—that is largely unknown outside a very small circle. The reader must be prepared to deal with a wide range of mysterious subjects, from secret societies to serial murder, from tiny ethnic churches to political assassinations, from organized religion to the most extreme forms of western occultism.

The most shocking part of this narrative will be the realization that it is all true.

Simon

Books Edited by Simon

DEAD NAMES
THE NECRONOMICON SPELLBOOK
THE NECRONOMICON

Coming Soon

THE GATES OF THE NECRONOMICON

DEAD NAMES

THE DARK HISTORY OF THE
NECRONOMICON

SIMON

AVON BOOKS
An Imprint of HarperCollinsPublishers

AVON BOOKS
An Imprint of HarperCollins*Publishers*
10 East 53rd Street
New York, New York 10022-5299

Copyright © 2006 by Simon
ISBN-13: 978-0-06-078704-2
ISBN-10: 0-06-078704-X
www.avonbooks.com

First Avon Books paperback printing: April 2006

Avon Trademark Reg. U.S. Pat. Off. and in Other Countries, Marca Registrada, Hecho en U.S.A.
HarperCollins® is a registered trademark of HarperCollins Publishers Inc.

Printed in the U.S.A.

10 9 8 7 6 5 4 3 2

To Lawrence K. Barnes, who believed
And to W. Andrew Prazsky, who did not
To W. Anthony Prazsky, who spoke the truth
about this world
And to Herman Slater, who spoke the truth
about the next

. . . spirit of the Sky, remember!

Acknowledgments

As a careful reader will surmise, some of the persons to whom credit is due prefer not to be mentioned by name in this work. As with my prior works, I refer to myself under the pseudonym Simon. At times, I attribute conduct to myself to protect the privacy of others referred to in the text. This includes some of the ecclesiastical personnel contacted by myself and my colleagues during the course of putting this small history together over the past year. Most of these gentlemen are worried about the impact this account will have on their own reputations, so their names have been omitted from the story.

There are others, however, to whom credit is due and who must be acknowledged here. This includes, first and foremost, Hugh and Mary Anne Barnes—the father and stepmother of Larry Barnes—who very kindly made their memories of their son available to me where my own memory was faulty or unsure. They also kindly allowed some of Larry's art to be reproduced in these pages.

I would also like to thank Frater Inominandum of the OTO, who very kindly made available to me copies of his excellent occult resource, *Behutet*; Michael Burgess, whose *Lords Temporal and Lords Spiritual* is an interesting guide to the world of Eastern Orthodoxy; to Judith McNally for her memories of the period; and to the surviving members of StarGroup One, now scattered around the country; to JC, editor extraordinaire, who helped make this book better than it was.

Spirit of the Earth, remember!

Timeline

1950: — William Prazsky born in June, and Peter Levenda born in October, in the Bronx.

1952: — L.K. Barnes born in May.

1963: — *November 22*: President J.F. Kennedy assassinated; Archbishop Carl Stanley of the American Orthodox Catholic Church accuses David Ferrie and Jack Martin—both bishops of the AOCC—as co-conspirators in the assassination.

1965: — Levenda enrolls in Christopher Columbus High School in the Bronx.

1967: — Levenda meets Prazsky at the high school; writes article on alchemy for school magazine, *Horizon*.

— They meet Filotej and create the Slavonic Orthodox Catholic Church in Exile.

1968: — *March:* Prazsky and Levenda celebrate their first public Divine Liturgy as the Slavonic Orthodox Church, in a Dutch Reformed Church in the Bronx.

— *June:* Prazsky and Levenda gate-crash Bobby Kennedy's funeral at St. Patrick's Cathedral in Manhattan.

— Prazsky and Levenda meet Archbishop Walter Propheta of the American Orthodox Catholic Church; meet Archbishop Hubert Augustus Rogers of the North American Old Roman Catholic Church.

TIMELINE

June: Both graduate from Christopher Columbus High School.

Prazsky and Levenda meet Father Andre Pennachio.

Rosemary's Baby opens.

1969: — *May:* Prazsky and Levenda go separate ways.

August 9-10: Charles Manson Family murders of Tate/LaBianca take place in Los Angeles.

September: David Berkowitz enrolls in Christopher Columbus High School.

Prazsky is accepted into the Ukrainian American Orthodox Church as bishop of the Slavonic Orthodox Church and as Ukrainian Bishop Hryhorij's successor (at age *nineteen*).

October 12: Prazsky consecrates Andre Pennachio as a bishop.

1970: — *April:* Prazsky incorporates Autocephalous Slavonic Orthodox Catholic Church of North and South America.

David Berkowitz joins Auxiliary Police in the Bronx.

1971: — *June:* David Berkowitz graduates from Christopher Columbus High School, enlists in Army.

1972: — *June:* Warlock Shop opens in Brooklyn Heights.

Simon meets Prazsky, begins spying on Fathers Chapo and Hubak.

Simon discovers *Necronomicon* at Prazsky's home; work on translation begins.

October 8: Archbishop Walter Propheta dies.

1973: — *March 16:* Chapo and Hubak indicted for rare book theft.

October 10: they plead guilty.

The Exorcist opens.

1974: — *June:* Berkowitz discharged from Army.

September: Berkowitz enrolls at Bronx Community College.

October 12: murder of Arlis Perry, believed to be by Son of Sam cult.

1975: *June:* Michael Carr of the Son of Sam cult meets David Berkowitz for the first time on Barnes Avenue in the Bronx.

October 12: Necronomicon completed; Larry's brother Wayne Barnes dies of heroin overdose same day.

1976: *Summer:* Berkowitz begins working as a cabbie in Co-Op City; Simon meets Larry Barnes for first time.

July 29: first Son of Sam murder.

October 13: John Carr of the Son of Sam cult discharged from USAF.

October 23: second Son of Sam attack.

November 27: third Son of Sam attack.

1977: *January 30:* fourth Son of Sam attack.

March 8: fifth Son of Sam attack.

April 17: sixth Son of Sam attack.

June 26: seventh Son of Sam attack.

July 31: eighth Son of Sam attack.

August 10: Berkowitz arrested for Son of Sam murders.

October 12: OTO Grand Lodge declared.

December 1: Necronomicon party at Inferno Disco in Manhattan.

December 22: Necronomicon published.

Close Encounters of the Third Kind opens.

Star Wars opens.

1978: *March 20:* OTO Caliphate registered in California.

November 19: Jonestown massacre.

TIMELINE

1979: — Second hardcover *Necronomicon* published.

— *December 16:* Harold Green and Carol Marron murdered in New Jersey.

1980: — Avon Books publishes *Necronomicon* paperback.

— *December 8:* John Lennon murdered.

1981: — Third hardcover *Necronomicon* published.

1983: — *May 13:* Producer Roy Radin murdered, believed by Son of Sam cult.

1984: — *January 6:* Bishop Anthony Prazsky commits suicide in church.

— *Summer:* Simon breaks with Magickal Childe and OTO.

1985: — *July 12:* Grady McMurtry, head of American OTO, dies.

1989: — *October 24:* Geraldo Rivera's "Devil Worship: Exposing Satan's Underground" aired.

1990: — *August:* Iraq invades Kuwait.

— *December 16:* Archbishop Andrew Prazsky commits suicide.

1991: — *January:* Gulf War begins.

— *November 1:* Craig Glassman dies in car crash, a Son of Sam cult-related death.

1992: — *July 9:* Herman Slater dies.

2001: — *September 11:* World Trade Center attack.

— *December 18:* Larry Barnes dies of complications due to heroin addiction.

2006: — *Dead Names* published.

DEAD NAMES

Introduction: Chapel Perilous

This is the testimony of all that I have seen, and all that I have learned . . .

It was Russian Christmas, January 6, 1984. A small party had assembled in the Pelham Bay home of father and son, Anthony and Andrew Prazsky. The singing of the Orthodox Divine Liturgy had taken hours, and the small church with the three-armed cross on the roof glowed with candlelight in the frozen, north Baychester night.

The address was on Hunter Avenue, in the last undeveloped section of the Bronx, huddled between the delapidated docks on Eastchester Bay, the forbidding forests of Pelham Bay Park, and the barren landscape that had once been an amusement park called Freedomland and which was now Section Five of the largest housing complex in New York history: Co-Op City.

Anthony Prazsky—a mechanic and maintenance worker by trade—was a short but stocky man of Slavic lineage whose parents had come to America by boat through Ellis Island at the turn of the century. Powerfully built, and with an upbeat, engaging personality, he had a passion for iron welding and made the medieval weaponry—lances, swords, morning stars—that adorned the walls of his small wooden house in the Bronx where he lived with his son Andrew and his ex-wife Petronella.

They lived next door to the church: a small, red brick building that Anthony himself had converted into a makeshift temple with Russian-style icons, brass censers, and an altar on which the *antimensia*—a cloth containing relics of a saint—was reverently laid every Sunday morning for the liturgical celebration. On top of that building was a great bronze cross with three arms or crossbeams, instead of the usual one. And one of the arms was crooked, at a slant. "What monstrous being," asked an elderly neighbor, out walking along the unlit, unpaved street one evening many years ago, "was crucified to that cross? What thing of earth or hell had . . . had *six arms*?"

"No," I replied. "Do not alarm yourself. It is only the fashion of the Asiatic churches. The top crossbeam represents the sign that Pilate ordered nailed to the top of the cross; the bottom crossbeam is rather more arcane, but refers to a tradition that the Victim had one leg longer than the other, so that the footrest at the bottom of the cross is slanted."

The suspicious old woman looked at me and again at the cross, and then shuddered and limped back to her hovel in that neighborhood of hovels.

Anthony excused himself from the gathering before dinner that Christmas and returned to the church alone on a mission known only to him. It was seven P.M.

It was dark, and still smelled strongly of incense. In the dimness, he could make out the icons on the altar screen—the *ikonostasis*—that separated the faithful from the celebration of the divine mystery that took place on the altar itself among the priests. Here he was surrounded by the emblems of a mystical faith that had its roots in Eastern Europe after the missionary work done by two Greek Orthodox saints, Cyril and Methodius, more than a thousand years ago. These were also his personal roots, for he had lived in this section of the Bronx for more years than he could count, during a lifetime of hard work and sacrifice.

As his son and his relatives and guests were occupied with conversation and Christmas cheer next door, Anthony Prazsky gazed with an unfathomable pain upon the icons, the candles, the altar. The sound of joy from the house rang hollowly in his head, like the soundtrack to a bad horror film. As he looked up at the rafters his eyes filled with tears.

His son, Archbishop Metropolitan William Andrew Prazsky, aka Archbishop Andrei, wondering what was taking so long, left the house, crossed the frozen street, and entered the darkened church. An icon of Jesus Christ Crucified above the altar—an icon showing the cross atop a small hill containing a skull and crossbones—was a reminder that the Church itself was built on death and sacrifice. But there was another, more brutal reminder, suspended in the air before the icon screen. His father, Bishop Anthony Prazsky of the Autocephalous Slavonic Orthodox Catholic Church, was swinging from the rafter, hung by the neck with a thick rope, dead. All around him the faces of the saints stared blankly in the shadows at the tragedy that had just taken place in their sacred midst.

The Archbishop screamed.

I did not hear of Anthony Prazsky's suicide until many years later, and by that time his son, Andrew, was also dead under suspicious circumstances. Other dead names were added to the grisly roster, including Herman Slater, Ed Buczynski, Larry Barnes, and many others, all too young, too gifted, too intense; yet sharing an esoteric faith that is shunned by the rest of polite society . . . The bodies were piling up, and no one knew of the connections between them—between them and a reviled, revered text known as the *Necronomicon*—except me.

It has been more than thirty years since the events I am about to describe. They involve a world—a demimonde—that is largely unknown outside a very small circle, and for that reason I will have to present some background information in order that the reader—who, I assume, is ignorant of these exotic matters—will better understand the context in which they occurred. The reader must be prepared to deal with a wide range of mysterious subjects, from secret societies to serial murder, from tiny ethnic churches to political assassinations, from organized religion to the most extreme forms of Western occultism.

The most shocking part of this narrative will be the realization that it is all true.

This book is the history of a phenomenon. Thirty years ago I sat in a small Brooklyn apartment surrounded by files, papers, documents, and books, looking down at a completed manuscript: the translation of a book that was believed by many not to exist. I had no idea at the time that the book I was working on was in any way groundbreaking. I only knew that it was a *grimoire,* a book of occult rituals and spells, and there had been so many published and available through other means that, to me, this was little more than my own contribution to the literature, albeit a unique one. The fruit of several years of coordination among college students, occultists, and linguists, the translation had finally taken shape and it wanted only my own Introduction to set the book in some kind of historical and spiritual context. I had no idea if it would ever be published; and, indeed, for a long time it looked as if it would not.

Today that book has sold nearly one million copies and has been downloaded—illegally—countless more times. It is available in Spanish and, illegally again, in other languages such as French, German, and Russian. It is notorious: praised by some as a powerful sorcerer's workbook, and denounced by others as a dangerous hoax.

While I was involved with the book, it haunted me: my dreams and my nightmares became a stage on which bizarre spectacles took place in a language I could not understand. I—and those around me—continued to experience strange visions and odd occurrences throughout the period the book was being printed and bound. And now, thirty years after its completion, most of those involved with the book from the very beginning are dead; none from natural causes. Most were young, some younger than I am now, when they died: one from hanging, one from poison, one from a lethal disease, another from addiction. None of them deserved to die the way they did; none were saints, but all were good people at heart: talented, generous, in tune with spiritual realities. It was perhaps this sensitivity to the Other World that doomed them; I cannot say for sure. So, in honor of my fallen comrades and to set their story straight—as well as to explain once and for all the history and characteristics of this most infamous work—I write the book you hold in your hands.

It is in part biography and in part autobiography. It is history, and it is mysticism. Because it concerns an underworld that is largely unknown to most readers, I have had to divide this work into two parts. The first part is a chronological history of how the book came to be in my possession, and of the other parties involved, and how the book came to be published in the first place. The second part is an occult explanation and clarification of the book's importance as amplified by myself and other experts in the field of ceremonial magic. It is designed to refute many of the misconceptions about the book that are current in the occult and New Age "community" both in print and in abundance on the Web.

The first section is concerned not only with the standard referents of secret societies and occult orders, but also with organized religion and the curious existence of a shadow world of clergy known as "wandering bishops." Although this was bluntly mentioned in the preface to the second edition of the *Necronomicon,* surprisingly, no one has picked up on it in the decades since then. Thus, it is important to explain this weird world of monks, priests, and bishops—including reference to their intelligence connections (connections that have been amply documented)—and to show why it is necessary to know about these people in order to comprehend the facts behind the discovery of the original manuscript in the early 1970s.

We will also look at the occult renaissance that took place in the United States at that time, with special emphasis on what was happening in New York City. This renaissance included what is now known as Wicca, the Ordo Templi Orientis or OTO, the pagan movement in general, the Church of Satan, the Process Church of the Final Judgment, and even the Son of Sam cult. This provides a context for understanding the importance of the *Necronomicon* historically, as many of these groups had very definite opinions about the book and its place in their worldview.

We will look at the lives of some of the most important players, such as Herman Slater, Larry Barnes, and others whose names have been taken "in vain" by critics and historians who did not know them or understand their place in this story. I hope my small contribution to this documentation— by the one person who knows the story from its beginning— will clear up confusion about the book and offer some comfort to the souls who have gone on before me, whose names and reputations have been vilified by the ignorant and the malicious.

I have kept silent for decades. During that time, the explosion of new technology has encroached on areas that were once reserved for the handwritten grimoire, the whispered chant, the secret handshake. Speculation on and about the origins of the *Necronomicon,* the principal players in its dissemination, and the aftermath of its publication has ranged from silly to slanderous. There is virtually nothing truthful about this subject in print or on the Internet. Pieces of the puzzle—some of which were openly mentioned in the various prefaces to the book—have been ignored in favor of baseless allegations concerning me, my motives, my associates, and the book itself. It is perhaps emblematic of the criticism as a whole that none of these charges are consistent with each other; that the various self-appointed experts in this case disagree completely except on one fundamental issue: that the *Necronomicon* is a hoax.

I hope that, when the reader is finished with this account—this *memento mori,* this *confessio,* this *summa necronomica*—that he or she comes away with the certain knowledge that no matter what the *Necronomicon* is, or isn't, it is most definitely not a hoax.

Simon
2005 e.v.

PART ONE

—o—

A List of Kings
Before the Flood...

1: Set and Setting

This story begins—as do so many others of our generation—in 1968. Specifically, on January 31, 1968: the Tet Offensive and, coincidentally, the pagan feast of Oimelc, one of the four cross-quarter days observed by the Celts of ancient Europe, and sacred as well to members of a new occult movement known as Wicca. Saigon would fall on April 30, 1975: Walpurgisnacht, another pagan holiday, another cross-quarter day.

As Walter Cronkite was giving the latest news reports from Vietnam and telling a shocked nation that he thought "we were winning this thing," a young man sat watching television in his living room in the Pelham Bay section of the Bronx in New York City and made a decision that he was not, under any circumstances, going to war. He could avoid it in any number of ways. He could go to college and thus take advantage of a stipulation that as long as he maintained a C average he could avoid being drafted. He could admit to the draft board that he was gay. He could feign illness, flat feet, or bad eyesight. He could flee to Canada or Sweden.

But there was another option.

Other than college students, homosexuals, and the physically disabled, there was another category of deferment: 4-D.

Ministerial. The clergy deferment. Priests are not drafted. And William Andrew Prazsky had a closet full of vestments: chasubles, surplices, Roman collars, cassocks. Not to mention chalices, ciboria, and relics of the saints. An ersatz mitre and homemade crozier. Some evenings, the odor of a curious sanctity—the result of burning Gloria incense in a gleaming brass censer, swung on chains in great arcs— would waft out of his bedroom and into the plain wooden house that he shared with his father and his elderly grandmother, both Czechs. His grandmother, Antonia, was a Czech immigrant. His parents were separated; his mother, Petronella, a Slovak and a Roman Catholic, lived alone in a Manhattan apartment on the Lower East Side. His father— William Anthony Prazsky—was a Presbyterian. Andrew grew up speaking both Czech, English, and Slovak. Tall, thin, dark, and with the fussiness of an old maid already at seventeen—oddly coupled with the coarseness of his background and upbringing, his father a mechanic for the Triboro Bridge and Tunnel Authority—he was a strange and easily identifiable sight at Christopher Columbus High School: a student with poor grades who dressed in a suit and carried a briefcase, and who constantly was seen hanging out at department offices, kissing up to teachers in the hopes of improving his grades through social networking. He knew that college was probably out of the question; he would never be able to maintain a C average on his own. He could not admit to the draft board that he was gay; it would have killed his father if he ever found out. He had no money for a trip abroad and would not have managed the life of a political expatriate very well in any event. He didn't know if he could fake an illness that would earn him the 4-F deferment, but he could fake something else. He could fake being a priest.

Already he had developed a snuff habit, and grew a mustache that he waxed faithfully like Salvador Dali: a walking social and cultural anachronism that went largely unnoticed in the turbulent Sixties, when so many other strange and nefarious deeds were being committed or at least contemplated. He would eventually forego snuff for cigarettes and his mustache for a full beard, but not until he had met another young man at Columbus High and thereby hatched a plan that would not only keep them both out of the Army, but uncover one of the strangest and most controversial books ever published.

Peter Levenda was born in the Bronx, like Prazsky, and in the same year: 1950. His father was an actor who studied at the American Academy of Dramatic Arts, but who had an earlier reputation as a segregationist during the Gary, Indiana, School Strike of 1945. His mother had studied dance and choreography. At the time of their marriage, his father was twenty-one and his mother only seventeen. Peter, their first child, arrived ten months later.

Peter had an uncommon intelligence, as noted by educators after a statewide intelligence test on which he scored extremely high. This was the 1950s, when various government and quasigovernment organizations were developing "special schools" for gifted children. Longtime collaborator and husband of fantasy author Marion Zimmer Bradley—Walter Breen—was one of these, selected by a group in New York City at the same time that Peter was being considered in Chicago. So was theoretical physicist Jack Sarfatti. What stopped any further progress, though, was the fact that Peter's father had been investigated by the FBI during the Gary School Strike and was considered a security risk.

Instead, in 1963, the family moved to Charlestown, New Hampshire: to a former prison farm on the top of Hubbard

Hill. The place had been owned by one Percy Whitmore, who was widely regarded as crazy by the local population. It seemed he was raising Morgan horses on his property when they were all taken in a TB test; added to that was the indignity of having power lines cut across his property. Like something out of the movie *The Ring,* this loss of his horses and the desecration of his land by the government led to a kind of nervous breakdown. Percy had a wife and daughter, and one day they simply disappeared and were never seen again. It would take a youthful Peter Levenda—many years later—to solve that particular mystery by accident, when he came across their unidentified graves during one of his long, solitary walks in the woods they owned: two graves, side by side, with simple slabs of granite to mark the spot and nothing else.

Later, during a renovation of the old, eighteenth-century saltbox house in which they lived, they uncovered a secret wall with shelves containing a collection of poisons: old glass bottles with the almost comical skull-and-crossbones warning signs on their labels. That same year, during a drought that had affected the entire area, a forest fire broke out on the farm, but it was quickly put out by volunteer firemen who rushed to the scene. All in all, it was a bizarre childhood.

Soon thereafter, they lost the property—work being hard to find in New Hampshire in 1963—and they wound up, first in a small apartment in nearby Claremont, New Hampshire, then back in the Bronx by late 1965. Peter was enrolled in Christopher Columbus High School, and a year or so later he would meet William A. Prazsky, who came from a similarly dysfunctional family and who shared Peter's Slavic heritage and had the same fascination with the occult.

Peter's involvement with the arcane began with copies of *Fate* magazine discovered in a local newsstand in Claremont. The Charlestown saltbox had seemed haunted to him, and he once described a feeling of absolute panic when alone in the nearby woods on a bright summer's day when suddenly the entire landscape became deadly silent: no singing birds, no chattering squirrels, only the feeling of some immense being standing somewhere near, just out of sight. It was a sensation of being watched by a powerful force, and it drove him out of the woods and back to the relative safety of the wooden house.

Later, after the move to Claremont, Peter made friends with George Harrison (not the Beatle, of course, but a local student), who shared his interest in the occult and in secret societies, an interest common to young boys of thirteen and fourteen. That was when he discovered *Fate* and the classified ads in the back pages for everything from crystal balls and Tarot cards to pamphlets on how to hold a séance or to tell the future. When his family finally moved back to New York, he had a small shopping list of books and curios he needed to further his eccentric studies.

Despite his uncommon intelligence, Levenda was a mediocre student at Columbus High, except for classes like English, history, and geometry. In English he was an honors student and editor of the school magazine. He developed a proficiency in French translation—something he had nurtured since he was still a preteen living in Chicago—and began studying other languages in his spare time. He had been sent to Catholic confraternity classes in New Hampshire by his parents, who evidently felt that he was in need of spiritual guidance, but wound up asking the priests and nuns many uncomfortable questions, mailing (rather than nailing) his own version of Luther's ninety-five theses to the door of the local church. In the Bronx, this type of formal religious study was abandoned, but at the same time he developed a strong spiritual sensitivity. Religion was fascinating to him, but he despised the reforms of the Second Vatican Council and filled notebooks with his scribbling on this and other ecclesiastical issues even as he pored over the works of Blaise Pascal, St. Augustine, and the Greek philosophers—all part of the *Great Books of the Western World* collection owned by his parents (and eventually hocked to pay debts). He felt that religion and occultism represented a kind of technology, a psychospiritual technology that, once stripped of dogma, could become a powerful force in its own right. An intense teenager, he wandered the halls of Columbus like a ghost, unsocialized and generally—except for editing the school magazine, a job he managed with little or no human contact anyway—a cipher.

And then he met Prazsky, and his interests in religion and the occult found a slightly wider audience.

In 1968, against the backbeat of the Vietnam War, hallucinogenic drugs, and the sexual revolution, there was another phenomenon spreading rapidly across the American landscape: fascination with Eastern religions and the occult. Since the values and utility of all American institutions were being questioned and resisted—from the sanctity of marriage to support for the government's war, to mainstream, consensus consciousness itself—it was only natural that religion would be subject to the same degree of cynical scrutiny. Organized religion was an institution like any other—the educational system, the bureaucracies in Washington, D.C., and the Pentagon—and the values of organized religion from conservative sexual mores to belief in God itself came under increasing attack. As we now know, there was also a dark underground to the Church, particularly to the Catholic Church: so many young men and some women had been sexually abused by priests that the corruption of the Church was known to many—not just to the victims, but also to their families and friends—a whisper campaign that would grow to a shout by the Nineties. The Church was not to be trusted; and as the young people drifted away from the Church and into the arms of the Eastern gurus, anyone who would embrace Catholicism, the Pope, and the bishops was seen as someone who was politically conservative. Indeed, the powerful Francis Cardinal Spellman of New York was known to support the Vietnam War as a spiritual struggle against godless communism.

In addition, the Church was already under fire for its role during World War Two and its silence in the face of the Holocaust; revelations were coming fast and furious that an agency of the Church had actually assisted Nazi war criminals in their escape to South America, the Middle East, and beyond.[1] Suddenly, the Church was no longer a magnet for idealistic young men who wanted to serve God; there were too many unanswered questions and, in the wake of the Second Vatican Council, too many concessions to popular culture by a Church that had no earthly sense of what popular culture was and how ridiculous their priests looked smiling benignly down on guitar-playing hippies in the sanctuary during Sunday Mass.

That same year, the Process Church of the Final Judgment was in full flower in the streets of Los Angeles. A controversial

---

[1] See, for instance, Peter Levenda, *Unholy Alliance;* Ladislas Farago, *Aftermath;* Aarons and Loftus, *Unholy Trinity;* and others.

sect—founded by disaffected members of Scientology—the
Process would become linked (however erroneously) with
Charles Manson, whose gruesome crimes in the Hollywood
Hills would shock the nation the following year. But in
April, Dr. Martin Luther King was assassinated in Mem-
phis by an unemployed white man, a drifter, who somehow
had sufficient funds at his disposal to allow him to travel to
Canada and Europe after the killing. Then, only a few
months later, in June, Senator Robert F. Kennedy was
gunned down in Los Angeles. The purported assassin? A
Christian Palestinian—Sirhan Bishara Sirhan—who had
become involved in Rosicrucianism and Theosophy in the
months leading up to the assassination. This, at the height
of the Vietnam War and the aftermath of the assassination
of President John F. Kennedy. It is safe to say that the country was in turmoil, and that the young were in revolt.

During this time, drawn by the growing spiritual vacuum
in the United States and the West at large, a British import
appeared on American television talk shows. The Beatles
had long prepared American audiences for British culture,
but they were perhaps not quite ready for this new export:
English witchcraft.

There is considerable controversy over the use of the term
"witchcraft," as Margot Adler has pointed out in her defini-
tive study of the subject.[2] It is an emotionally charged term
that can be used either as a pejorative in the usage of Church
and State, as something sinister and thrilling in the screen-
plays of Hollywood and horror writers, as an anthropological term referring to an informal set of superstitions and

---

[2] Margot Adler, *Drawing Down The Moon: Witches, Druids, Goddess-
Worshippers, and Other Pagans in America Today* (New York: Viking,
1979)

vaguely occult practices . . . or as another name of the pagan
religion, Wicca, in which the practice of magic takes second
place to the celebration of a purely pagan faith. Folklorist
Charles Leland attempted to show the survival of a pagan
goddess-worshipping cult in Italy in his *Aradia,* published in
1899. Margaret Murray picked up the thread in her *Witchcult
in Western Europe* in the 1920s. But it was not until Gerald
Gardner virtually exploded on the scene in the 1950s and
1960s that "witchcraft" or "Wicca" truly became what it is
today: a religious and cultural phenomenon in which magic
plays a complimentary role.

Gardner had attempted to prove that witchcraft was an ancient cult that had survived two thousand years of Christianity, its members seeking out the lonely places of Europe and
worshipping in secret. In a sense, he agrees with the Church
that the Craft existed and that it was pagan and worshipped a
Horned God; he differs from the Church only in that his
Horned God is not Satan, Prince of Darkness, but Cernun-
nos, a god of Nature and Fertility. He claimed to have been
initiated into just such a coven of witches in England, and
his Book of Shadows was supposedly a working ritual manual containing spells and rites used since ancient times.

Sybil Leek—a British witch from the New Forest—had
already managed to put a matronly face on "the Craft."
Obese and jowly, with purple clothing, arcane jewelry, and
oddly named pets, she wove a spell of pop astrology and
homely nature remedies that appealed not only to the young,
but also to women of a certain age who saw in Ms. Leek the
possibility of feminine empowerment. It was largely due to
Sybil Leek that we first became acquainted with the concept
of witchcraft as divorced from satanism: while Ms. Leek
and her fellow witches would worship a nature god and goddess (and while that nature god might indeed have horns), it

was not to Satan that they prayed but to the virile male potency of Nature itself: a god older than Jesus, older than Jehovah.

This idea was not wholly unique to Ms. Leek. Who can forget the film *Bell, Book and Candle,* starring Kim Novak, Jimmy Stewart, and Jack Lemmon, about a coven of witches operating through a front in a New York City nightclub? That film premiered in 1958, setting the stage for the American occult revival of the 1960s in which witchcraft would be considered less threatening and more glamorous than the Inquisition would have had us believe.

While Sybil Leek was a great promoter of witchcraft, she did not have an elaborate organization which aspiring American witches could join. Leek was a personality unto herself, selling books on popular occult subjects and appearing on television talk shows like an overweight Martha Stewart coming down from a month-long acid trip. To fill the need of the spiritually starved American public, another British citizen would join the fray. This was Raymond Buckland, and with him "Wicca" appeared in force on American shores.

Raymond Buckland arrived in the United States in 1964—the same year that saw the premiere of the television sitcom *Bewitched,* starring Elizabeth Montgomery as another in a line of attractive, inoffensive blonde witches—at a time when the British witchcraft revival was taking place based largely on the writings of Margaret Murray, Charles Leland, and finally Gerald Gardner and the imposing personality of Sybil Leek.

When it comes to Gerald Gardner, though, the controversy intensifies. An Englishman who spent a considerable portion of his life in Southeast Asia—in Sri Lanka (what was then Ceylon) and especially in what was then known as

Malaya and Singapore, becoming in the process an expert in the wavy-bladed Malaysian knife, the *kris*—he returned to England and became involved in Western-style mysticism. Befriending a variety of occultists, he claimed to have become initiated into a coven of witches. Witchcraft was against the law in England at the time, so no one could claim to be a witch without risking prosecution; instead, Gardner wrote an occult novel, *High Magic's Aid,* which was about witchcraft without actually proselytizing for it. When the witchcraft laws were repealed in the 1950s, Gardner then went on to write several more books about the Craft and became in time the most public exponent of witchcraft in the West, so much so that an entire branch of the faith bears his name: Gardnerian witchcraft.

The problem with Gardnerian witchcraft is that its Book of Shadows—the "manual" and collection of rituals and myths used by a coven of witches—is almost completely modern, containing poetry by Kipling and rituals by the notorious British magician Aleister Crowley, and in some cases derived from the fin-de-siècle English occult society the Golden Dawn. Evidence surfacing in the past twenty-five years or so demonstrates that Gardner was a member of Crowley's occult society, the OTO or "Ordo Templi Orientis" (Order of the Eastern Temple), a masonic-like group that believed it had solved the mystery of the link between sexuality and magic, and that Gardner actually paid Crowley to write some of the rituals included in the Book of Shadows. Thus, any claim that Gardner may have made as to the age and authenticity of his cult are suspect; at least one writer is of the opinion that Gardnerian witchcraft is but an informal branch of Crowley's OTO.

That did not stop Raymond Buckland from becoming

America's strongest link back to British witchcraft, however. Moving to the quiet Long Island suburb of Brentwood, down the line from Ronkonkoma on the LIRR, Buckland was married to the rather more ethereal Rosemary, a witch high priestess whom many considered to be the genuine article. Her husband, with his more sinister appearance, replete with devilish goatee and a hearse parked in his suburban driveway, seemed more like a showman on the order of Anton LaVey, the man who was destined to make the Church of Satan a household term in 1966. Buckland was a great popularizer of witchcraft in the United States, and indeed occasionally appeared opposite Sybil Leek on the American television circuit, as they each verified each other's claims to be a genuine witch.

Try as he might, though, with his doctorate from the University of London and his many published works on witchcraft, he could not exert much control over the explosion of the Craft in the United States. Perhaps witchcraft itself, by its very nature, was not amenable to a centralized organization. The usual explanation given to this author was that a decentralized operation was much more secure in the event that the "burning times" came again. No database of members, no hierarchy to enforce adherence to the rules, meant no one could crush the Craft. Today, as we struggle with decentralized terrorist cells—and with the Patriot Act giving law enforcement agencies the power to collect information on our reading habits from our libraries—we can understand the wisdom of this approach even as we deplore the lack of verifiable documentation to support all those various claims to legitimacy.

Much more likely, however, was the realization that the Craft was whatever one made it: that it was closer in nature to a Dungeons and Dragons style role-playing game than it was to a church; indeed, the card game Magic came under just such opprobrium by the concerned parents of Pound Ridge, New York, when they decided that the "game" was closer to an occult practice than to, say, pinochle.

Different witchcraft groups began to form and to stump for members. The Alexandrian covens were arranged around one Alex Sanders (or Saunders), who took Gardnerian witch-craft and gave it a more medieval feel, with the profligate use of rituals found in the grimoires: the workbooks of the sorcerers and magicians. It was to the Alexandrian form of witchcraft that, it was claimed, Sharon Tate—ill-fated wife of *Rosemary's Baby* director Roman Polanski—had been initiated during the filming of *Eye of the Devil* in London. That Polanski used the services of Church of Satan creator Anton LaVey in bringing the Ira Levin novel to the screen has been alleged and challenged; that the Church of Satan once featured Manson Family member Susan Atkins as a vampire emerging from a coffin during one of its filmed "black masses" is, however, an incontrovertible fact, thus bringing *Rosemary's Baby,* the Manson Family, the Church of Satan, and the murder of director Roman Polanski's wife by the Manson Family around full circle.

Traditionalist Witchcraft was another group, this one breaking down into ethnic tribes: Irish Traditionalist, Welsh Traditionalist, etc. They took their inspiration from the clas-sics of Celtic antiquity, such as the *Mabinogian,* although their rituals do not differ very much from the Gardnerians (as an example), using many of the same rituals inherited from the Golden Dawn, a famous British occult society of the late nineteenth and early twentieth century which num-bered William Butler Yeats and Aleister Crowley among its members. And, while they claimed to be Irish, or Welsh, and so on, they accepted members from any race and ethnic group. The Traditionalists insist that they are the remnants of covens that predate the creation of "Gardnerian" witchcraft, but internal evidence shows nevertheless that they have adopted many of the Gardnerian "innovations" since then.

Buckland, after a falling-out with some Gardnerians, formed his own brand of witchcraft, known as Seax, or "Saxon," witchcraft, something that never became as popular or as widespread as Gardnerianism, possibly due to his estrangement from his more charismatic wife, Rosemary. Then there were Gavin and Yvonne Frost, whose peculiar form of witchcraft was monotheistic and with a heavier emphasis on sexuality than their competitors. There were many at one time who refused to recognize the Frost version of witchcraft as being witchcraft at all, although from the point of view of the history of religions, it is doubtful whether *any* of these groups—the Frosts, the Gardnerians, the Alexandrians, etc.—could rightly be said to represent *real* witchcraft. After all, it is difficult if not impossible to discover what real witchcraft is if the only evidence one has is the Gardnerian Book of Shadows with its poetry by Kipling and its rituals by Crowley. That there are covens of thirteen members with a high priest and/or high priestess may owe more to Hollywood than the New Forest.

Those Americans seeking a spirituality that was not Asian (Buddhist or Hindu), however, and moreover one that incorporated a healthy amount of occult practice and proactive involvement in the world—including spell-casting and sexuality in its various forms—found witchcraft more to their liking. There is no sense of self-denial in witchcraft—or "Wicca," as it became known, a nod to an Indo-European root meaning divination and sorcery—and no fakirlike abstinence, renunication, or Buddhist "visions of sorrow." Witchcraft is Western, European. Its very name has resonance reaching back a thousand years. Witchcraft is supposed to be joyous and mysterious at once, with an undeniable appeal to the readers (and writers) of fantasy and science fiction. It was not as intellectually demanding as the elaborate and complex requirements of ceremonial magic (which is a technique more than a religion anyway, and not designed for attracting large movements of followers). The size of the covens was small enough that relative underachievers could attain positions of prominence, and the multiplicity of covens meant that widely various forms of witchcraft could be created and maintained with relative ease, each accepted as valid by the others. To those involved in Golden Dawn style ceremonial and high magic ritual, there was something irredeemably blue collar about the Craft; to those involved in the Craft, there was something a little too strenuous and demanding about ceremonial magic, which was for loners anyway and not really designed for the beer blast mentality of some of the wilder covens. Further, ceremonial magic was heavily infused with Judeo-Christianity; it seemed impossible to be a traditional ceremonial magician and a pagan at once. Certainly, if one took the notion of Wicca seriously enough, one could not in good conscience practice rituals in which the Hebrew God was invoked, or angels summoned by use of Qabalistic formulae. The grimoires had been written by men working within the Judeo-Christian tradition in medieval Europe and the Middle East. There was nothing pagan about them, except perhaps for their basic assumptions that (a) reality could be manipulated and (b) there are hidden forces in the world that link seemingly unrelated objects and events; ideas familiar to Renaissance philosopher

Giordano Bruno, for instance, and either of which could get one burned during the Inquisition.

If there ever was such a thing as a purely "pagan" grimoire, however, then all of these philosophical and religious obstacles could become irrelevant. After all, magic existed in the world long before Judaism and Christianity. Even initiatory magic of the Golden Dawn variety, with its levels of awareness leading from ordinary consciousness to a kind of "superconsciousness" at the higher, more Olympian strata, was typical of some pagan religions. Initiatory degrees of this kind could be discerned in some of the ancient Egyptian codices, for instance, and there were mysterious rituals practiced among the Eleusinians that teased at the corners of madness and ecstasy. The Sumerians, Akkadians, and Babylonians worshipped at temples that were dedicated to the planetary deities and often consisted of seven levels, each level assigned to one of the seven visible "planets": Sun, Moon, Mercury, Venus, Mars, Jupiter, and Saturn, a kind of Ur-Qabala that formed the inspiration for the occult systems that were to come, those of Robert Fludd, Athanasius Kircher, Paracelsus, Bruno, and the Rosicrucians on the one hand and the early neo-Platonists on the other. But there seemed to be a break between the ancient magicians whose occultism was much more complicated and intellectually sophisticated than Siberian shamanism, for instance—but that never seemed to have been written down or formed the basis for a continuous secret society in the same way that the Knights Templar were said to have been the forefathers of the Freemasons, who in turn gave birth to the Golden Dawn and other modern occult societies—and the carefully articulated occult philosophy of the Middle Ages. There were hints in the writings of Plato and Pythagoras that such an occult system existed; Pythagoras himself claimed to have been initiated into an Egyptian secret society and pledged to keep silent about its rites and mysteries. The occult philosophy represented by the Emerald Tablet of Hermes Trismegistus—a classic of neo-Platonist occult thought—was never more than just that: a philosophy, minus the actual ritual technology.

Instead, the pagan "witches" were left with some charming ideas like "drawing down the Moon," and casting a circle, and invoking four watchtowers in the four cardinal directions, and observing an occult calendar that revolved around the solstices, the equinoces, and the four "cross-quarter" days that evenly divided them . . . but with no all-encompassing form of practical occultism to span everything from astrology to cosmology to spiritual initiation to ritual magic. The American occult revival of the 1960s seemed divided between the witches and their sometimes scandalous sabbats in which naked people posed for reporters and photographers holding daggers and smiling, and the more secretive magicians who burned pots of incense in suburban basements, wearing elaborate robes decorated with Hebrew letters and waving swords, summoning elemental forces to do their bidding and calling on Jehovah and Jesus for assistance . . . and protection.

Groups like the Church of Satan and the Process Church of the Final Judgment were not pagan; while the Church of Satan was openly satanic, deliberately invoking the antithesis of Jesus and Jehovah, the Process Church worshipped all three. Church of Satan members practiced ceremonial magic in various forms, but the slant was always . . . well, satanic. There was an agenda, a political viewpoint, to everything they did. The activities of the Process Church were somewhat more mysterious, and became even more so in the late Sixties and early Seventies. Scientology was a stepchild of Aleister Crowley's OTO, created by a science fiction writer (appropriately enough) who had been involved in magic and occult practices with the OTO in postwar California. The Process Church was founded by disaffected members of Scientology; so there was a kind of apostolic succession from Crowley to Gardner and Alex Sanders on one side, the "pagan" side, and to Scientology and the Process on the other. The most notable element of Crowley's legacy, however, was short-changed by both of these strains: ceremonial magic. Too unscientific for Scientology, and too Judeo-Christian for the witches, it languished during the American occult revival, being practiced only by a handful of Golden Dawn wannabes, a few of Crowley's followers—some members of the OTO—and by many more individuals privately, in secret, alone in their basements or studio apartments. Indeed, it may be said that ceremonial magic was designed with the solitary practitioner in mind, whereas witchcraft—particularly of the Wicca variety—was meant to be celebrated in groups. Aleister Crowley went so far as to create a magical order, a secret society known as Argentum Astrum, which was slyly structured to provide an "Order" in which solitary practitioners could thrive: in which each member knew only the one who initiated him and the one he would initiate in turn. It was the ideal "cell" structure, something both Communist agents and Arab terrorists could understand: in case of capture, a man could implicate only two other members, and would know nothing of the overall strategy and composition of his group.

  Magic, however, promised something more to its practitioners. Magic promised contact with Dark Forces, with demonic beings and angelic hosts, heightened states of consciousness that were the result not of drugs (or not *only* of drugs) but of *techniques,* methods of sensory manipulation that would enable the magician to strum the strands of the web of existence, playing reality like a harp.

2: The Cathedral of Starry Wisdom, Inc.

In the midst of all this activity a startling development took place in the world of books and libraries,
of churches and cults. On March 16, 1973, two Eastern Orthodox monks were indicted for perpetrating a series of
thefts of rare books from libraries and private collections all
over North America, the largest such heist in American history. Fathers Steven Chapo and Michael Hubak had a very
odd pedigree, and I was able to meet both of them long before their arrests by federal authorities:

I was asked to infiltrate their operation by the archbishop
of the Autocephalous Slavonic Orthodox Catholic Church of
North and South America, Inc.

Archbishop Andrew Prazsky was then about twenty-two
years old. His father, Bishop Anthony Prazsky, was still
employed by the Triboro Bridge and Tunnel Authority as a
mechanic, but nearing retirement. Things were looking up
for the Prazskys, and they had cultivated some influential
friends.

One of these was a member of the Royal Canadian
Mounted Police, a woman who worked for their intelligence-
gathering division. Another was a Syrian Orthodox priest,

known to me only as "Father Fox," and he had intelligence connections all over the world. Father Fox spent time in Northern Ireland, where he was once detained for running guns; he spent time in Vietnam, for reasons unknown to me. He had a wife and child in the Bronx, to whom he wrote infrequently. He was a graduate of Fordham University and could converse in Russian and Arabic. He was clearly an intelligence asset, and perhaps he freelanced. Fox was involved with something called the Greek Order of St. Denis of Zante, a chivalric or knightly order that numbered many prominent politicians among its members.

According to Andrew Prazsky, it was Father Fox who set up Chapo and Hubak for their arrest.

The story is long and involved, so I will keep it as short as possible. When it was all over, Chapo would refer to me as a "ferret," an indication of my role in the affair. When Chapo and Hubak first met me, they did not know that I was already aware of their criminal enterprise, for they had given many stolen books and manuscripts on the occult to Archbishop Prazsky as a bribe to keep him quiet and to ensure that he continued to support their efforts from behind the scenes.

Bishops at Large

Much of what has been written about the Slavonic Orthodox Church and the two felonious monks (and there hasn't been very much) has been confused and largely speculative. Church names are confounded in the newspapers and other published reports, as are the names of the prelates involved. Often, clergymen of these denominations have more than one name anyway—a secular name and a sacred one—and this adds to the confusion, especially among journalists and historians who are not familiar with Eastern Orthodoxy, and most especially not with those groups whose leaders are dismissed as *episcopi vagantes,* or "wandering bishops," that is, bishops either without credentials or with very suspect ones. Prazsky's ecclesiastical origins were identical to those of the most notorious wandering bishops in the land and, indeed, shared lines of apostolic succession with such bizarre forebears as David Ferrie, Jack Martin, and Carl Stanley: gentlemen believed by New Orleans District Attorney Jim Garrison to have been involved in the JFK assassination conspiracy. Prazsky's story, however, is even more bizarre and astounding.

Christopher Columbus in the late 1960s was pretty much like other New York City high schools of the period. The Vietnam War was being felt among the student body like an impending hurricane, about to take the roofs off the worlds of all the young men about to graduate. The sexual revolution and the availability of a wide variety of drugs—principally marijuana and LSD—was also having its inescapable impact. Students for a Democratic Society (SDS) were holding meetings in the school, and the teachers themselves—under the unswerving hand of Al Shanker—had gone on strike one semester, thus delaying the opening of school for several days.

Columbus High School is located in the Bronx, close to Fordham Road and Pelham Parkway. In the 1960s this area was largely Jewish, and students from the high school would occasionally hang out in local delis, eating potato knishes and slurping colas, criticizing their teachers or parents and wondering how to avoid the Draft. One of Columbus's most famous alumni was Christine Jorgensen, the transsexual. Another was David Berkowitz, now serving time for his role in the Son of Sam murders.

While there was a sexual revolution going on in the

country, homosexuality was an issue that many ignored. The students at Columbus who were gay in those days tended to associate only with other gays, if indeed they could identify each other. As it happened, these social outcasts would surround themselves with others who may not have been gay but who—for whatever reason—were themselves outcasts as well.

Such was the case with William A. Prazsky.

Born in June 1950 to second-generation Slavs, Prazsky was tall, thin, and effete. He affected a Daliesque waxed and pointed mustache while still in high school, and carried a snuff box with him wherever he went and, on occasion, a sword cane. He had a passion for antiques, religious iconography, and sacred music. In short, he was a dandy of the old school, made all the more startling by the fact that his father was a short, gruff, and enormously strong man who worked in the maintenance department of the Triboro Bridge and Tunnel Authority. Anthony Prazsky's idea of good music was recordings of country and western tunes on electronic organs; his favored cuisine was a TV dinner on a tray in front of the television and a can of peaches. His favored pastime was welding.

Anthony Prazsky built a large collection of medieval weaponry in his shop at work. Maces, lances, axes, coats of arms, swords, helmets . . . the entire panoply of Middle Ages brutality was on display in his home. To visit the family's foyer, where much of this equipment was kept, was like walking into a torture chamber. Well made and heavy, these were not mere ornamental pieces that could be mistaken for the real things. They were solid and functional, and would have been a hit at any Renaissance fair.

William Prazsky, his only child, was instead rather more wispy and effeminate, something which probably did not escape his father's attention and that may have contributed to the elder Prazsky's dedication to the art of medieval weaponry. William Jr. cherished the ornamental splendor of religion, and managed to develop a collection of chasubles, surplices, stoles, and other Catholic impedimenta over the years. He also had a keen interest in books on religion and, as a sideline, the occult. He hung out in the Foreign Language department at Columbus, and tried to cultivate relationships with the teachers there, pretending to a knowledge of Italian and Latin he did not possess. Academically, his record was poor, and his intellectual abilities were limited to those topics that appealed to his artistic nature. He had a hatred of studying and of school in general, and tried mightily to avoid actually sitting in a classroom. His written English was equally poor, and he was easily distracted. He wore suits to school and, with his mustache waxed to perfection, probably seemed to be one of the teachers to anyone passing by who did not know better.

He had few friends, but those he did have were like-minded souls who were members of the Third Order Franciscans, a kind of lay order for religious and monastic-minded Catholics. They swapped information on where to buy Roman collars and cassocks, and which bishop's ring was the gaudiest or most tasteful. Prazsky might have pursued this sad and solitary existence were it not for the appearance at Columbus of a number of extraordinary individuals who would quite simply change his life.

One of these was Stanley Dubinsky, an extremely talented and creative writer and poet with a gargantuan appetite for life and a keen sense of the sardonic. Then there was Peter Levenda, another writer who would one day earn a modest degree of fame as an historian of the Nazi era. It was Levenda who, as a teenager, would suggest to Prazsky that they form a religious corporation. It was Dubinsky who argued in favor of an atheistic view of the world that had no room for churches and religions. Between the two of these young men—and a number of other friends in the school and vicinity—Prazsky's worldview was being formed.

The three friends met almost by accident one day. Levenda was the editor of the high school "literary/arts" magazine, *Horizon.* For that publication, he had written a short article on alchemy that focused on the legendary scientist Van Helmont and the idea of transmutation. Ambitious stuff for a teenager in high school in the 1960s. One day, in an otherwise unused classroom, Levenda began to explain the mechanisms behind operations of ceremonial magic, a system used by medieval magicians to contact spiritual forces, including angels and demons, and which is still used today throughout the world. His listeners included a few other students, notably among them Stanley Dubinsky, who found the discourse fascinating even though he did not particularly agree with the point of view of the lecturer that the system "worked" in some way; the important thing was it was different, intelligent, and even amusing. Dubinsky then went on to contact another bizarre friend of his, William Prazsky— whom he called "Billy," to the latter's irritation—and invited him to meet this Levenda, who seemed as interested in matters spiritual and religious as he was.

Levenda's family tree was exotic, to say the least, and his own turbulent adolescence seemed to mirror that of his parents. In fact, he seemed a Sixties version of Harry Potter (and with his owlish glasses and quiet, conservative appearance, even more so) both in background and in aspiration.

One thing he had in common with Prazsky was the fact that his parents were also separated. More important, though, was ethnicity. Prazsky's parents were Czech and Slovak, and Levenda's father was Slovak. So Levenda was half Slovak, like Prazsky. It was a common bond, and an important one.

Prazsky found Levenda's impromptu lectures on the occult stimulating. This was a person who shared some of his own quirks: Eastern European *melancholia,* deep interest in religion and the occult, and a loner personality. Levenda did not fit in with any of the cliques at Christopher Columbus, and wound up with a few friends who could only be described in today's argot as "geeks" or, more kindly, "nerds." These were the outcasts of school society. Even as the editor of the school magazine—due to his high scores in English and skill as a writer and critic—Levenda was virtually anonymous at the school. His parents by this time were having serious problems, and his father would move out of the house before he graduated. Prazsky, on the other hand, had an aspect of his personality that Levenda did not share and about which he was not even aware in the beginning: he was gay.

The experience of being homosexual in a world where men are expected to be burly, muscular lovers of sports, guns, and easy—straight—sex can be a confusing one for a young man. Social isolation takes place early on, and as that occurs, some adolescents become fascinated with the obscure, the unpopular, the neglected, the outré. Identification with the feminine side of one's personality can lead to interest in the outward trappings of ritual: the flowing robes, the heavy jewelry, the clouds of incense, the ethereal music. The dead languages.

Prazsky had developed all of these interests and more. He loved antiques and collected what he could with money he cadged or, on occasion, stole from either one of his separated parents. He played Gregorian chants on an old stereo at all hours of the day and night. He began smoking cigarettes while still in high school, and during school hours he took snuff, delicately placing a few grains on his hand and snorting it, afterward using a lace handkerchief to wipe his nose. The reader is reminded that Prazsky was sixteen years old at the time, and living in *the Bronx*.

He spoke Czech and Slovak, but these were not glamorous or romantic languages to know and, anyway, they reminded him too much of his parents and his actual, vulgar origins, so he affected a knowledge of Italian and Latin. Latin was alien to his father, who was a Protestant. His mother, however, was Catholic, and it was to Catholicism that Prazsky turned when he first became interested in ritual. A psychoanalyst might say that it was his mother's Catholicism and Prazsky's adoption of the trappings of the Catholic faith that were somehow related to his homosexuality; and that his subsequent conversion to Eastern Orthodoxy was an attempt to reconcile his mother's ritual-laden faith with both his parents' ethnicity.

It is certain that Prazsky resisted the reforms instituted by the Second Vatican Council, for he much prefered the stately ritual of the old school. As in the case of his friend, Peter, folk masses with pale hippies playing acoustic guitar in the sanctuary left him cold. He wanted satin robes and jeweled mitres, swinging censers and amethyst rings . . . and the authority that a priest had over his congregation, the spiritual authority and acceptance that—for a struggling homosexual in 1966—was denied to him everywhere else.

Due to the Church's strict laws concerning celibacy for its priests, seminarians usually find themselves divided into two groups before they are ordained: the jocks and the gays. In order to sublimate sexual feelings as much as possible,

the jocks can be seen playing aggressive games of basket-
ball, football, and other sports at all hours; the gays have it
somewhat easier, if more clandestine—they can have sexual,
even romantic, relationships with each other, as long as
these relationships do not come to light. Recent revelations
concerning the sexual abuse of young boys by Catholic
priests is perhaps witness to this situation; what is not revealed by these cases, however, is the degree to which some
priests engage in sexual relationships with each other, away
from their unsuspecting congregations and the prying eyes
of the hierarchy.

Prazsky was well aware of all this as a young man in high
school. By the time he was nineteen years old he had already
developed a sexual relationship with an older man, another
priest who will appear later on in our story. Before that, however, he had been approached by teachers at Columbus who
were notorious among the students as being either gay or
simply pederasts who preyed on children. One was a teacher
who actually abused his students in front of the class on occasion, believing that no one noticed what he was doing.
And there was yet another teacher, a young blond man with
an apartment in Manhattan, who became one of the first to
help create the Slavonic Orthodox Church.

As Levenda and Prazsky began to hang out after school in
the Jewish delis around Fordham Road, they shared their
knowledge of ritual and religion. Prazsky was far more involved in Roman Catholicism than Levenda; he frequented
meetings of the Third Order Franciscans and had a friend
there, Tony, who lived in the Yorkville section of Manhattan
with another, younger man—a troubled youth with fantasies
of violence—who was supposedly an heir to the Dodge

fortune. Prazsky was thus able to get into Manhattan's St. Patrick's Cathedral easily, for instance, invading areas that Levenda had never seen, and this was impressive. Further, Prazsky had a complete collection of ritual vestments in an ancient wooden wardrobe closet in his room: everything from the plain black cassock and Roman collar of the parish priest to biretta, chasubles, surplices, stoles, a gold monstrance (used for exhibiting the Holy Eucharist during special ceremonies), a chalice, paten, and other instruments. All dressed up and nothing to bless.

Levenda, meanwhile, had been approaching the concept of religion and the Church with a scholar's intensity. Prazsky noted that Levenda was an honors student in English and History, and asked him to help him with his homework. This usually resulted in Levenda writing Prazsky's papers for him. As the two young men neared graduation age, however, they had other things to worry about. One was college. The other was the Vietnam War.

Levenda had no financial means to go to college. His parents were separating, his father drank his salary every week, and his mother was unemployed. As a result, he spent very little time in school. He stayed home with his mother one or two days a week, allowing one of his other siblings to go to school in his place. The three children thus rotated their school attendance, since one of them was forced to stay home and attend to their sick mother.

Prazsky, on the other hand, had the wherewithal to go to college due to his father's long employment at the Triboro Bridge and Tunnel Authority and the fact that their home in the Pelham Bay section of the Bronx was now appreciating in value. The largest building project in New York City history was taking place literally across the street from their house: Co-Op City. The parking garage for Section Five of Co-Op City would be built on their doorstep, driving up the value of their messy, ramshackle home.

Levenda and Prazsky realized that the only means at their disposal of staying out of Vietnam was to attend college and obtain college deferments. This posed special problems for both young men, as Prazsky—who could afford the tuition fees—could not function as a scholar and would never be able to maintain a decent enough grade point average to keep his deferment; and Levenda—who was more than capable of maintaining his grades in college—could simply not afford to go, since his first priority after graduation was getting a job and earning enough money to support himself and thus relieve somewhat the economic burden on his separated parents.

Prazsky did not want to go to college in any event, not unless there were no other options. So, like jailhouse lawyers, they read whatever they could find on the selective service system, and suddenly the solution to their problem presented themselves: the 4-D, or ministerial, deferment, available only to clergymen.

While military service would seriously disrupt Levenda's personal program of religious and mystical research, he did not want to enter a Catholic seminary, fearing that their regulations and strictures would not permit him to continue studying the occult, a field that—to him—seemed to offer the best information about technologies for consciousness expansion and self-transcendence.

Prazsky was also reluctant to enter into a real seminary for it would have seriously curtailed his other activities; plus it was unthinkable for him to begin at the bottom. He had already wandered around the school in a suit, waxed mustache, sword cane, and silver snuff case. How could he give

all that up and become a lowly seminarian? They would certainly take away his snuff and cane. Besides, there was no
way he could handle the coursework. He still hadn't learned
how to spell.

For years Levenda had wondered what to do with his life
after school. His interests were all too arcane for the real
world. What kind of job would he have, if he was successful
in avoiding the Draft? He had always wanted to be a writer,
but had no illusions that he would make a living at it, accept-
ing early on that he would probably "write for the drawer"
for years before gaining entrée to the literary world. Instead,
like many young people, he scoured the classified ads in the
backs of magazines and newspapers looking for the secret
keys to his future. He found an ad for the Universal Life
Church, and joined for five dollars, receiving in return a card
identifying him as a validly ordained minister ... and a
booklet on how to get rich betting on the horses. He showed
Prazsky his minister card, and of course Prazsky was interested. Levenda began to read up on the legal requirements
for churches and church corporations, and it slowly dawned
on him that there were no legal impediments to them creating their very own church.

Unknown to either of them at the time, they had entered
upon a road that was well-traveled. Most people know that
there are bogus universities where one may purchase a "degree" for a few hundred or a few thousand dollars. What one
gets for this money is a piece of paper, no more. Admittedly,
it can be a beautifully printed document, but it is not worth
the paper it is printed on. It looks real and may impress others who do not have actual degrees, but it is worthless. People buy these bogus degrees in order to pad a résumé, hoping
that an employer will not investigate further and discover

that the "university" is what is referred to as a "diploma mill": a business set up for the express purpose of issuing false documents, usually established from an anonymous mail drop or post office box.

Many are not aware, however, of the existence of bogus clergy and bogus orders of nobility. That there are churches that function as "bishops mills" is largely unknown outside of a small circle of specialists in this field. The bogus university is easy to identify: they usually have no faculty, no staff, and no campus. A bogus church is somewhat more difficult to characterize, since a *legitimate* church can be anything from a cathedral to a storefront. In many cases, legitimate churches even operate from peoples' homes. So, how does one identify a bogus church?

There are several avenues open to investigation. In the first place, bogus churches usually have no congregation to speak of. They have clergy, sometimes hundreds of priests and bishops, but they far outnumber any congregation. In the second place, bogus churches are often eager to prove that they are not bogus. What genuine church does that? The bogus church "proves" its bona fides by issuing documents demonstrating its legitimacy, its "apostolic succession."

Now, a Protestant church may or may not be bogus. That is usually up to potential congregants to determine. But in the case of "Catholic" or "Orthodox" churches, the issue is far more serious. These churches place a great deal of emphasis on ritual and on the sanctity of their sacraments. The regulations concerning who may perform these rituals and under what circumstances is largely a matter of Canon Law. If the church operates within these strict guidelines and can prove an unsullied pedigree of bishops going back to the first Pope, Saint Peter, then one may assume that it is canonical and therefore not bogus. This may seem to be a simple matter, but often it is anything but simple or clear-cut.

In addition to bogus churches, there are bogus nobles. That is, bogus orders of chivalry, of knighthood and titles like baron, marquis, count, and duke. There are legitimate lines of nobility, of course, and legitimate orders of knighthood, such as the famous—or infamous, depending on your point of view—Knights of Malta. But there are many, many false orders that have been established for the express purpose of separating credulous Americans from their American dollars.

The reader may be interested to learn that, often, those who create bogus orders of knighthood are also involved in bogus churches, and that sometimes these same individuals may be involved in bogus universities as well.

It is an underworld that few knowingly encounter in the normal course of their daily lives, for how many of us come across knights and counts and dukes on the subway, or in fast-food restaurants, or in our schools or churches? Yet, they exist. In some cases they have come to the attention of government authorities both in America and abroad, and not only because the dignities they award are intrinsically worthless, but because their nobles and bishops and deans are actually agents of foreign intelligence organs. And therein lies our tale.

There is a long, hundred-year history of bizarre churches and sects that grew up around the more established Catholic and Orthodox denominations. These are either splinter groups that broke off from the parent due to some conflict or disagreement or simply because of internal politics; or they are groups that sprang fully formed into existence from the feverish dreams of the socially maladapted. In terms of

Eastern Orthodoxy, we also have the situation that the Cold War was being fought through the churches as well as through the normal channels of government and espionage agencies. This clandestine relationship between Orthodox churches and American and foreign intelligence operatives is one that has not been adequately explored, and when Levenda and Prazsky began their quest for the perfect venue for their own cult, they would come up against another: the cult of intelligence.

Levenda's taste in religion at the time ran to the austere, mystical church that would be low on ornaments but high on intensity. Prazsky ran to the other extreme: a lot of ornaments, gold, and jewels, and not much more than that. The one thing they both agreed upon was: it had to be a real church, legally incorporated. They were not sure how they were going to use this as a vehicle for earning a living—that was not the first thing on their minds—but they were sure that it would provide them with a forum for their interests and possibly, very possibly, a means out of the Draft.

Who would recognize these two teenagers as real priests, though? And who would ordain them, lead the church, and lend it credibility? Further, exactly what type of church would be best? Certainly not Protestant: not enough ritual. It couldn't be Catholic, obviously, for New York City's Cardinal Spellman would have something to say about that! Besides, there was something missing now in Catholic ritual. It had become less mysterious, more mundane. That did not appeal to either of the two boys.

Travels around New York City and meetings with Tony and other Third Order Franciscans alerted them to another option, and so it is with some trepidation that we find these two souls on the doorstep of the Russian Orthodox Church

Outside Russia, commonly known as the Synod or, to New
York City clergy, as Ninety-third Street.

And the ill-fated Brother Victor.

The Synod was something of an anachronism. It was the
headquarters of clergy and hierarchy of the Russian Orthodox Church who had fled Russia after the Revolution in
1917. They were accompanied by some members of the
royal family who managed to leave with sizable fortunes in
artwork, jewelry, and other collateral. The family bought a
large building on the corner of Park Avenue and Ninety-third
Street that had been originally built for a railroad magnate,
and converted half of the building to church use. This half
became the cathedral and monastery. The other half of the
building was retained as a residence for the royal family
themselves. The émigrés also established a school on the
premises, St. Sergius, and this is where the desperate duo
encountered Brother Victor.

Visiting the Synod on a Sunday morning when the beautiful Eastern Orthodox Divine Liturgy is celebrated in full regalia in a ritual lasting some three hours—during which time
no one sits, since there are no chairs—the two young men
stood respectfully and watched as bishops with long flowing
beards and colorful vestments swung ornate censers, and a
choir famous for their professional-quality singing chanted
the entire service in Russian. It was like something out of
Doctor Zhivago. This is it, they thought. This is where we
have to be. This is . . . well, *cool*. The two were dressed in
black suits and Roman collars, looking like Catholic seminarians if not actually priests, and this caught the attention of
some of the parishioners.

Standing respectfully to one side, the two tried to keep a

low profile since the entire experience seemed extremely Russian and extremely exclusive. The Russian faithful do not appreciate gawking bystanders, so Prazsky and Levenda tried to look solemn and attentive and very, very polite.

They were approached by a young monk with a blond, wispy beard who introduced himself as Brother Victor and as the man in charge of the school. They spoke briefly for a few moments, and then made plans to meet later on during the week. (When Prazsky and Levenda did not have class!) They introduced themselves as Father Elefterij and Father Petro. Thus was a legend born.

Petro is, of course, the Slavicized form of "Peter." *Elefterij,* however, is another story. The word comes from the Greek and means "freedom." The two young men had watched a curious film called *The Magus,* starring Anthony Quinn and Michael Caine, based on the John Fowles novel, and during one of the scenes depicting a Greek revolt against the Nazis, the Greeks are heard to yell this word as a battle cry. Prazsky seized on it and assumed it as his nom de guerre. He would eventually drop Elefterij and revert to his second name, Andrew, in the years that would follow, but the Slavonic Orthodox Church had come into being, almost by accident, during that first, fateful meeting at the Cathedral of the Russian Orthodox Church Outside Russia.

This church—usually referred to by its acronym, ROCOR—was heavily invested in anti-Soviet (and later pro-Nazi) intrigue from the 1920s on. During the Cold War, persons as illustrious in their own way as George deMohrenschildt—the mentor of accused presidential assassin Lee Harvey Oswald—and other members of the "White Russian" community around Oswald in Dallas had ties to ROCOR. Founded by aristocratic Russians fleeing the 1917

Revolution, it was a hub of anti-Communist espionage activity and since 1952 was headquartered in New York City.

As the two boys polished their act, studying Church Slavonic—which is to Russian Orthodoxy as Latin is to the Catholic Church—and memorizing the traditional prayers and chants in that language, they also began to accumulate the proper wardrobe. The attire of Orthodox clerics is markedly different from the Western-style dress of Roman Catholic priests and bishops. In the first place, the Eastern-style cassocks are much more voluminous and are called *riasa*. The priests wear cylindrical, rimless stove-pipe hats—called *klobuks*—which are familiar to anyone who has seen *Zorba the Greek* or *Doctor Zhivago*. These *klobuks* are often draped in veils as well.

Prazsky, being the more handy of the two, began to make these hats himself. At first he simply made them of stiff dressing material and visited several dry goods stores, looking for the proper black material. After the first few attempts, however, he began to get the idea that they should be made on proper hat blocks, and had several made to order in Lower Manhattan: some for *klobuks,* and some for the magnificent mitres that are the envy of ecclesiastics everywhere. Mitres are the crowns worn by bishops in both the Orthodox and Catholic churches, but the Orthodox mitres are round, where the Catholic mitres are pointed and narrow. Traditionally, the Orthodox mitres are quite heavy, but Prazsky was able to make this headgear using lightweight materials: a real advantage in hot summer weather . . . as well as on some of the more thin-necked bishops. Eventually, later on in his career, he was able to sell them to other bishops of his acquaintance and wound up taking orders from churches around the country, since they were very much in demand.

* * *

During this time, Levenda began seeking ways to incorporate their new church, which was to be called the Slavonic Orthodox Church. There was a precedent for this creature.

Czechoslovakia was a kind of artificial country that had been created at the end of World War I and the dissolution of the Austro-Hungarian Empire. Two regions—one Czech and one Slovak—were joined together to form a single nation. The problem was that they had different languages, different cultures, and different religions. The Czechs were predominantly Protestant, and the Slovaks were largely Catholic. There was, however, an Orthodox church in Czechoslovakia—neither Protestant nor Catholic—and it figured prominently in a key event of the Second World War.

The country was under the iron rule of one Reinhard Heydrich. An SS officer of bitter reputation, he ran the occupied territory with savagery and hatred. Eventually, a team of paratroopers was sent in to assassinate him. They succeeded in this mission, and afterward hid in an Orthodox church in Prague. The assassination of Heydrich caused the Nazis to react with ferocity, and they massacred an entire Czech village—Lidice—in retaliation. The Orthodox church in question was raided by the Nazis, and entered into World War II history, being effectively closed down after the raid.

This was the church that Levenda and Prazsky "joined" in 1967, and for them it was a stroke of genius. The church had no existence in the United States, except for a handful of scattered faithful and clergy who had since joined other denominations. The headquarters was behind the Iron Curtain, in Prague, if it even still existed. Since beginning their quest for a religious "home," they had learned that virtually every other country in Eastern Europe had an Orthodox Church with a solid presence in the United States—every country, that is, *except* Czechoslovakia. As they happened to be Czech and Slovak themselves, this was an irresistible opportunity. There was literally no one to stop them from claiming the title as their own, and thus they formed a religious corporation in its name.

Before they could legitimately claim valid ordination as priests, however (a sticking point with both of them, as legitimacy might later prove to be an issue), there had to be a bishop to ordain them. That proved a bit more difficult until Filotej was found, living in an apartment in Spanish Harlem that was decorated in blinking Christmas tree lights the year round.

Filotej—or Bishop Filotej, as we should call him—was a DP: a "displaced person" from somewhere in Eastern Europe, no one was quite sure where. He had his own way of speaking English (which he invariably referred to as "new English"), and was an engaging character, full of life and the kind of desperate optimism one sometimes finds in people who have endured unspeakable hardships. Short, balding, and fond of schnapps—which he drank from tiny, gaily colored glasses—and roasted capons, he spoke a kind of pidgin Czech, Slovak, Russian, Croatian, and perhaps Romanian, a melange of idioms that was impenetrable to the uninitiated. He spent time after the war living at Grottaferrata in Rome, a Greek monastery that housed a number of Eastern European refugee clergy at the time. Though it was a Catholic institution, Eastern rite clergy were admitted as well. (What is known as the "Eastern rite" is a reference to the Orthodox style of Divine Liturgy—what the Catholics refer to as the Mass—performed by Eastern clergymen who belong to various of the Eastern Orthodox churches that allied themselves with Rome and accepted the Pope as their spiritual leader.)

The name "Filotej" means "friend of God," and this was how he was known.

Filotej was probably the last surviving clerical member (in the United States) of what had once been the Orthodox Church of Czechoslovakia. It was Filotej who, in extremis, ordained Levenda and Prazsky into the priesthood. It was certainly a bizarre beginning, with Christmas tree lights twinkling in the summer heat and a stuffed capon roasting in the oven.

Thus armed with a sense of legitimacy and purpose, the duo descended upon the world of organized religion with a vengeance.

The first to feel the burn was Brother Victor.

He had invited the two young men up to the school on various occasions, and they would show up in clerical garb, robes flowing. They must have looked ridiculous, but Brother Victor never rebuffed them. He was good for tales of gossip and intrigue behind the monastery walls of the Synod, but even more valuable were his impromptu lessons on Orthodox theology and protocol, which the two drank up greedily. He must have thought that these men were devoted, if ill-prepared, religious who had to be taken at least seriously enough to lead in the right direction.

It would prove his undoing.

Shortly after one such meeting—which must have taken place sometime in 1968—Brother Victor had an accident. After being told by the Church hierarchy that he could not associate with Levenda and Prazsky, he still met with them on one occasion in defiance of the edict. A few days later he fell down an empty elevator shaft at the monastery on Ninety-third Street, and broke both his legs. All attempts by the boys to reach him were fruitless. They never saw Brother Victor again.

As the two boys became more polished in their ecclesiastical attitude and attire, they succeeded in finding incorpora-
tors who would help them set up the Slavonic Orthodox
Church. One was a teacher at the high school who was gay
and had a crush on Prazsky. Blond, single, young, and with a
large apartment in Manhattan, he was also interested in the
occult but more interested in having the two boys hold naked
séances. They demurred, but eventually he signed the incor-
poration papers. (The boys themselves could not do this
since they were still minors.) Other signatories included one
of Levenda's parents and one of Prazsky's.

Thus set in legal motion, Prazsky went on to do what he
did best: order stationery.

Prazsky's talents in arts and crafts could not be denied.
He had a flair for the artistic and creative, and accepted only
the best in everything. For church stationery, he headed
downtown to a specialist engraver in Manhattan who designed a superb Orthodox cross—the kind with three bars
instead of only one—and raised black lettering in Old English type. It read: "Slavonic Orthodox Church in Exile—
Bishop Filotej—Father Elefterij—Father Petro." It was
printed on heavyweight parchment and cost a small fortune,
which Prazsky embezzled from his father.

Next was the purchase of regalia.

Prazsky had been accepted into college, which was necessary for his deferment until a clerical one could be obtained.
His eighteenth birthday was in June 1968, so he faced an
earlier danger of being called up for the Draft than Levenda,
who came of age later in the year. Getting accepted meant
that he had—at least for the first semester—a deferment
from the Draft, but it wouldn't last long.

Prazsky set about getting his hands on as much college
stationery as possible. Using his prior experience with the

Slavonic Church engraver, he began to cleverly forge everything from school transcripts to report cards and bulletins in an effort to deceive his father into thinking that his only son was doing well. Even more important were the bills for each semester, which Prazsky managed to duplicate and send to himself every time he needed more money for . . . stuff.

After the first semester in school, Prazsky no longer needed to attend since he had copies of all the necessary forms, but he needed the cash: he had to bribe his way into a world that offered tremendous opportunities for a man of his abilities.

But first he needed jewelry.

Ecclesiastical jewelry and regalia can be quite expensive as well as hard to find, if you are Orthodox. Prazsky located a manufacturer in Greece that made everything from *panagias*—the heavy, jewel-encrusted medallions Orthodox bishops wear around their necks—to a spectacular crozier, the huge gold staff carried by bishops, which in the Orthodox Church is a rod with two entwined serpents, a caduceus, representative of the rod of Aaron as well as the common symbol for medicine and the Greek god Mercury. It is also a symbol of occult initiation, and this was not lost on Levenda even if it was on Prazsky.

For what Prazsky was doing—at the age of eighteen—was proclaiming himself a *bishop* of the Slavonic Orthodox Church!

Levenda and Prazsky went down to JFK International Airport to pick up and clear the shipment from Greece through Customs, a shipment that contained everything an Orthodox bishop needed to look . . . Orthodox. It was Prazsky's money, so Prazsky was the bishop. This had not been discussed with Levenda, of course, who was doing all the work to keep Prazsky from flunking out of school on the one hand, and incorporating the church on the other. Levenda, however, was not interested in titles or regalia, but in how the church would be run.

As they schemed every day on ways to find a suitable location for their church so they could perform the Divine Liturgy on Sunday—going down to Greek shops in midtown Manhattan to source censers, incense, charcoal, and other objects needed for the services—they enlisted the aid of Stanley Dubinsky once again to serve as a kind of altar boy, as well as Tony from Yorkville and a number of others. They inveigled the pastor of a local Bronx church of the Dutch Reformed denomination to let them use his church on Sunday, and actually joined a North Bronx clergy association. At the same time, they were still pursuing their occult studies. It was a very busy spring of 1968, and then the unspeakable happened: the assassination of Senator Robert F. Kennedy in June.

Icons were being destroyed: first, the fabled icon of American military might during the Tet Offensive, which was largely a propaganda victory for the Communists. Then the murder of two of America's most vocal peacemakers and idealists, Dr. Martin Luther King and Senator Kennedy. It was not a good time for poets and pacifists, and this message was not lost on Prazsky and Levenda. They would graduate high school that month, only a few weeks after the Bobby Kennedy assassination. And William Prazsky would turn eighteen and face the Draft.

The night before the funeral for Bobby Kennedy, Prazsky and Levenda—both still only seventeen years old—decided on a bizarre plan of action. Sitting in the Prazskys' delapidated wooden home, Prazsky wondered if attending the funeral Mass was possible, and if it would gain them attention among the other Orthodox clergy to the extent that they would be "recognized" or, barring that, that they would be visible enough that the mere fact that they were in attendance would prove their legitimacy as priests.

Levenda—still in shock over the assassination and seriously considering the possibile existence of an assassination conspiracy—thought Prazsky's idea both insane and callous. The last best hope for America and the renewal of Camelot was lying in a coffin in the central aisle of St. Patrick's Cathedral in Manhattan, and Prazsky was plotting a way to exploit the event for himself.

"Well," Prazsky said, "let's go and see, anyway."

Levenda had no objections to going to the Cathedral, but he had no illusions about being able to get inside the church. It was impossible. The tightest security New York City had ever known was in place. Another Kennedy had been assassinated, and only months after Dr. King had been killed. There would be Secret Service coming out of the walls. It just wasn't possible to get close to the coffin bearing the slain senator.

They dressed in their by now typical clerical garb: a standard Roman collar and cassock for Levenda, topped by a *klobuk* with veil; an Orthodox *riasa* for Prazsky over his blue jeans, and the obligatory *klobuk* and veil. In addition, Prazsky carried a wooden cane with a brass ornament. They boarded the number 6 IRT subway train out of Pelham Bay Park looking like a couple of extras for some obscure Chekov production and headed downtown to the Cathedral.

As expected, St. Patrick's was surrounded by heavy security that night. Police barricades were everywhere. But Prazsky—due to his Third Order Franciscan connections—knew how the Cathedral was connected to the Chancellery of the New York Archdiocese, and decided to try that approach.

They walked up to the Chancellery, which was not heavily guarded, if at all, and managed to bump into a bishop who was wandering around in his red cassock and surplice, as if he had just finished performing some ceremony inside. Prazsky did all the talking and introduced themselves as Orthodox clergy from the Slavonic Orthodox Church. Prazsky was tall, at least six feet, wore a mustache, and was dressed like an Orthodox priest, and *who else* would dress like that *except* an Orthodox priest? That explains somewhat the reaction of the bishop who told them how to get into the Cathedral the next morning for the Mass, and even escorted them to the entrance to the Cathedral from the Chancellery, so they could view the coffin and pay their respects that very evening.

Suddenly, the two boys found themselves in an extremely tense situation. If discovered, who knows what would have happened? Would they be arrested? Or shot on sight? After all, those flowing robes could be concealing any manner of weapon, from riot gun to pipe bomb. The tall, stovepipe *klobuks* themselves could easily hide a hand grenade or two, or an Ingram MAC-10.

Gulping, they proceeded in the direction pointed out to them by the bishop and found themselves eventually standing before the coffin of Senator Robert F. Kennedy.

Before them, kneeling in a pew, were Senator Kennedy's widow, Eunice, and the widow of President John F. Kennedy herself, Jacqueline Kennedy Onassis.

The two interlopers made some nervous benedictions in Church Slavonic over the coffin, knelt for a few moments in another pew, and then made haste to leave, Prazsky complaining all the while that he did not have a camera to capture the moment for posterity. Levenda was shaking; they had breached security and touched the coffin of his hero.

But for Prazsky it was not enough.

As the two made their way by subway back to the Bronx, Prazsky decided that tomorrow they would attend the funeral Mass. Levenda, too dazed to argue, nodded agreement. Arriving home late that night at his family's apartment on Revere Avenue, the old black-and-white Zenith television glowing with a bluish light as his mother slept on the couch, he stumbled into bed and fell asleep immediately, the enormity of what they had done not yet sinking in.

The next morning, in a rented limousine (which, they felt, would give them greater authority in passing through the barricades), they drove straight through to the Cathedral.

The police and Secret Service in attendance at the barricades saw the limo and did what bouncers and doormen everywhere do: they passed it on through. Prazsky and Levenda then proceeded to the Chancellery entrance, which was by now heavily guarded by both NYPD and federal agencies. Before them stood Roosevelt Grier, the former football player and Kennedy supporter who had been one of the men to jump Sirhan Sirhan at the scene of the assassination. They nodded at each other and exchanged pleasantries, while a Secret Service agent—identifiable by the lapel pin they all wore and the radio receiver in his ear—came up to them and asked, "Russian Orthodox representatives?" to which Levenda replied, in his best Slavic-accented English, "Slavonic Orthodox representatives." The agent nodded and began to lead them through what he called "a rather circuitous route" from the Chancellery, outside along a wall, and into the church itself, at which time he handed them off to another agent, who was accompanied by a Catholic prelate in charge of seating arrangements.

Prazsky and Levenda were the last "clergy" to arrive. This meant that they were placed at the ends of their respective pews . . . facing each other . . . *inside* the sanctuary!

To those who are not Catholic and are not of a generation to understand what that means, allow me to explain:

The two boys thought they were simply going to be seated somewhere in the church to watch the funeral. Prazsky, however, had gussied himself up as a bishop, wearing a heavy panagia and cross around his neck. Levenda was in his plainer outfit, but wearing a heavy cross around his neck as well. They appeared to be high-ranking clergy (at least Prazsky did), and they were admitted into an area of the church that was normally off-limits to anyone *but* clergy and their assistants: the sanctuary.

This is the part of the church that contains the altar where the Mass is performed. It is separated from the congregation by a communion rail with a gate, from which three steps descend onto the main floor. Inside the sanctuary at the time were the highest-ranking clergymen in America from Catholic, Protestant, and Orthodox denominations: archbishops, cardinals, etc. Little did they know that they were sharing pews with two seventeen-year-old high school students in homemade costumes.

Levenda sat in his pew in the front, facing the altar, trying not to tremble too noticeably under the unrelenting heat from the klieg lights. Across from him, on the other side of the altar, Prazsky attempted to stifle a smile. Other clergy began staring at them, wondering who the hell they were, but it was too late. The service had already begun.

Levenda felt a tap on his shoulder.

Fearing the worst, he turned slightly to see Andy Williams—the singer whose rendition of "Moon River" was famous at the time—asking him, "Am I on yet?" Levenda had no clue, so he shook his head no and returned to the service, sweltering under the heavy lights and casting quick glances out into the congregation where he could see the leaders of the free world gathered to pay their respects to the idealistic young senator who had won the California primary a few days earlier.

Levenda has said that what he learned from that experience was to "brass it out." Caught in a situation from which there is no possible escape and in which there is considerable danger to oneself, it is best to relax, gain as much self-control as possible, and keep an eye on the exit at all times. This he did.

Prazsky, on the other hand, learned another valuable lesson: you can fool some of the people some of the time, and that "some of the time" is usually enough.

They stood and sat at all the appropriate places. During the recitation of the Apostle's Creed, they observed the correct Orthodox practice of omitting the *filioque:* the phrase "and from the Son," which has caused so much dissension and death between Orthodox and Catholic denominations since the eleventh century, because the Orthodox believe that the Holy Spirit descends from the Father only, whereas the Catholics believe the Holy Spirit descends from the Father *and the Son.* This attention to detail is what contributed to their credibility as Orthodox priests for so long.

They listened to Ted Kennedy's poignant eulogy for his slain brother, reciting that phrase so beloved of Bobby, "You see things as they are, and say why? I dream of things that never were, and say why not?" (A beautiful sentiment, of course, but one that comes from the mouth of the Devil in George Bernard Shaw's play.)

Then Andy Williams stood up and went to sing the "Battle Hymn of the Republic." He was finally "on." So was Levenda and his co-conspirator, Prazsky.

Because of where they were seated, as the last ones in, they would be the first ones out.

Prazsky and Levenda, the two high-school-student gate crashers, *would lead the procession out of the Cathedral.*

This was an event being covered by all the nation's television networks, and much of the world's media as well. The cameras were whirring and the kleig lights burning. All eyes were on the first two clergymen to approach the senator's catafalque and begin the recessional. Who were they? What were the television journalists saying about them?

Levenda did not dare glance in Prazsky's direction. Instead, as Andy Williams began singing, Levenda began walking. In fact, he walked so fast that a Catholic clergyman in charge of ceremonial protocol sidled up next to him and begged him to slow down! Levenda dropped his pace a bit, and as Williams finished singing, Leonard Bernstein—in the choir loft above the main entrance to the Cathedral—struck up the Hallelujah Chorus from Handel's *Messiah.* This, as the great bronze doors of the Cathedral swung slowly and sedately open to reveal the statue of Atlas carrying the world on his shoulders across the street in Rockefeller Center. And here were Prazsky and Levenda, leading the way out of the ceremony with that majestic music behind them and the whole world, literally, before them.

As Levenda would later tell his friends in the years since, "It was better than a graduation ceremony." In fact, neither he nor Prazsky attended their high school graduations, nor did Levenda's photo appear in the high school yearbook.

They had not graduated yet, but they had clearly left their school years behind them.[1]

As the two left the Cathedral, they sought desperately for a way out and onto the street before they were asked any questions by security personnel. They took a path around the side of the church that they knew from their previous visit and nearly ran down Jacqueline and Rose Kennedy, who were taking the same route. Once again the two startled boys managed to say a few words of consolation before they continued on around the back of the church.

They had discharged their limo when they arrived—it cost them eighteen dollars, including the tip—and so they took the subway back to the Bronx and the incredulous stares of their parents and friends.

They had done it. They had breached the tightest security New York City—and possibly the country—had ever known, and had not only managed that, but also the incredible feat of sitting next to the altar during the ceremony, cheek by jowl with the most powerful clergymen in New York, and leading the procession out of the cathedral in front of America's political and social elite, under the eyes of the Secret Service and the world's press. And they were still seniors in high school, with no money, no jobs, no prospects, and the war in Vietnam looming large in their future.

A little later that summer, during another gate-crashing adventure where they invited themselves to the consecration of

---

[1] Ironically, Levenda always had a hard time leading church processions during his primary school years. Sister Agatha would shake him mercilessly when he failed to take the right twists and turns; as the shortest boy in school, he was always in front of the line (size places), so the burden of memorizing the procession plan invariably fell on him, and he never got it right. He wondered if Sister Agatha was watching that day.

the Armenian Cathedral in New York—an event that was presided over by the Catholicos of Armenia (the spiritual leader of the Armenians, and a man who had to get permission to leave what was then Soviet Armenia to come to the United States for the ceremony)—and attended by Mayor John Lindsay of New York City and his family, with whom they spoke as they stood in the Catholicos's dressing room prior to the service, they met an individual who would have an indirect effect on their lives: Bishop Lawrence Pierre of the American Orthodox Catholic Church.

Bishop Pierre—a heavyset black man redolent of lavender toilet water—handed them a card with his Church's address. Neither Levenda nor Prazsky had heard of such a Church, but it intrigued them and they followed up on it in the coming weeks. Had they been privvy to Warren Commission files and the files of the Garrison probe in New Orleans, however, they would have known that the American Orthodox Catholic Church was at that time being investigated for its possible role in the assassination of President John F. Kennedy.

There is no space here to go into all the background on this organization and its involvement in the Kennedy assassination case. Briefly, therefore, the American Orthodox Catholic Church (AOCC) had its origins in Eastern Orthodoxy, which was in disarray after the Russian Revolution. In the 1960s, Bishop Carl Stanley was one of the Church's leaders in the Midwest. He had participated in the consecration of Jack Martin and David Ferrie, two of the more notorious members of what New Orleans District Attorney Jim Garrison decided was a conspiracy of anti-Castro Cubans, right-wing zealots, intelligence agents (and others) to murder the President. Stanley himself, according to documents in the National Archives, was a convicted felon with a substantial rap sheet. He was under investigation by the FBI after the assassination, evidently because Stanley *himself* had reported on his relationship with Ferrie and Martin and his suspicions that the two men were involved in killing the President. Garrison picked up on these threads during his own investigation in 1967–68, and cast a wider net: eventually, he would be seeking to depose wandering bishops as far afield as Canada, including one Earl Anglin James, who had consecrated the bishop who consecrated Stanley in the first place. From the aristocratic Russian Orthodox Church Outside Russia to the somewhat sleazier American Orthodox Catholic Church, the ties to the Kennedy assassination were numerous and suggestive.

One of Stanley's associates, and the man who would take over the AOCC as its "patriarch" a few years later, was Bishop Walter Myron Propheta. Stanley was based in Kentucky at the time, and Propheta in the Bronx. It was only inevitable that Levenda, Prazsky, and Propheta should meet, and that took place in the summer of 1968, courtesy of Bishop Pierre.

Propheta was a hard-line anti-Communist who had supported Dewey during the campaign against President Truman.[2] A Ukrainian by birth, he had been a priest with the Ukrainian Orthodox Church—another staunchly anti-Communist organization, since the Ukrainian people had suffered tremendously under the Moscow regime, which had tried to exterminate their language and culture along with a number of their political activists—and had left that Church

---

[2] For a full discussion of the AOCC, Propheta, and "wandering bishops," see Levenda, *Sinister Forces, Book One: The Nine,* (Eugene, OR: Trine Day, 2005).

to form his own congregation. The reasons for this are a little murky, and may have had more to do with politics than religion, since leaving the Church led by Bishop Bohdan and joining a suspect group that has been dismissed by most commentators as a kind of "bishops mill" could not be seen as a particularly intelligent move.

The key word here is "intelligent," for it seems that the AOCC—particularly under Propheta—was just that: a front for an intelligence organization. As suspected by Jim Garrison, the AOCC was hand in glove with a number of covert intelligence operations being run in the United States and abroad, the Church providing "cover" in the form of authentic-looking religious documents, clerical outfits, and a widespread network of wandering bishops who for the most part were all rabidly right-wing. David Ferrie and Jack Martin were only the tip of the iceberg, for Propheta found himself involved in everything from the Biafran civil war to the Italian elections in the 1960s. One of his successors is now believed—by Italian military intelligence—to have been involved in money laundering for Serbian terrorists during the latest crises in Bosnia and Kosovo.[3]

Indeed, the AOCC was not the only such "wandering" denomination so involved. The Old Roman Catholic Church had connections to intelligence activities at home and abroad as well, including a famous hypnotist who was said to have been the man who "programmed" the assassin of Robert F.

---

[3] This would be the late Bishop DeValitch, a Serbian count with the AOCC who had ties to an infamous Serbian war criminal known as *Arkan* or "Archangel." DeValitch's church had provided money laundering and other services to Arkan and his Serbian warlords, according to SISMI, the Italian military intelligence organ. Prazsky and Levenda knew DeValitch personally as a charming and aristocratic gentleman, cultured and sophisticated, but with a whiff of Dracula about him.

Kennedy, Sirhan Sirhan.[4] When Levenda touched the coffin of Senator Kennedy in St. Patrick's Cathedral, had he unconsciously closed the circuit of wandering bishops involved in the Kennedy assassinations? (Ironically, it would be the energetic team of Prazsky and Levenda who would help form stronger links between Propheta's AOCC and the North American Old Roman Catholic Church under Bishop Hubert Augustus Rogers in Brooklyn's Brownsville section, when Prazsky was looking for a safe haven should the relationship with AOCC not work out).

The two seniors graduated high school in June 1968, only weeks after their "debut" at the funeral Mass for Senator Robert F. Kennedy. Wearing their religious costume, they would ride for free on mass transit (bus drivers rarely charged clergymen in those days), raise money as needed by blessing graves (a practice in which they would stand around in cemeteries on special occasions, such as Memorial Day or Mother's Day, and wait for people to approach them to ask for a blessing on a loved one's grave; this usually resulted in a donation of some kind, anything from a few coins to five dollars), and scheme for ways to expand their empire.

Levenda was in favor of continuing as they were, building a proper church, attracting a congregation, etc. Prazsky, however, had no use for congregations unless they were going to worship him. Plus, the Draft was blowing in the background. Prazsky was safe for the moment with a student deferment, but that wouldn't last more than the first semester. He needed cash to finance his scheme to build a "real"

---

[4] See William Turner and Jonn Christian, *The Assassination of Robert F. Kennedy,* (New York: Thunder's Mouth Press, 1993).

church that would serve as the buffer between him and the dirty, demanding world at large.

His solution was to forge a variety of documentation showing that he was attending Long Island University in an effort—hugely successful—to embezzle money from both his separated parents for nonexistent tuition and books. This money was then diverted to other, more worthy causes, as we have seen, such as antiques, ecclesiastical robes, and jewelry. Levenda's resources were somewhat more strained. His father had moved out and his mother was still unemployed, so money was very tight.

At the same time, they were both involved in studying the paranormal.

That two young men who were involved with setting up a church should simultaneously be preoccupied with the occult and the arcane is not as strange or contradictory as it may at first appear. Such combinations have a long and distinguished pedigree. The revered spiritual master G.I. Gurdjieff had studied to be an Orthodox priest before he became one of the Western world's most famous gurus. High-ranking members of the Theosophical Society were also bishops in a breakaway Old Catholic denomination. The OTO—one of Aleister Crowley's societies—also runs a Gnostic Catholic Church that was created by a group of wandering bishops in France. The history of occultism is replete with such examples. Prazsky's interest was purely mundane: if he could find treasure, or knowledge of things that others wanted to keep secret, he was in. Levenda's interest was more scientific: does magic work? Or, more accurately, what *is* magic? Is it psychology? Is it psychobiology? Is it some form of encrypted physics? Is it, like alchemy, an encoded system that can only be understood by actually practicing it?

Levenda continued to study occultism, looking for clues to the existence of hidden forces in nature, while Prazsky waited for the results. In the meantime they had other fish to fry.

The Bishops' Mill

Consulting the card presented to them by Bishop Pierre in front of the Armenian Cathedral that summer of 1968, they decided to try their luck and go calling on Walter Propheta and the AOCC. The church was headquarted in the Bronx, near Arthur Avenue and the Bronx Zoo. The two young men showed up one Sunday morning at the bizarre little "Cathedral of the Holy Resurrection," which was decorated with icons drawn in crayon. This is not to say that they were childish-looking cartoons, but expertly executed icons that seemed at first glance to have been painted in oils. There was Propheta in command of the ceremony, assisted by Bishop Leonard—an alcoholic who was fond of urinating out of windows—and Bishop John Christian Chiasson, a Canadian-born man, short and spry, with a wispy beard, perfect Canadian French, and a prancing, effeminate manner.

On any given Sunday, one could find various clergy of odd denominations showing up to entertain or be entertained by the infamous Propheta. This Sunday was like any other, and Prazsky and Levenda made their appearance known to Propheta and his cohorts. This was not difficult, as the two recent high school graduates were the only congregation in the church.

Churches of the "wandering" variety as a rule have no congregations. No one is really interested, not the local Christians—who already have their own denominations, be it Catholic, Protestant, or Orthodox—nor the bishops themselves, who have no use for congregations and all the fuss and

bother they represent. These men are not interested in saving
souls or promoting the Word of God. They are interested in
how good they look in a mitre and chasuble, or how genuine
their documents are . . . or appear to be. In Propheta's case,
there was another wrinkle. A congregation could be cumber-
some when it came to the intelligence work his group was doing. His operation could not stand a great deal of scrutiny,
and valuable time would be wasted if he had to worry about
births, deaths, and tormented souls. It was far easier to send
out Bishops Leonard and Christian every day to beg for donations among store owners in various towns outside of New
York City: in Westchester County, Connecticut, and New
Jersey. Propheta would stay home in the Bronx and cultivate
his own interests in relative peace while his henchmen
would bring in roughly five hundred dollars a week (in 1968
dollars) going door-to-door, raising funds for an orphanage
that did not exist.

(The American Orthodox Catholic Church had a long history of this. In 1945 three men who claimed to be clergy of
the Church were arrested on charges of raising money for a
nonexistent "mission" and for misrepresenting themselves
as related in some way to members of then Archbishop
Spellman's Roman Catholic Committee of Laity. A material
witness in the case, George Lanoway, aka Thomas Ryan,
was an ex-con with a rap sheet, mostly for burglary, going
back to 1916.)

In short time, both Prazsky and Levenda would find themselves on the well-worn panhandling route alongside Bishops Leonard and Christian, but not before being reordained,
and in Prazsky's case, being consecrated by Archbishop
Walter Propheta.

This is a common occurrence among the wandering bishops, who are never certain whether their previous ordinations

and consecrations are "valid." They go from church to church, sect to sect, getting reordained and especially reconsecrated in order to collect as many certificates as possible, thus proving that they are "real" bishops—in the sense that they would be recognized as such by Rome or, at the very least, by the Patriarch of Constantinople. In the case of the two high school grads from Columbus, this was done by Propheta, who claimed—naturally—that he had valid lines of apostolic succession and that his ordinations and consecrations were the best in the business. Whether he actually did is a matter of some conjecture even today.

Prazsky was consecrated; that is, made a bishop. He had decided to represent himself as a bishop of the Slavonic Orthodox Church, and Propheta had gone along with the idea, never realizing that the "bishop" was hardly more than a baby. As for Levenda, he suddenly found himself outranked by a kid whose homework he had to do to get him through high school. The whole idea of a partnership on equal terms was now fast disappearing as Prazsky elevated himself to greater and greater heights of sacerdotal frenzy. A rift was beginning to appear in their friendship, and it would take the arrival of yet another would-be bishop to emphasize the differences between them.

In the summer of 1968 a Liberal Roman Catholic priest made the obligatory appearance at the Cathedral of the Holy Resurrection in the Bronx. Father Andre Pennachio was a show-business cleric with 1950s-style matinee idol looks. He had friends and contacts throughout New York City's entertainment industry and indeed made a cameo appearance in Francis Ford Coppola's megahit, *The Godfather,* as a bishop overseeing the baptism of Michael Corleone's godson. In 1968, however, Pennachio was seeking advancement in his priestly status.

He had business cards and other paper litter attesting to the fact that he was a chaplain for the Department of Corrections, as well as a chaplain for the Teamsters Union. He claimed personal acquaintance with Joseph Konowe, a Teamster official in New York. He also introduced friends to cartoonist Harry Hirschfield, psychic and astrologer to the stars (including most especially Peter Sellers) Maurice Woodruff, comedian Lenny Kent, actress Thelma Carpenter, and a host of other B list celebrities. Prazsky and Levenda met them all, and more. While Pennachio was being held at arm's length by Propheta—for reasons that were never made quite clear—Prazsky latched onto him like a limpet.

At about this time, Prazsky also managed to inveigle his father to join the ranks of the wandering bishops. William Anthony Prazsky thus became Bishop Anthony Prazsky of the Slavonic Orthodox Church *and* the American Orthodox Catholic Church, thus giving the Prazskys veto power over Levenda, should it ever be required.

The four of them—Andrew Prazsky (who was by now foregoing the name Elefterij), Anthony Prazsky, Peter Levenda, and Andre Pennachio—began to scheme to set up their own ecclesiastical operation. With the two Prazskys as bishops, they only needed a third to retain a degree of autonomy, since Canon Law requires three bishops to ensure the consecration of a fourth.

Pennachio wanted desperately to be that bishop, and campaigned for it shamelessly. He set up a committee to raise funds for his consecration ceremony, something unheard of among the wandering bishops who generally become consecrated in relative obscurity. This would not be the case for the more flamboyant Andre Pennachio, who wanted a Broadway spectacle if possible; something in line with Andrew Prazsky's taste for public exposure and adulation. They also needed office space somewhere from which to manage the fund-raising effort away from Propheta's acquisitive gaze, so Pennachio came up with a location in downtown Manhattan: the offices of a company I shall call "DM Industries."

It was a strange choice. DM Industries was an import house specializing in wrought-iron outdoor furniture and sold only to the trade. There never seemed to be any customers visiting the showroom, however, and the offices themselves were luxurious. The owner, Harry K, was a flashy salesman type who wore a lot of gold jewelry and expensive suits. Pennachio, Prazsky, and Levenda spent hours at the office creating press releases, more stationery, and phoning potential sponsors, and never saw a single customer or heard any phone calls coming in. Pennachio knew what was up, but kept that mostly to himself until the whole thing exploded in May 1969.

Until that time, things went swimmingly for the four. Anthony Prazsky got a kick out of wearing ecclesiastical garb, but was really only at home when he was welding something or fixing someone's plumbing, which he eventually did at the cathedral of the Old Roman Catholic Church in Brooklyn, a venerable institution that owed its pedigree to some of the first wandering bishops in America, and with which Andrew Prazsky was forming relations, using his father's skill as a maintenance man as entrée. Andrew himself was glorying in his bishop status and fawning over Andre Pennachio, who was outrageously gay and enjoying every moment of his developing relationship with Andrew. To his credit, he did not suspect that Andrew Prazsky was only eighteen years old at the time.

Pennachio kept an apartment on the Grand Concourse in the Bronx, a spacious place with two bedrooms and a large,

sunken living room. He was married to a wealthy female patron who was nowhere to be seen: a marriage of convenience?
That made it possible for Prazsky and Pennachio to share
more than intimate glances and dreams of episcopal splendor.

They could be seen visiting a Manhattan nightclub called
The Living Room when comedian Lenny Kent was performing. Or at the retirement dinner for a naval officer in the
Brooklyn Navy Yard. Or at the television studios of Channel 5
in New York, where astrologer Maurice Woodruff had his
own show, predicting great things for Pennachio on the air.
Pennachio then introduced his young protégés to famous
sports personalities: wrestlers and prize fighters like Rocky
Marciano and Antonino Rocca.

It was Antonino Rocca's presence that gave the show away.

At a meeting held at the Brotherhood Synagogue in
Manhattan—a joint Jewish-Presbyterian site located in
Greenwich Village—Rocca met with Rabbi A. Allen Block,
Prazsky, Levenda, Pennachio, and others. Rocca detailed his
involvement with both American and Israeli intelligence at
this meeting, telling his astonished listeners that he was running agents in Beirut for the CIA, and running Phantom jets
illegally from Europe (principally Luxembourg) to Israel to
help build up the Israeli Air Force. He boasted that he had
men killed out from under his command in Lebanon, but that
he always managed to survive. He reassured the rabbis present that Israel would always remain secure and that the U.S.
government would always find a way to support Israel regardless of the domestic political situation.

What was Antonino Rocca—the Italian-Argentine heavyweight wrestling champion—doing telling these relative
strangers all this information? How much of it was true?
Why would he make up such a story, and why was he meeting

rabbis in the Village in 1968–69? Levenda, from whom this story was obtained, does not have any answers to these questions but insists that the Rocca episode was of a piece with the rest of the Pennachio saga, for DM Industries was also not quite what it seemed.

In October 1968, Peter Levenda came of age and was now eligible for the Draft. To Pennachio, this was a minor nuisance that could be remedied easily. He made a few phone calls, and weeks after Levenda formally registered for the Draft and was categorized as 1-A, the two met with a colonel of the Selective Service System at his office in downtown Manhattan. This particular colonel cultivated an Allen Dulles persona: replete with elbow patches and meerschaum pipe. He waved away the concerns of the two men, and like magic Levenda was now listed as 4-D, the coveted clergy deferment. He had beaten the Draft.

There was, however, a catch.

It was understood that Levenda would be acting as part of the "team" of right-wing, anti-Communist agents at the AOCC and available for such . . . assignments as needed.[5] This was not so much a formal request or *quid pro quo* as it was a suggestion. That the colonel meant business, however, will become clear later on in our story.

This was the time of massive anti–Vietnam war demonstrations and protests. Levenda was sympathetic to the aims of the demonstrators, a position that was not shared by his fellow "clergymen," who were all pro-military and anti-Communist. This is not to say that Levenda himself was a Communist or a Communist sympathizer; far from it. He

---

[5] This meant acting as an informer on the various churches and bishops with which he had contact, and to cooperate in whatever duties he was asked to perform. Most of these were mundane and had no obvious intelligence function.

did, however, believe the war was wrong. The assassinations of those political leaders who would have led the country away from Vietnam, from race hatred, and from social and political inequality, filled him with loathing and distrust of the powers and forces behind the scenes of American politics. He attended meetings of various antiwar groups, but found that most of them were too self-involved to be effective. Instead, he listened to members of the Weather Underground, the Black Panthers, the IRA, and other more radical organizations. And one day, leaving his home in the Bronx, he found himself being photographed by the driver of a car parked across the street from his family's apartment building on Revere Avenue.

These were also the days of the Red Squads and other covert action groups that spied on Americans who opposed the war. Levenda had been careful not to sign petitions, because he felt that, first, they were pretty useless as weapons for change, and second, signing them only served to identify the signatories to the Red Squads. He did not know how he'd come to be on someone's list, but there he was, staring into a telephoto lens. It would not be the last time.

As the politicking increased around Prazsky and Pennachio, Harry K's secretary let it slip to Levenda that he was being singled out for dismissal by the two men; that, in effect, they were planning to use him until the fund-raising efforts were accomplished and Pennachio consecrated, then find a way to get rid of him—to "cook his goose," according to the secretary. This information was only a confirmation of what Levenda had already suspected, and rather than allow himself to be exploited, he simply resigned from the church.

As far as he was concerned, except for the draft deferment, it had largely been a waste of time anyway. He was no further along in his studies, he was not making any money, and his home life was a shambles. It was time to get serious about his career. This happened in May 1969, but not before Levenda was elevated to the rank of Abbot on March second of that year.

With these dubious credentials under his belt, Levenda felt that the time had come to say good-bye. He simply disappeared from the intrigues at DM Industries . . . and then the insanity began.

Phone calls came day and night from persons connected to DM. Harry K himself called Levenda at home, trying to find out how much he knew and whom he had told. When everyone was satisfied that Levenda was not going public with what he'd seen and heard around either DM Industries, Andre Pennachio, or Walter Propheta, they breathed a sigh of relief and left him alone. The next phone call came from an American priest working for the Russian Orthodox Church Outside Russia, who in effect offered him a job working for him at his church in Connecticut. Although Levenda had never met the man or even known of his existence before that day, somehow the priest had his home phone number. It was a blatant attempt to keep him under some kind of surveillance or control, so he met the priest at a Chinese restaurant in the Bronx and basically told him that he was no longer interested in being involved with the heavily politicized Orthodox churches. The priest accepted his refusal and was heard from no more.[6]

Later that year, however, he received a letter from the Selective Service System, telling him that his 4-D deferment had been revoked. Levenda responded with a thinly veiled

---

[6] Oddly, another approach was made, this time concerning the Syrian Orthodox Church, but it seemed to have originated from an organization potentially hostile to American interests. Levenda again declined.

threat to expose what he knew, and the deferment was reinstated and remained on the books until the end of the Draft after the war.

Except for one brief and important episode, this was the end of Levenda's full-time involvement with the churches. Prazsky, however, went on to greater glory and in 1969 was reconsecrated by Archbishop Hryhorij ("Gregory") of the Ukrainian Autocephalous Orthodox Church (UAOC), a more prestigious and credible Orthodox Church with a valid pedigree. Hryhorij himself had been consecrated during World War II in Poland as he and some other members of the Ukrainian hierarchy fled to the leathery embrace of the Nazis as a means of opposing the native Ukrainian Orthodox Church, with its ties to Mother Russia and the Communist regime. It was an excellent move for Prazsky, for it legitimized him in the eyes of the other Orthodox, and Hryhorij actually made Prazsky his *successor*.

In 1970, and on the basis of these new changes, Prazsky formed another corporation, this time the Autocephalous Slavonic Orthodox Catholic Church of North and South America, Inc. This would be the church to which Fathers Hubak and Chapo belonged at the time of the rare book thefts that netted, among other valuable tomes, the *Necronomicon*.

I became involved with Prazsky's newly formed Autocephalous Slavonic Orthodox Church in 1972. At the time, he was busy spreading himself around the various ethnic Orthodox churches—Old Calendar Greek, Serbian, Syrian, Ukrainian—in an effort to further legitimize himself and to create a valid organization. He seemed to have been largely successful at this endeavor, attracting a number of prelates who were more or less legitimate and who had active congregations. Among them were monks and priests who, unlike their leader, had university educations and were fluent in a number of Eastern languages.

One of these was a man we mentioned at the beginning of this chapter, Father Fox, a myterious priest with intelligence connections. Fox had been all over the world during the course of his career, and ticket stubs and other paper litter shown to the author reveal his travels to Vietnam during the war, as well as to Middle Eastern countries and various European locales. This was a very busy priest. He also had a wife and child in the Bronx, to whom he wrote sporadically, and a close relationship with the Syrian Orthodox Church, which was the last denomination for which I have any record of Fox's involvement. But for a while he had a relationship with Prazsky and the Slavonic Orthodox Church, and this is what led, I was told, to the Hubak and Chapo affair.

Fox's relationship to Prazsky is not known to me in any detail. What is known is that Prazsky had in his possession a suitcase full of Fox's personal papers from which the above brief summary was extracted. This suitcase (given to him by Michael Hubak) was something of a hot property, and it went from hand to hand until it eventually vanished along with a number of other, unrelated, documents. Fox's existence, however, can be confirmed through newspaper accounts of his arrest at the Northern Ireland border and with the Syrian Orthodox Church and Fordham University.

That Fox might have been an intelligence agent of some kind is not too far-fetched. His travel records, his fluency in important foreign languages (important during the Cold War particularly), his ability to switch denominations as it suited him, and his demonstrated capacity for arms smuggling, all point to an intelligence function. It is assumed that he briefly joined up with Prazsky because of this intelligence agenda. Prazsky's name had become well-known in the circles frequented by Fox, and—during the Cold War—any church that had ties to Eastern Europe was targeted for penetration by domestic and foreign intelligence agencies. Prazsky's church claimed a Czechoslovak heritage, and in 1970 this was tantamount to claiming that you were a front, at least part-time: but for which side?

Michael Hubak (whose family name has been spelled "Hubiak" as well) was forty-five years old in 1972, and had been around Eastern Orthodoxy for awhile. Although the *New York Times* articles on the rare-book thefts identifies him as a member of Prazsky's church, by the time of the arrest he had already flirted with the Russian Orthodox Church Outside Russia and other Orthodox denominations. He was well-known to Father Fox, and the rumor current at the time of his arrest was that he and Fox had fought over a love interest, and that being set up to take the fall for the rare-book thefts was Fox's way of getting even. I have been unable to verify the truth of that rumor, except to say that Hubak and Fox were known to each other before the arrests and disliked each other intensely.

It is not known exactly when young Steven Chapo first teamed up with Hubak, but when I met the team at Prazsky's request in 1972—pretending to have a background in bookbinding—they were operating a "chapel" above a top-less bar on Hillside Avenue in the Jamaica section of Queens, New York. The chapel was ambitiously called "St. Stephen's Monastery," but was actually a one-bedroom apartment with windows overlooking the street and the flow of custom to the bar. In the rear of the apartment, in the kitchen, was a large device atop the stove that was used to steam the library watermarks from the books. Another device was used to eradicate any ink stamps that might have been found to indicate the book's lawful ownership. In the front of the apartment was the chapel itself: a modest table serving as an altar and a few icons. The rest of the apartment contained piles of . . . books.

These piles were sometimes quite large and quite old. In some, maps and illustrations had been removed for separate sale. This is a crime of some magnitude in the eyes of book lovers and collectors. To destroy a book in order to sell off individual pages is beyond belief. I reported all this to Prazsky the next day, who nodded sagely as if he suspected it all along, and then he showed me *his* collection.

3: The Discovery of the *Necronomicon*

Prazsky was adept at handling social situations, especially when his audience were men of like-minded nature: other schemers, preferably in ecclesiastical robes, preferably gay. Outside of that milieu he was not so popular or successful. He was also not educated enough to handle some of the day-to-day work required of a church—even a church as dubious as his—and he noticed the lack of a Levenda to help him prepare press releases, write up the rituals, write and send letters to other churches, government agencies, and the media. He couldn't hire someone to do this; in the first place, the Prazskys were not that wealthy and they did not have an actual congregation whose donations would pay the bills. In the second place, Prazsky trusted no one.

As stated, Levenda left the church in 1969 after the DM Industries affair, and Prazsky had rushed to consecrate Andre Pennachio a bishop on October 12, 1969, the birthday of Aleister Crowley (as well as Columbus Day, a convenient date for an Italian-American priest being consecrated by an occultist bishop). Pennachio, however, disappeared soon afterward, evidently after a falling out with Prazsky, whose thirst for control had extended over Pennachio to the extent that Pennachio felt insulted, if not humiliated, at his cavalier treatment by the nineteen-year-old "bishop" and paramour.

By 1972, however, Prazsky was attempting to patch things up with Levenda, who by then had had several jobs, his own apartment, and was independent and self-supporting, a bourgeois existence that Prazsky secretly despised. Levenda's involvement with the Warlock Shop began as soon as the store opened, in June 1972. He lived in Brooklyn Heights and had worked there awhile for Spencer Memorial Presbyterian Church, using Rabbi Block of the Brotherhood Synagogue as a reference. The shop had become a magnet for all of us, including two other clergy of Prazsky's church, Fathers Jay and Roger, two gay Slavonic Orthodox priests who were renovating a tumbledown brownstone in Fort Greene, not too far from the Warlock Shop. This accident of geography would prove fortuitous, for it introduced Jay and Roger to us and thus provided another link back to Prazsky. Levenda was cautious in his dealings with Prazsky, and frankly, never trusted him again. He came to learn, however, that his former friend had developed quite an occult book collection through his strange and complex relationship with Michael Hubak and Steven Chapo.

Before the arrests of the monks in 1973, we had occasion to examine Prazsky's collection in some detail. In order to entice us with his plan for spying on Hubak and Chapo—and for dragging Levenda back in to handle the bothersome paperwork that was piling up, including applications for knighthoods and other paper dignities that had to be translated from or into a variety of European languages—he opened his barrister-style bookcases and removed volumes of rare and antique books on occult subjects. Many of these were also in foreign languages, and while Prazsky was conversant in Czech and somewhat in Slovak, and could muddle through the Church Slavonic alphabet for liturgical purposes, when it came to Latin, Italian, French, and German, he was at a loss, especially if the books were printed hundreds of years ago and required a specialist's mastery of the tongues.

Many of these volumes—worn and dusty as they were, with fragile pages and worm-eaten covers—were of little use to a practicing occultist of today. They were old studies of astrology, palmistry, and other forms of divination whose novelty lay more in their handsome line drawings and engravings than they did in actual information. For an historian of the occult, they would have been invaluable, but Levenda was interested more in whatever unique references he could uncover and specific details concerning the methods used by the medieval sorcerers and magicians in their rites. Some of the titles were well-known to us in English translations or in readily available foreign language editions, such as those by Alan Kardec on spiritualism, or the first three books of Cornelius Agrippa (held by Prazsky in a handsome German printing). The twenty-two-year-old, an archbishop now, had other items in his collection that were far more interesting to us, although they were a mystery to Prazsky himself.

One of these, to make a long inventory short, was a handwritten manuscript in a large cardboard box like the type libraries use to hold precious books whose bindings are falling apart. The mouse-gray box was tied with green string. When we untied it, we beheld a pile of loose pages, written in demotic Greek. The title told us the package we held in our hands was called *Necronomicon*.

We did not know what it was.

Prazsky, attempting to appear cosmopolitan and literate, sounded out the name. He assumed, as we did, that it had something to do with the dead, *nekros* being the Greek prefix meaning "dead" or "death," as in *necropolis:* a city of the dead, a cemetery.

"Nekro?" he said, between puffs of a cigarette that was lingering dangerously close to the dry and somewhat brittle manuscript. "Death? *Nomikon? Nekronomikon.* Dead Names," he pronounced, with more authority than he had. The suffix *nomikon* does not mean "names" in Greek, as it sounds in English or Latin, but refers instead to "law" or "legal." The suffix, however, has a wider application. In the case of a word like *astronomikon,* for instance, the idea is "pertaining to" as in "pertaining to the stars," a suffixed form of *astronomia. Nekronomikon* could simply mean "about the dead" or "pertaining to the dead." But somehow the Prazsky "translation" stuck, and we began to refer to the book among ourselves as "Dead Names."

We were interested in looking through the pages, and removed the box to the desk in Prazsky's office, setting it down carefully and lifting the pages out one at a time.

As Orthodox clergymen, we had a working knowledge of Greek. The Russian (Cyrillic) alphabet is a derivative of the Greek alphabet, as is the alphabet known as Church Slavonic. The Cyrillic (or Kyrillic) alphabet gets its name from St. Cyril, who was a Greek missionary involved in the conversion of the Slavs to Christianity. As the Slavs had no written language at the time, St. Cyril invented an alphabet for them based on his own language. Thus, it is not too difficult for a reasonably educated Russian Orthodox layman or priest to read Greek writing. The problem, of course, is not so much in reading the alphabet as in understanding the grammar and vocabulary. We realized we would not be able to translate the thing on the spot, and simply turned more pages until we came to the strange drawings and seals in the rest of the book.

These were compelling and exotic. While they shared something in common with seals and sigils we had seen in other grimoires, these were pointedly different in many respects. There was something oddly asymmetrical about them, and the total lack of Hebrew writing was itself an indication that we were holding something rare, indeed.

Most European grimoires available to the general public have strange seals and sigils. Many of these can be found to contain at least a few Hebrew or Roman letters. The seals in this manuscript did not. But one of the seals contained Greek letters that spelled out INANNA. We could sound it out, but did not have a clue what it meant. It sounded a little like a "barbarous name," that is, a seemingly meaningless grouping of sounds whose pronounciation—like that of a Hindu mantra—holds within itself an occult efficacy.

It was Levenda who finally realized what that name meant, but he said nothing in front of Prazsky.

Prazsky was not that eager to find out what the manuscript was. He felt that it was strange and unusual, to be sure, but the other volumes in his possession were so much more interesting and beautiful to look at. After some negotiation, we managed to wrest the box away from him for a short time so we could have some of it translated. There was a quid pro quo, of course—that we continue to spy on Hubak and Chapo in Queens, and that Levenda do some office scutwork at the Slavonic Orthodox Church in the Bronx. This arrangement was informal but nonetheless ironclad. At least it allowed for a more complete examination of the manuscript in relative peace.

We had offered (halfheartedly) to find an expert and have him or her come to the church office to look at the manuscript in Prazsky's presence if he so desired, but that would have cramped his style and he demurred. He trusted us with the book because after all it was stolen, we knew it was stolen, and we knew who stole it. We were not about to go blabbing to the media or the police. Hubak and Chapo had not been arrested as yet—that would not take place for months—and so we felt a little like accessories after the fact even having the book in our possession. Also, Prazsky knew that Levenda would be much more interested in the grimoire itself than in "dropping a dime" and calling the police. The book was relatively useless to Prazsky because it was not beautifully bound or illuminated. He was not so stupid as to think it was valueless, but at the moment he had far more valuable items in his collection. We would have to be very careful about who could see the book, or even who could know we had access to it. At the time, that did not seem like a terribly onerous responsibility because as far as we knew the book was only an interesting grimoire with an uncertain pedigree. Looking back, we were wise in keeping its existence as secret as we did.

Critics of the *Necronomicon* have insisted that the monks—Hubak and Chapo—who had stolen so many books from around the country did not steal the *Necronomicon* because it was not mentioned in the handful of news stories that accompanied their arrest. Naturally, the news people focused on the ancient atlases and other extremely valuable works that had been missed by the libraries and collectors because a dollar value was easy to assign to these items. The media *never* published an entire inventory of the swag, which included more than eighty "ancient books, atlases and *manuscripts*"[1] since November 1970 from Yale University

---

[1] Lawrence Fellows, "Two Unfrocked 'Byzantine Priests' Held in Yale Rare-Book Thefts," *New York Times,* March 17, 1973, 1 (emphasis added)

alone. And there are many libraries in the United States that have files on Hubak and Chapo and the rare-book thefts, for the two men scoured the nation in search of rare and valuable commodities in both public and private collections. The list of universities reads like a college directory: the University of Chicago, Fordham University, Dartmouth, Harvard, Northwestern, Notre Dame, and others. Indeed, neither Hubak nor Chapo would have known what the *Necronomicon* was beyond an interesting occult curio. Their focus was on the expensive printings, the elaborate maps, the heavy illustrations that would fetch top dollar from collectors. They stole the occult works on behalf of their mentor and sponsor, Prazsky, because that seemed to be his interest and the best way to keep him happy and satisfied. Further, neither monk revealed to the media the books that were held by Prazsky because they would need him later. They had already given the authorities quite a list, in their desire to cooperate fully. (It is my belief that they also kicked back some of the money they earned to Prazsky, as he was chronically short of cash.) In addition, and as Prazsky related it to me, some of the materials in his possession did not come from university libraries but from unnamed individuals, some of whom would not have been able to go to the police to report them missing without drawing unwelcome attention upon themselves.

These were criminal elements who had an interest in the occult as strong as Prazsky's; even stronger, for they were actively involved in cult practices. They were wealthy and could afford to purchase (or otherwise obtain) rare grimoires and other occult works in addition to the normal prey of collectors: rare Bibles, atlases, Asian scriptures, ancient pornography, and erotica. The individuals behind the famous Son of Sam cult were included in this category of well-heeled private collectors. Whether the *Necronomicon* manuscript itself came from one of these collections or from a university collection is unknown to me, since Prazsky certainly would have never revealed any information of this kind. What is known is that the cardboard box in which the manuscript was contained did not bear the title *Necronomicon,* but only what appeared to be a lot number on a small white label, with a European form of the numeral 7. My assumption is that it was a box among boxes in someone's private library, or perhaps in a university collection, that had been identified by some other means, such as "Greek manuscript of unknown author" or something like that. Levenda's theory was that the manuscript had been stolen in Europe—hence the number 7 with the horizontal line drawn through it—during the race of the German armies through the East during the war, at which time they seized entire collections of art, books, and manuscripts from public and private collections in Poland, Czechoslovakia, Hungary, Russia, Ukraine, etc. Much of this loot has never been recovered and languishes in secret archives and private collections all over the world. A theft of any one of these items would go unreported by its owner, for its provenance is shaky at best and would lead to large troves of ill-gotten treasures better left undisturbed by the glare of public scrutiny.

It was Levenda, sitting in Prazsky's office in the Bronx, who realized that the Greek inscription on one of the seals—INANNA—was indeed the name of an ancient Sumerian deity. His excitement was due to the supposed fact that no one who authored a manuscript this old could have known about Inanna, since nothing was known about the Sumerians until well *after* the manuscript had been written. (I say "supposed fact" because now it is known that some peoples in the Mideast and India have kept the weak flame of this knowledge alive and flickering in their own hermetic traditions, but we were not to know this until much, much later.) We could not be sure that this meant anything at all; perhaps it was a coincidence that the name was also a Sumerian goddess: it could have meant something entirely different in another language. We just didn't know.

We had also never heard of the fictional *Necronomicon*, since we had not come to the occult through comic books and fantasy magazines, but through other avenues. That honor went to Herman Slater of the Warlock Shop, for when we told him what we had found, he nearly had a heart attack.

The Horror of Red Hook

In June 1972, in a tiny, narrow wooden storefront building near the corner of Atlantic Avenue and Henry Street in Brooklyn Heights—a store wedged between two larger brick buildings and looking as out of place as its new tenant—a strange man with a cast in his eye, a pronounced limp, and a handsome black seluki named Ptolemy, set up shop. His store carried a variety of dusty herbs in even dustier glass jars on rickety wooden shelves nailed to white-washed, exposed brick walls, a handful of worn pamphlets on crystal-gazing and tea-leaf reading in rusted magazine racks, some Tarot decks, a few black, hooded robes on hangers . . . and a human skull in the window. The Warlock Shop was in business.

Herman Slater was the owner and proprietor of this decidedly bizarre establishment at the edge of a neighborhood that from time to time boasted residents like Norman Mailer, Norman Rosten, Brad Steiger, Claire Bloom, Walt Whitman . . . and H.P. Lovecraft. In fact, Lovecraft had lived only two blocks away during the very brief time he was married and not living in Providence, Rhode Island. It was his sojourn in Brooklyn that was the inspiration for one of his famous short stories, "The Horror at Red Hook," Red Hook being a neighborhood somewhat to the south of Brooklyn Heights and along the docks that leer out over the East River.

In 1972, Atlantic Avenue was also home to a large Arab community and hosted restaurants serving cuisine from Morocco, Lebanon, Yemen, and other regions of the Middle East. There was a music store specializing in recordings of Fairuz and other popular Levantine stars, a shop selling spices and Arab pastries, and another with brass lamps and the carved blades of the *khanjar* knife. Above one shop was the local headquarters of the Red Crescent Society, the Islamic equivalent of the Red Cross; and in some of the back rooms money was raised to help the Palestinian refugees . . . and the PLO. It was a street located in New York City, but which really existed at the edge of Lovecraft's own paranoid universe. Now, with the addition of the Warlock Shop, it was as if he had never left Brooklyn; had never died in 1937 in Providence, Rhode Island, but had instead gone retail at the outskirts of loathsome Red Hook.

As he told it to me, Herman Slater had first encountered the stories of H.P. Lovecraft while he was recuperating from hip surgery. He devoured stories of gothic horror as well as science fiction and fantasy, but mostly horror. Herman had suffered from tuberculosis in his hip and the replacement surgery had given him a limp. He also had an eye that stared off into space at roughly right angles to the rest of his face, so that you never knew where exactly he was looking: at you, or somewhere else. Herman Slater was also gay, a flagrant homosexual when he wanted to be flagrant, a flaming queen when he was in the mood, a transvestite in gay revues wearing mounds of taffeta and satin and layers of stage

makeup that made his Henry Kissinger–like features look by
turns matronly and auntlike . . . or positively frightening.
While he was devoted to gothic horror and the occult, he was
also a window to the world of the leather bar and the bathhouse, in the days before AIDS made all of it dangerous; in
the days when the threats came more from police raids on
Christopher Street gay bars than from the act of love itself.
Herman Slater was a denizen of the demimonde, the nether-
world, whether of sex or of religion, or even of politics. (In
his youth, he had interviewed neo-Nazis such as occultist,
and fascist, James Madole of the National Renaissance Party
in New York.)

Balding, limping, cockeyed, gay, and a pagan warlock . . .
Lovecraft could not have created Herman Slater, not even in
his wildest imagination. Yet, he was probably one of the
most decent, most genuine human beings this author has
ever encountered. Perhaps it was his "outsider" status—to
borrow a term from Colin Wilson—that made him particularly sensitive to the vulnerabilities of others and more ac-
cepting than most. He was also an inveterate gossip, a
troublemaker for the sake of making trouble whom no one
could stay mad at for very long. It was no accident that the
truce in the famous "witch wars" of the early 1970s was settled in the back room of the Warlock Shop, with some of the
most prominent members of the Craft of various disciplines
in attendance.

To those who are interested in this fascinating moment of
New York City history, I can do no better than to refer them
to issues of an occult magazine, *Behutet,*[2] which provides an
oral history of Herman Slater, the Warlock Shop, and its
successor, Magickal Childe. It is probably the most accurate

---

[2] See the Web site www.thelesis.org, especially numbers 10 and 11.

and informative of all the reports I have seen. What I will give here is only a summary, for it is necessary to know something about this man and his influence over the American occult community to understand the history of the *Necronomicon*.

We can start with the witch wars.

The witch wars came about due to a tremendous amount of infighting among the leaders of various witch covens as these early groups attempted to define "witchcraft" in terms of their own version. For instance:

The Gardnerian groups adopted the "skyclad" practice of conducting their rituals—their monthly lunar esbats and their eight major sabbats—in the nude. This was due to Gerald Gardner's own idiosyncracy, and indeed, the term "skyclad" comes from Gardner's sojourn in India and Malaya, where Kali is sometimes worshipped as a goddess "clothed only in the sky." (Somehow, the American Gardnerians were under the assumption that "skyclad" was a particularly charming Britishism among hereditary witches.) The Traditionalists—the Irish, Welsh, etc.—conducted their rituals clothed, in ceremonial robes. The Hereditaries—those who claimed to have been born into witchcraft and raised by witches—often conducted their rituals in street clothes and in fact often did not consider their practices religious at all but more along the lines of traditional healing, cursing, etc.

Another bone of contention was determining who was a "real" witch and who was not. This was fought over which version of the Book of Shadows was genuine and from whom—from which particular high priestess—it was received. (This is similar to the fights over "apostolic succession" that preoccupy members of the various "wandering bishop" denominations in Europe and America.)

Further, some members of some covens were banished

from their groups for various reasons. One of these reasons was often cited as "not in harmony"; for example, so-and-so was "not in harmony" with the high priestess. This may have been due to personal problems between them, or a suspicion that a member was agitating politically against the high priestess, or any number of other issues. (In most of these covens, the high priestess was the ultimate authority, the high priest being the one who "drew down the Moon" into the high priestess so that she became possessed by the Goddess.) These banished persons often went and formed their own covens, or joined other covens, which were then assumed to be somehow at odds with the previous coven, and then magical spells were cast against each other in a kind of occult warfare.

Then there was the basic insecurity of all of the various witch covens in America at the time: which tradition was "real" and which was invented? Some covens declared themselves to be more real than others, and this led to obvious resentments between them.

And then disaffected members of one or more covens began to break off and form entirely different "traditions," such as Minoan, Etruscan, Egyptian, and others. These groups were based on close reading of popular histories of various ethnic and religious entities, even though the creators of these groups had no ethnic or other link whatever to the originals.

The last problem for the witchcraft revival in America was the decision by some of these witches to recognize or become somehow affiliated with satanic cults. While this happened rarely, it did happen that some "witches" broke off and joined the Church of Satan or some other such cult viewed with opprobrium by the pagan community at large. Others became involved with ceremonial magic, a practice that some priests and priestesses tried to discourage since magic was considered (a) Judeo-Christian and (b) somehow dangerous to those not properly trained in the three degrees of witchcraft, the third degree being that of the high priest or high priestess itself.

There was also the question of "gay" witchcraft. If Wicca, as properly understood by those creating it, was a blending of the male and female polarities of nature—as represented by the God and the Goddess, the Priest and the Priestess— then what was the rationale for a gay coven in which all members would be either men or women? Some of the covens—particularly those in and around Long Island, New York, where part of the allure of witchcraft was romping in the nude with your neighbor's wife—were against the idea of a totally homosexual coven; yet, a gay member of a straight coven could often be considered "not in harmony" with the group and would eventually leave.

All of these issues became irrelevant as the blossoming of various covens covering every possible permutation sexually, ethnically, and otherwise took place, but not before emotions ran high and the various factions found them-selves "at war" with each other. Witches burned telephone wires as well as candles during this period, and Herman Slater found himself the clearinghouse for all of the fighting and gossip.

As the most famous store of its kind in the United States—Slater was interviewed frequently by local and na-tional news media, particularly around Halloween—as well as in the world, where his shop was reviewed in Italian, Spanish, French, and German newspapers and magazines, he became a kind of de facto spokesman for witchcraft. He developed long and enduring friendships with some of the most important leaders, and his live-in lover, Ed Buczynski, was a high priest of the Welsh Traditionalist variety.

Ed was a charming, charismatic young man with the blond good looks and raunchy attitude of a rock star. The two could not have been more opposite in physical appearance, but between them they were a magnet for Wiccan politicking and gossip. Another local celebrity was Leo Martello, the promoter of Italian witchcraft, or *strega.* Martello claimed Sicilian origins and was the author of popular books on witchcraft, psychic self-defense, and other themes; a kind of Mediterranean Sybil Leek. Martello was also gay, which gave him some common ground with the group that was forming around the Warlock Shop. There was also Mary Nesnick, Lady Theos and Phoenix of Long Island, Gavin and Yvonne Frost, Patricia and Arnold Crowther, Alex and Maxine Sanders; the unruly pagans around publications like *Green Egg, Nemeton, Pentagram,* and others, like the pagan newsletter for young people, *Mandragore;* and of course the Bucklands. British representatives like the Crowthers and the Sanderses communicated by mail and phone; the Frosts were generally not present at the Brooklyn store since they were avoided by most members of the Craft, but the others were common sights around Brooklyn Heights at the time of the "witch wars." Buckland himself had complained, in print, about the lack of *bona fides* of many of the covens that were pretending to be "real" witches. The claim of Alex Sanders to be a real witch, initiated as a child, was suspect since his Book of Shadows was largely a copy of the Gardnerian version, which itself was an invention. What was taking place was the painful and gradual realization by everyone involved with the Craft that modern Wicca was based largely on a kind of hoax perpetrated by Gerald Gardner. That no one could claim to be a real witch as such was finally commonly understood, but was the Gardnerian Book of Shadows a forgery or an invention?

Did it matter?

Eventually, by late 1973 and early 1974, the witch wars came to an uneasy truce in the back room of the Warlock Shop, Herman Slater presiding like a Jewish matchmaker over the proceedings. Rosemary Buckland's influence was both elevating and calming; her husband, Raymond, quiet and thoughtful. As the highest-ranking Gardnerians in terms of actual proximity to the late Gerald Gardner himself, their influence held tremendous weight. Gradually, the covens stopped fighting with each other—except for the occasional skirmish that developed more as a result of personal "disharmonies" among members than any real doctrinal differences—and learned to live and let live. It was realized that solidarity among pagans in the face of government and religious persecution was more important than any theological hair-splitting over robed versus skyclad or Gardnerian versus Traditionalist. Some pagans in the United States, particularly in small-town America, were "outed" at their jobs and had come under discrimination, several attempting suicide, some successfully. Others had been fired, ostensibly for their pagan beliefs. And, of course, there were the gay witches who had already suffered discrimination in their lives due to their sexuality and who were particularly sensitive to the potential for persecution and a return of the "burning times." This was during Vietnam, when there was already an anti-establishment movement in America. The idea that government might actually crack down on witches—as absurd as it seems today—was considered a very real possibility then, with both the Manson killings and the Kent State massacre fresh in everyone's minds.

As the political climate in the United States turned from the Vietnam War to the the Watergate scandal, there was increasing tension in the pagan groups due to a fear that American police or intelligence agencies had been spying on them. From Red Squads to "mind control," every government organization became suspect of trying to penetrate the cults. News reports showing that the FBI, for instance, had successfully infiltrated right-wing hate groups like the Ku Klux Klan raised the stakes for the pagans. Neo-Nazi groups like the National Renaissance Party—a political sect with an openly occult agenda—had tried to form alliances with both the Klan as well as the Church of Satan. Thus, were FBI agents or informers involved in infiltrating the covens as well?

This type of paranoia—whether with basis in reality or without—fueled a certain type of occultist because, after all, occultism is by its very nature paranoid. Occult theory posits the existence of hidden forces and invisible connections in the world of reality, forces that can be manipulated by the skillful magician. Thus, if I can manipulate these forces— goes the story—then obviously so can others. Who are the "others" and what are they up to?

Herman Slater's favorite customers were not the witches. Normally, their purchases were few: a blank notebook to use as a diary or to create a coven's Book of Shadows; some herbs; some candles. Very few books. And the Gardnerian "skyclad" covens didn't even use robes. They all used some ritual implements, such as a pentacle for "drawing down the Moon," but these were shared by the whole group. Aside from a personal knife, called an "athame," individual witches were not obligated to own this equipment themselves. The big buyers, in Herman's experience, were the ceremonial magicians.

Magicians—although they normally tended to operate alone and not in groups—needed a lot more equipment: robes, candles, incense, swords, knives, etc. And a lot of books. The thirst of magicians for books is unquenchable. They need rituals, and the search for rituals that are easier to perform or more powerful than others is ongoing. Some medieval rituals require lengthy and expensive preparations that most modern-day magicians either cannot afford or cannot meet due to arcane regulations. Also, there is always the fear that a certain ritual has somehow been compromised by having been translated incorrectly or incompletely. Some of Herman's customers wound up spending thousands of dollars in his store on equipment and books over the course of several months. Some of the equipment was in the form of consumables like candles and herbs, but for the most part they were high-ticket items like magic swords and heavy, occult jewelry fashioned of specific metals, from gold and silver at one end to tin and nickel and copper at the other. Herman also sold magic mirrors, to be used for divination and speaking to spirits, as well as a comprehensive collection of crystal balls. His selection of Tarot decks was second to none in the city, and every time a new form of divination was available—runes or I Ching coins or a host of other forms—the first place to carry it was the Warlock Shop.

Eventually, a market in ready-made occult seals was developed. These are based on the exotic designs that can be found in such medieval spellbooks—grimoires—as the *Black Pullet*, the *Red Dragon*, the *Keys of Solomon*, etc. Fashioned as jewelry, an aspiring magician could purchase one or all of these and use them in rituals—after the proper consecrations and incantations, of course. Satanists would come into the shop and order statues of the Goat of Mendes (a famous Satanic icon), reverse pentagrams, and other intimidating jewelry and statuary, as well as Anton LaVey's famous *Satanic Bible.*

During this time, in the early 1970s, Herman asked me to source grimoires for him. Knowing of my ability in foreign languages, his strategy was that I would locate European grimoires in their original tongues. I would find these being sold in foreign language bookstores in New York City, and they were often quite expensive. One such store was located at Rockefeller Center, and they could always be counted on to have some grimoires stashed somewhere in their shelves. These editions were usually quite small in size, smaller than a digest, rather more like a prayerbook. They were available in French, Italian, Spanish, and Latin. And, of course, the New York Public Library had a few. The Rare Book Room of the Forty-second Street Main Branch had some valuable editions of Trithemius, one of which became a slim, photocopied volume Herman published called *Magickal Alphabets,* with an introduction in both English and German. I had painstakingly copied the relevant alphabets myself after a few afternoons spent at the library. Another became a book on runes.

He would sell some of these grimoires in his shop to those who could read and understand them in their original language; at the same time, I would translate them for English-language publication. These eventually included the *Black Pullet* and the *Red Dragon,* mentioned above; but the most infamous contribution to the literature was, of course, the *Necronomicon.*

Herman was the logical person to consult on the topic of the mysterious Greek manuscript. He was not an antiquarian or an expert on occult texts, but he would have an idea of the worth of the thing and might even know another expert who would be able to shed some light on the provenance of the book, or at least give it some kind of historical or magical context. We did not want to show him the book, fearing he would make off with it or hand it around to whoever would be in the store at the time: old lovers, current lovers, prospective lovers. We also did not want to expose what was obviously a physically fragile artifact to the careless hands and noxious herbal fumes of the shop. However, there was no other way around the problem. Herman would actually have to see the manuscript before he could suggest what to do with it and tell us if it would be worth anyone's while to go to the time and expense of getting it translated.

With great trepidation, I carried the box into the shop on Henry Street in late 1972, only six months after the opening of the store.

There was a clang of the cowbells that Herman used as a door chime, and the smell of burning incense. Herman himself was modeling one of his ceremonial robes with the hood over his head. With his unique facial construction with the one staring eye, he looked like a character actor from the old film, *Horror Hotel,* about a modern coven of New England witches. We chatted about this and that, and then I showed him the box.

"What do you make of this?" I asked, untying the green string.

His eyes widened at the sight of the old manuscript.

"What is it?" he asked. "How old is it?"

"It's some kind of grimoire. It's written in Greek, but it's difficult to decipher. Some of it doesn't even appear to really be Greek, even though Greek letters are used. I guess it's quite old. Six, seven hundred years at least. Maybe more."

"Where did you steal it?" he asked, mischievously enough, but my heart skipped a beat.

"Uh, I didn't steal it, actually, but someone else might have. I really can't hold onto it for very long in any event. I just wanted to know if we should bother with trying to get it deciphered or translated. I mean, is there a market for something like this? It will take a while to get the thing done. I mean, look at it. There are a lot of pages here, and I haven't even counted them or even seen them all. And I don't know how long I can keep it before I have to give it back. Is there someone we can show this to, someone with a keen sense of discretion?"

Herman thought about it a minute.

"Well, there's a Crowley collector on the Upper East Side. He spends a fortune buying Crowley first editions and Golden Dawn diaries. He's loaded. He might know what to do with it, but he'll probably want to buy it."

"I can't sell it. It's not mine. Anyway, it looks interesting. I wish I had enough time to look at it."

"Why don't you photocopy it?"

"I thought of that, but the pages are so fragile, and anyway I would have to do it myself. I couldn't take it to a printer to have it done. And I don't have access to a photocopy machine right now."

We stared down at the box, shifting some of the pages to look at others. Herman was entranced by the drawings.

"What does it say on the first page? Does it have a title?"

"Yeah, but I'm not even sure it is the title. The first word, here, is a Greek word, *Necronomicon.*"

"You're full of shit!"

Herman didn't shout this so much as he whispered it in awe.

"What do you mean?"

"You must be joking."

He must have realized that my blank stare was genuine, for he lowered his voice and motioned me into the back room, through the beaded curtain, and into the kitchen, where he had a small, round, zinc-topped table with wrought-iron chairs.

I went inside and sat the box down on the table.

"Are you sure that's what it says? *Necronomicon*?"

"Sure. Of course. Why would I lie about that?"

"I mean, it doesn't really say 'necrophilia' or 'necromancy'?"

"Herman, it's very clear. *Necronomicon*. You can see for yourself, the capital letters are not that different from the Roman alphabet."

"Someone is putting you on. This has to be a fake. There is no *Necronomicon*. It's a kind of joke. It isn't real."

"Then what's this?"

"I have no idea. Maybe somebody is just trying to put you on." As he said this, however, he voice trailed off and his eyes grew narrow. I could sense a native shrewdness, something I knew Herman had in abundance, a quality he shared with Prazsky.

"But it doesn't matter anyway."

"Herman, I really don't know what you're talking about."

"Don't they teach you anything in seminary except how to perform oral sex on bishops?" Herman had the greatest respect for me and my position within the Church, but he also had a wicked sense of humor and knew that he could not get a rise out of me anyway, so he sometimes baited me with jokes of the "Cardinal Spellman died because he ate a poisoned altar boy" variety.

"What, Herman? *What?*"

"The *Necronomicon* was a book invented by H.P. Lovecraft in his short stories. You know Lovecraft?"

My face was a stone of incomprehension.

"The father of gothic horror and eldritch tomes? What, you never heard of Lovecraft?"

I shook my head.

"Oy. A ceremonial magician who never heard of Lovecraft. He was a short story writer way back in the twenties. I used to read him a lot when I was laid up because of my leg. He wrote about eldritch tombs and monstrous beings who were summoned with a sorcerer's book called the *Necronomicon.* It doesn't really exist."

We glanced at the box on the table between us.

"It does now," we both said at once.

Without knowing any more about the book other than its title, Herman urged me to have it translated at once. He told me that people had been looking for the *Necronomicon* since its first appearance in a Lovecraft short story in the 1920s. He said that booksellers would list the book in their catalogues as a kind of joke, and still get thousands of orders for it. Herman did not know if "our" *Necronomicon* was "the" *Necronomicon,* but he knew it didn't matter. Not to him. If he could list a *Necronomicon* in his catalogue—one that he could actually ship—he would make a fortune. Not only that, but the prestige of the Warlock Shop would skyrocket.

As long as it wasn't a hoax.

And as long as I could somehow provide a cogent translation, something printable and salable.

I knew nothing of the publishing business. I knew even less of the retail trade. But I knew liturgics, had a smattering of ancient languages, and had been a student of religious history. I could organize the thing, at least. I had friends who could fill in the missing pieces, if the project was interesting enough. Herman had not offered any money up front for this project; frankly, he was broke, and struggling to make the store a success in its first year. He could not bankroll the project. But he was interested in cutting a deal whereby he would get fifty percent of the take and split the rest with me. I could split my fifty percent with whomever would be assisting me in translating and editing the book.

I went home with the box under my arm. I would have to call a few people, discreetly, and see what could be done.

The weeks and months that followed were hectic, to say the least. Herman was eager to have a completed English manuscript in his possession so he could flog it to various publishers. He was already letting it slip to close friends that he had an angle on the *Necronomicon,* and this was making my life even more frustrating and nerve-wracking. In addition, I was faced with an almost insurmountable task: how to attract quality people to work on this project when there was almost no chance that they would be financially remunerated for their work, and absolutely no chance that their intellectual contribution could be openly credited? Also, how was I to keep the project secure from the prying eyes of other occultists and fellow travelers? The manuscript itself would be in danger from theft (ironically), and we could lose a potentially valuable commodity. In addition, I would have to face the ire of Archbishop Prazsky, and I was not sure I wanted to take that chance.

I also was not sure that I wanted to share any of this project with Prazsky. If he felt there was a profit to be made from it, he would involve himself in the project to such an extent that we would not be able to complete it. I could not draft an agreement between us, since it involved stolen goods. I had no written agreement with Herman either, or with anyone else on this project for the very same reason.

Current in the media in those days was the story of Clifford Irving and the Howard Hughes "autobiography." It had been a hoax, to be sure, but Irving had sold the property to a New York publisher for a hefty sum while pretending that Hughes had authorized the work and contributed to it. When it was discovered that Hughes had nothing to do with it, the resulting scandal would find Irving himself in prison and suffering from a reputation that would not go away from then on.

This cautionary tale was very much on my mind in the first few months of the *Necronomicon* project. The only solace I could take from it was the fact that the *Necronomicon* was very much a solid mass of manuscript and not the figment of a novelist's imagination; but the legal twilight zone in which I was working was worrisome. It imposed a severe limitation on what I could say and do.

At the same time, the manuscript itself lay there like cardinal sin in a box.

There was definitely a sulphurous air about it, an odor of something opposite to sanctity. The very name of it, a name speaking of death, was enough to give one pause. It was, to the ceremonial magic I knew from the grimoires, like a shiny leather bustier to a formal wedding dress: it was rock and roll, Billy Idol's "White Wedding," to the grimoires' "Wedding March." It spoke of another world; not just the heaven and hell of the grimoires and of my own religion, but of a world more ancient than either of these: a world between night and day, between the visible and the unseen. It was asymmetrical, out of whack and out of context, something . . . other.

To most people, magic itself is strange enough, but to me

it was only the ghost in the sacerdotal machine, the technology of ritual. The *Necronomicon,* however, stood outside that system; it spoke of another machine, and of another ghost that haunted it. I knew I would have to test drive this Greater Vehicle myself one day, once I knew where to find the controls.

In the meantime, my casual inquiries were beginning to bear fruit.

Levenda had suggested that there was a definite Sumerian and Babylonian influence in the book. At that time, the best-known resource for the potential Sumeriologist was the University of Pennsylvania, an institution that had been studying the Sumerian civilization for decades and that boasted a good library on the subject. We would have to act fast, for Prazsky was agitating for a return of the manuscript and Levenda was tired of dealing with him.

Levenda made a few calls and tried some social engineering to locate an undergrad or ideally a grad student who was in need of a few dollars and could keep silent about the job we were doing. The money would come from my own pocket, since I could see that the pressure was on us to do something soon. Rumor had it that arrests in the case of Michael Hubak and Steven Chapo were imminent; I did not know how that would impact our situation, but I did not want to be caught short—or with the manuscript in my possession—when it did.

At the same time, I spoke to a few members of my own congregation and located two persons who were educated in the type of Greek represented by the *Necronomicon.* I separated the manuscript into three sections, omitting the title page so that no one would know the name of the book, and gave one section to one person to translate and another section to the other; the third would be kept for a little later on, and given to the first person. I felt that this way there was no opportunity for anyone to have worked on the entire book; for some reason, that seemed like a common-sense security approach. Looking back on it now, of course, it just seems silly.

One of these persons was a young and talented woman who studied Biblical Greek and who moonlighted as a waitress in a diner on the West Side. She is known as "Papaspyrou" in the Acknowledgments section of the *Necronomicon,* and since she has since married and changed her name I feel no hesitation about identifying her here. The other was a gentleman who prefers to remain anonymous, even today, so I will not further identify him except to say that his knowledge of Greek was both native and rooted in our ecclesiastical tradition.

Even between the two of these talented individuals there were whole sections that came out as nonsense. It was obvious that some of the incantations were not in Greek at all, but in some other language that had been transliterated into Greek letters. It was here that Levenda's work paid off, for he was able to identify these barbarous sections as prayers in Sumerian, rendered phonetically. His association with students at the University of Pennsylvania led him to source material on the subject, which verified his initial suspicions that the manuscript represented what was essentially a workbook of Sumerian magic.

This was an astounding revelation, and it did not bode well for our success. For one thing, academia would immediately scoff at such a suggestion. The Sumerian civilization had disappeared under the Semitic Akkadian and Babylonian invasions and had not been rediscovered for millennia. There is no way that a book written in the eighth or ninth century AD could speak of Sumeria, much less record incantations in a language that had been lost for thousands of years; at least, this was the conventional wisdom. The only conclusion that could be drawn was that somehow we were being played with. Not for the first time, I wondered at the provenance of the mysterious book in my possession.

The translators worked slowly, page by painstaking page. As each page was complete, I put it carefully back in its box. Naturally, they would have to refer again and again to those pages in the course of their work, and I did not want them handling the fragile parchments, so I finally began the process of photocopying most of them and letting the translators work from the copies rather than the original.

Not all of the pages could be safely copied, and I could not take them to a professional printer, so I managed to work with a liquid copier at the church's office. The drawback to this method was that the copies were not always very clear, and they degraded with time. In less than ten years the ink had disappeared from the pages and I was left with a mass of useless, curled and shiny paper. But I had solved one problem—I could get the manuscript back to Prazsky before he began screaming at me—and when I did, it was just in the proverbial nick of time.

The following month, March 1973, the nefarious team of Hubak and Chapo was arrested by the FBI.

A few weeks earlier we had concelebrated the Divine Liturgy at Prazsky's church in the Bronx. Remember that neither Hubak nor Chapo were aware that I was actually a member of Prazsky's church. Prazsky had a sadistic streak, and his idea for that Sunday's commemoration of the death and resurrection of Christ was to have me appear at some point during the liturgy for pure shock value, stunning Hubak and

Chapo with the realization that I had been part of Prazsky's operation all along.

The manuscript now safely in its box in Prazsky's office, I was swept along into this dubious operation. Solemnly, I put on the heavily brocaded vestments of an Eastern Orthodox priest and prepared to celebrate the ancient form of what the Catholics call the Mass and what the Orthodox call the Divine Liturgy.

The Divine Liturgy is a mystical event. The preparatory rituals themselves are profound with meaning, as one of the celebrants stabs a loaf of blessed bread with a golden knife and another pours water and wine into the chalice, commemorating the moment the lance pierced the side of Christ on the cross.

Prazsky let Hubak and Chapo perform this part of the ceremony, and I came in later, vested, and waited in the wings for the public part of the service to begin. In the Divine Liturgy there are several processions that lead out of—and back into—the sanctuary through a set of doors in the icon screen. One of these processions involves the clergy carrying the Book of Gospels, while other members precede the Book with censers, candles, etc. As the clergy left the sanctuary area, I entered and stood before the altar, ready to begin the next cycle of prayers.

Hubak and Chapo entered after the procession and saw me standing there, dressed completely in priestly vestments, intoning the next chant in Church Slavonic. Hubak immediately turned on his heel and left, ripping off his vestments, while Chapo stood and stared.

I never saw Hubak again. Chapo stayed behind to find out what was going on. After the service, when he realized that I had been a Prazsky "infiltrator," he spoke with me briefly to get the details of how they had been fooled into believing

I was an innocent walk-in who happened to have a background in bookbinding. Chapo, though visibly shaken, still managed to keep his composure and call me a "ferret"—someone who had insinuated himself into the Hubak and Chapo operation and "ferreted out" information about the crimes they had committed. Chapo did not understand that I had very little to do once I was introduced to them; they had freely and openly discussed with me details of their criminal enterprise.

The elements of their arrest had already been put into place by that time. According to the *New York Times*, which reported the story on March 17, 1973, Hubak and Chapo were "unfrocked." This, of course, was not true. Hubak and Chapo had never been defrocked or unfrocked. In fact, much to my surprise, when Hubak got out of prison, Prazsky took him back and eventually consecrated him as a bishop in the Autocephalous Slavonic Orthodox Catholic Church. This could only be due to the fact that Hubak had something on Prazsky, and I suspect that the hidden stash of occult books—whose existence was probably never revealed to the authorities—had something to do with it.

Michael Hubak—as "Bishop Raphael"—could be seen in newspaper articles in the Ukrainian newspapers in the 1980s, assisting Prazsky in consecrations of other bishops. I wonder how many of these men of God realized that the man consecrating them to the highest position in the church had been an indicted felon, a thief who stole and defaced ancient and very rare books for profit.

This was the character of the Prazsky episcopate. He had alienated the best and the brightest, the men who could have most advanced the cause of Orthodoxy and Christianity, and kept around him the sycophant and the criminal. In any case, these events had an alarming effect on my project for

Herman Slater. When news of the arrests of Hubak and Chapo became common knowledge, I put a hold on the progress we had been making in the translation and editing of the manuscript, fearful that the authorities would be knocking on all our doors.

Of course, the original manuscript was back in Prazsky's possession. There was very little chance that anyone would come looking for me concerning the *Necronomicon* since I was only known in those circles by a pseudonym, but I wasn't taking any chances. This was the time of Watergate, and the full scope of federal spying on American citizens was becoming known to one and all. I had no way of knowing how much the authorities knew about Prazsky's church, which was, after all, an Eastern European sect with ostensible ties back behind the Iron Curtain. Indeed, as part of Prazsky's entourage, I had attended ecumenical services at the Russian Orthodox Church—Moscow Patriarchate—one Easter Sunday where we played a game of "spot the KGB agent." (Moscow used the Russian Orthodox Church on Ninety-seventh Street as a means of moving KGB agents into the country, disguised as priests. There is one way for a genuine priest to spot a phony, and that concerns a special prayer that is recited at a specific time during the Divine Liturgy. If the prospective priest does not know this prayer, or says it incorrectly without the appropriate gestures, then he is not genuinely ordained. It is believed that the Russian Church in Moscow neglected to train the agents in this particular prayer in order to permit their overseas churches to recognize the spies and isolate them from the population.) Thus, I became a little paranoid, wondering how much the authorities knew about Prazsky, about the church, about my own church, and about . . . me.

One should realize that many of the denominations with

which I had been involved over the years—especially the American Orthodox Catholic Church—had been fronts for intelligence operations. As mentioned earlier, District Attorney Jim Garrison of New Orleans had suspected as much during his investigation into the Kennedy assassination. All of us knew about the dark and sinister presence of intelligence operatives and agendas within the church. Even decades later the name of the AOCC would come up again, this time in connection with a money-laundering scheme involving Serbian terrorists and mass murder.

At any rate, I put the project on hold temporarily. This was not what Herman Slater wanted to hear, and he started pressuring me to complete the manuscript and get it ready for publication. He had a prospective publisher in mind, an individual who had come to the shop from out of state and was known as a customer who dropped a lot of cash each time he visited, buying up books, robes, jewelry, swords, etc. Herman wanted something to show this guy, so I worked up a mock proposal with just enough of the original manuscript to give the flavor of what we were working with. As it happened, this potential publisher disappeared with the proposal and was never heard from again.

Hubak and Chapo copped a plea to the charges of book theft in October 1973, and eventually did time at the federal penal institution at Danbury, Connecticut. When Hubak came out a short time later, he was received back into the arms of the Slavonic Orthodox Church and eventually made bishop: a circumstance that made me realize there was a lot more to the Prazsky-Hubak relationship than had been known back in the 1970s. He died some years later, after a stint in Cairo working as an English teacher and, it is said, a theology instructor for the Coptic church under Pope Shenuda. The present whereabouts of Steven Chapo are unknown to me.

* * *

I pulled together the informal team that had been working on the project, and the hard work of translation was completed in late 1974. There was a lot of background work to be done, research in the religious and occult practices of ancient Mesopotamia, and Levenda was instrumental in that. By the time 1975 began, I had most of what I needed. I was no longer in touch with Prazsky and was busily involved with my own affairs. Herman Slater was planning his move to Manhattan, where he would have more room to devote to his mail-order business (which was growing enormously) as well as additional space for classes in the occult. Until then I had been conducting them in various places around the City, usually apartments rented or owned by students who kindly offered them for the purpose.

These classes sometimes included the performance of occult rituals, more in the way of instruction than anything else. As classes progressed, and as some of the students became more advanced in their work, we began to experiment with the rituals in the *Necronomicon*. It was this preliminary training program that led me to believe that the book contained important information for the magician, and that the rituals and chants were extraordinarily powerful in the hands of a trained occultist. Most students approached this subject with a sense of trepidation, and later many of them were of the opinion that the rituals should not be "overworked"; that is, used in any kind of daily or otherwise routine practice. The gods invoked by these formulae had not been summoned, we believed, in hundreds of years. They represent an area of the human psyche that is largely untapped, if we are to believe the theories of Jung and others for whom the gods are *archetypes*: icons of deep, unconscious psychological traits. In the West, we are used to the symbols of Greek mythology, such as have been utilized by Freud and his school to represent psychological processes (the Oedipus complex, as an example). Jung went further and discussed occult and alchemical emblems and their relationship to psychological integration. But here we had gods, goddesses, demons, and myths that predated all of these; that were born in the distant memory of prehistory. What psychological processes might be represented by Inanna, Marduk, Tiamat? Is there a Nergal complex?

As we struggled with these questions, both intellectually and through the medium of ceremonial ritual, other events were taking place that gave all of us a sense of immediacy . . . and of impending doom.

4: The Children

In an editorial in *Earth Religion News*—a periodical published by Herman Slater and the Warlock Shop—volume one, number four, 1974, it declared that "THE WAR OF THE WITCHES . . . is over." By that time everyone had stopped fighting with each other and denouncing one another as heretics and gotten down to the more serious business of building covens and occult networks across the country.

These networks included some of the leading lights of neopaganism, numbering the Church of All Worlds, the Pagan Way, the Church of the Eternal Source, and other popular groups among its informal membership. There were still feisty witches out there, such as Sicilian witch Leo Martello with his acerbic wit and disdain for white-bread paganism, but in general people stopped arguing with each other over whose tradition was the purest. As it turned out, of course, virtually all of these "traditions" were modern inventions.

The groups that were not part of the witch wars were actually the most worrisome to us at the time. These included the Church of Satan, the Church of Scientology, and the Process Church of the Final Judgment. Although their individual members were no strangers to the Warlock Shop, it was hardly likely that they would hobnob with the witches or care one way or another about coven politics. They had other concerns, and from about 1974 on these concerns became national news.

The Exorcist had opened in 1973, and this brought about a general reawakening of consciousness where occultism was concerned. The arc went from fear of demonic possession to interest in satanism. The Church of Satan was only the most prominent of these groups. There were others. One of these, Maury Terry refers to as The Children.

1974

On February 4, 1974, newspaper heiress Patty Hearst was kidnapped by the Symbionese Liberation Army and her brainwashing ordeal began. On June 30 the mother of Dr. Martin Luther King was shot and killed by Marcus Wayne Chenault. On August 9, President Richard Nixon resigned from office rather than face an impeachment process over Watergate; it was also the fifth anniversary of the Sharon Tate murders. On September 27, Manson Family member and convicted felon Susan Atkins had a vision of Jesus in her cell and became a born-again Christian. On November 13, Robert DeFeo Jr. would commit what are now known as the Amityville murders.

And on October 12, 1974, a young woman—Arliss Perry—was murdered in a church at Stanford University in California.

The murder was ritualistic in nature, the body of the nineteen-year-old found facing the main altar diagonally from a side alcove, with a candle placed between her breasts and another inside her vagina. Her blue jeans had been placed across her spread-eagled legs in a V-shape, suggesting a diamond or perhaps the unicursal hexagram (an occult symbol developed by Aleister Crowley), and she had been beaten, strangled, and stabbed behind her left ear with an ice pick. The body was found beneath the sculpture of a cross. The gruesome homicide was unsolved, and it would be years before Terry would connect that crime with a series of other murders plaguing New York City a little while later: the Son of Sam killings.

During the Satanic Cult Survivor craze of the 1980s, it was widely believed that there existed a vast underground satanic network in the United States that was responsible for the kidnapping and murder of thousands of children every year. Eventually this hysteria was calmed by the presentation of a few facts, most notably the statistics on the number of kidnapped and missing children; subtracting the numbers of children "kidnapped" by one of their parents in a custody case, or the numbers of runaways who wind up on the streets of our major cities, the resulting number of "missing" children is quite small.

A network of satanists can exist, however, and it appeared—during the Son of Sam investigation—that it truly *did* exist, although not to the extent promoted by tabloid journalism.

When Prazsky and Levenda were busy studying the grimoires—and Levenda was lecturing informally in available classrooms at Columbus High School—they attracted the attention of a number of like-minded souls in the vicinity. Some of these young men attended séances in the Prazsky home; others accompanied the two high school students on various rituals in the woods. These men would form the core of the group that enlisted David Berkowitz later on when jokes would be made about Prazsky's weird home in Pelham Bay, likening it to "Pelham House" in the Hammer film, *The Satanic Rites of Dracula* (1971), which was the headquarters for a satanic cult plotting world domination. Maury Terry, in *The Ultimate Evil,* writes at length about the Brooklyn Heights cult and the Yonkers cult, but omits mention of the cult that operated with impunity in Pelham Bay Park, a short walk from the Prazsky home: a cult that was familiar to John and Michael Carr of the Son of Sam murders, and eventually to David Berkowitz.

While neither Levenda nor Prazsky would ever dream of calling themselves "satanists"—particularly since their goal was to create an Eastern Orthodox Church—others were not so squeamish. In the antiauthoritarian era of the 1960s, satanism seemed like a logical extension of the antigovernment, antichurch attitude of the young. Couple that with drugs and sex, and you have the makings of an underground movement.

Berkowitz attended the same high school and lived in the same neighborhood as Prazsky and Levenda, beginning in 1969. By 1970 he was already serving as an auxiliary police officer at the Forty-fifth Precinct in the Bronx, and as an unofficial volunteer fireman at Co-Op City. In 1971, after graduation from Columbus High School, he enlisted in the Army and wound up in Korea.

Around this same time, his father—Nathan Berkowitz—remarried. His wife, Julia, had children of her own, one of whom was a self-professed witch who began to teach David about the occult. After his honorable discharge from the Army in June 1974, Berkowitz wound up back in the Bronx, on Barnes Avenue, and got various odd jobs, including as a taxi driver in Co-Op City. This was during the period when the Autocephalous Slavonic Orthodox Church was growing—in stature, if not in congregation—in Co-Op City, led by the ceremonial magician manque, Andrew Prazsky.

There are rumors that Berkowitz and his fellow occult enthusiasts knew Prazsky and the church, and had attended occult ceremonies there in the 1970s, both before Berkowitz went to the Army and after his return. It *is* certain that some of Berkowitz's future acquaintances did attend rituals at Prazsky's home and at the Freedomland site. There may be some truth to the rumor that Berkowitz did as well, since, upon his return from Korea but before his discharge from the Army, he spent some time at Fort Knox in Kentucky, when he seems to have become a "born again" Christian and to have engaged in street-corner preaching on behalf of his newfound faith.[1] This vacillation between mainstream Christianity and the occult was typical of Prazsky's interests as well, and his Slavonic Orthodox "cathedral" near Co-Op City, where Berkowitz worked as a cab driver, was a visible affair, complete with a huge three-armed Orthodox cross on top of the building that would have been a magnet for someone like Berkowitz, who would have seen this as something exotic and strange. At any rate, his religious conversion does not last, because by the end of 1974 he is back in the Bronx, and by mid-1975 at the latest he was developing contacts among what would become known as the Son of Sam cult at the Barnes Avenue address, principally with Michael Carr (a Scientologist who had many of the same interests as Prazsky, especially regarding coats-of-arms and phony titles of nobility).

At the same time, a few boroughs away from Co-Op City, the Warlock Shop opened in Brooklyn Heights in June 1972. I visited the shop then, after having passed it one summer's day after a sojourn among the Maronite Rite Lebanese

---

[1] This has an odd parallel to the early life of cult leader Jim Jones, who preached on street corners as a youth in his native Indiana.

Catholics along Atlantic Avenue, and found the environment
like something out of a Polanski film. I left my contact information with the proprietor, Herman Slater, and offered to
teach some students the rudimentary elements of the practice of ceremonial magic. Slater thought my clerical background and presence just the sort of thing to attract a small
but elite group of serious students, and he began to advertise
my classes quietly.

Some of these classes—begun in the fall of 1972—were
held at the St. George Hotel in Brooklyn Heights, on Clark
Street; the same hotel where some scenes from *The Godfather* were shot, and up the street from where other scenes
from *The Sentinel* and *The French Connection* were filmed.
Later, classes were also held at the homes of various students around New York City.

The Brooklyn Heights location was convenient for
me, since I was involved with a small church located on
Amity Street just below Atlantic Avenue. An odd building,
it had served various functions over the years as a dance
hall, a meeting hall, and—during the early 1970s—a church
for yet another Eastern Orthodox denomination. Western
Rite services were held there: Roman Catholic–style liturgies
celebrated by Orthodox priests, an approach that was fash-
ionable at the time for it attracted congregations who might
otherwise have been put off by the lengthy (three hour) Divine Liturgies of the Orthodox variety, which are always
sung, and usually in exotic languages that the average American would have a hard time comprehending, such as Greek,
Arabic, Russian, Church Slavonic, and other alien tongues.
As a priest, I had celebrated both types of liturgy; while I
preferred the more ancient Orthodox form, there was something to be said for the comparative simplicity of the Roman
variety. The church on Amity Street was not set up for a true

Orthodox service anyway, since there was no *ikonostasis* (icon screen) or the other elaborate furnishings required by the rites.

The Amity Street church, though, had other associations, and in the years after the opening of the Warlock Shop a few blocks farther north, it became known as a center for occult practices. Several times, the church had to be reconsecrated because of the satanic rites performed there. Cultists would break into the church in the dead of night and use the altar for their own ceremonies. In the morning we would find the wax stains of black candles, occult inscriptions written in animal blood on the altar and on the floor of the sanctuary, and other evidence of a satanic nature.

When investigative journalist Maury Terry began to look into the Sam cult, he wrote obliquely about the Warlock Shop and the Amity Street church. It was well-known to us that a satanic element had been attracted to the shop; after all, it was virtually the only place in New York City where it was possible to walk in and purchase any amount or kind of ritual paraphernalia, from human skulls and entire, articulated skeletons to every type of herb, candle, incense, implement, and book. At one time Herman Slater must have had at least twenty different types of ceremonial swords available, many dozens of the sacrificial athame knives, silver chalices, silver and brass pentacles, and different styles of heavy silver jewelry fashioned in designs ranging from "biker chic" skulls and demons to accurate representations of magical seals and symbols taken from the different grimoires.

Berkowitz is known to have visited the shop, but more importantly, the other members of the Sam cult were drawn to it like flies. It was not only a good place to shop for hooded robes and swords, it was also a convenient place to pick up the local gossip, learn about new "recruits," and spy on other cults. The homosexual aspect of the shop's ownership also provided entrée into yet another demimonde: this one of leather bar, bathhouse, and Mafia-controlled S&M clubs in the City; relationships that Slater openly admitted and described to me with something like amusement. (These were the pre-AIDS days, and gay culture was vibrant and campy—and at times dark and dangerous—in ways that are not understood today by those who were not around at the time. Slater would show me photographs of himself and his friends in drag—quite outrageous drag—performing their "gay revue." Brooklyn Heights in those days was known as the largest gay neighborhood on the Eastern seaboard and probably the largest in the United States outside of San Francisco. Further, there were several older, wealthy, and successful men who lurked around the gay scene in those days, and who had other agendas for their young lovers, which included everything from filming their sexual sessions on handheld 8mm cameras to other, even less savory practices.)

When the Son of Sam murders began to take place, those of us around the occult milieu in New York knew very well that more than one person was responsible for them. We also knew that there was a Brooklyn Heights connection, even after the shop moved from the Heights to Manhattan's Nineteenth Street, since so many occultists lived in Brooklyn Heights by that time: Wiccans, Satanists, and magicians of every variety. There was a small cult operating out of a brownstone on Hicks Street, and another on Henry Street, north of Montague. Classes were still being held on Clark Street, and coven meetings were taking place at various locations in the Heights. So, when the murders began, we knew they were not the actions of one killer; we understood the occult calendar being used, and we were aware of the activities of just such a cult that had a base of operations in Brooklyn.

These were not people with whom we socialized. In most cases—except that of one or two young women who were affiliated with Brooklyn Polytech and Pratt Institute (both located not far from the Heights)—we did not know the cultists personally. We only knew of them through second-hand sources. But as the years went by, and as the investigation into the Sam murders was reopened, we discovered that everything we had heard on the street in those days was true. That a branch of the Process might have been involved was a persistent rumor in those days. That the Sam cult was involved in drugs and prostitution—including gay prostitution—was also known to us. That they were responsible for sacrificing dogs—principally German shepherds— was a fact, since a warehouse near the Brooklyn Bridge was known to have been used for rituals of that sort. There was also an assumption that organized crime was behind the cult, and that they used the cult as a kind of "cutout" for carrying messages and, eventually, committing murder-for-hire.

One couple that met a sad end at the hands of the cult was known to me personally, since they had asked me to visit their Brooklyn apartment to talk to them about ceremonial magic and occultism. This was Howard Green and Carol Marron, who lived on DeKalb Avenue. Carol Marron had a job at the Pratt Institute, and had been living with Howard Green, an older artist and painter, since the shop opened in 1972. They were among the many people who approached me for instruction, except that they were asking for personalized training and initiation, and I had always steered clear of that type of involvement, preferring to stay aloof from any hint that I was somehow creating a cult or offering a spiritual solution that could be obtained from my hands alone. This created many problems for me with individuals who were desperate to be told what to do and to find a guru; my insistence that ceremonial magic was for individual self-initiation did not please this type of seeker, but I have always found spiritual "teachers" to be dangerous and have resisted the temptation to create a cult of my own, hence my anonymity and use of a pseudonym.

After the publication of the *Necronomicon* in December of 1977, Green and Marron were known to be hanging around Herman Slater's new Magickal Childe bookstore in Manhattan. They kept pretty much to themselves, and were discreet in their inquiries, but someone in the Sam cult latched onto them, probably through the store. I never saw them again.

Their bodies were found off Route 80, near Paterson, New Jersey, on December 16, 1979.

They had been drained completely of blood.

The day before their murders, they were believed to have paid a visit to a cult member living in Washington Heights, a neighborhood at the far northwestern end of Manhattan. Washington Heights was another area known for cult activity, and I personally knew practitioners of African magic who lived in a high rise near the George Washington Bridge, as well as members of the OTO, who had apartments near the subway line. None of them were suspected in the deaths of Green and Marron, and quite rightly. They had nothing to do with them. But the area was heavy with occult groups, which overlapped with drug dealers. (As we would eventually learn, to our horror, the so-called Matamoros cult of northern Mexico was just such a mélange of drug dealers and occult practitioners.) Even *Necronomicon* co-publisher Larry Barnes was known to frequent the area, less for occultism than heroin, and I unwittingly accompanied him on one such run in his leased Lincoln Continental, a conspicuous ride in those streets. And Washington Heights is a short drive south from Yonkers, which is where David Berkowitz moved in 1975, where the Carrs lived (Michael and John, both Sam cultists), and where some of the Sam cult activities took place in Untermeyer Park.

It's important to remember that in those days drugs were commonplace. Marijuana was smoked by the bushel, and for a brief period it had even been decriminalized in New York City. Hashish and hashish oil were common; opium was chic; and cocaine use gradually grew to viral proportions, running a swath through our best and brightest. Larry Barnes was as addicted to cocaine as anyone I had ever met; in fact, in order to get his printing projects out on time, he would lay out piles of cocaine in his office so that his shop workers could snort a few lines and thus be reenergized enough to do three or four hours of overtime in the middle of the night. Thus, one could not successfully isolate drug use among certain individuals and then track the source back to one or two dealers. There were so many drugs, and so many people using drugs in all sorts of situations, that it became impossible to figure out who was supplying whom. Small vials of cocaine passed through many hands on the way to the final nose. Even such elite restaurants as the Odeon in lower Manhattan became infamous for scenes of coke use by the staff and patrons. The restrooms alone became unisex drug dens where men and women indiscriminately went to snort a few lines and return to their superbly cooked meals, meals often prepared by a coked-up chef and served by coked-up waiters. Add to this mix the pre-AIDS sexual behavior of sophisticated and often bisexual urbanites, and you had a world that was swimming in sensations, humming just below the visible horizon of the city's workforce. Beautiful and accomplished young women—actresses, dancers, writers, painters—became coke whores virtually overnight. Successful young businessmen found themselves working impossible hours just to support an enormous coke habit in the days when the drug went for three hundred dollars a gram. Their dealers were often cultists who pushed the drugs through their connections in the worlds of music, art, business, the courts, and the clubs. Low level cultists became dependent on upper echelon cult members for their continued supply . . . and their continued credit as their ability to work normal hours to earn enough money to pay for their increasingly expensive habits seriously decreased over time. All of this, of course, came to the attention of organized crime, which did not hesitate to exploit these weaknesses for their own purposes.

Drugs, sex, and the occult. In New York City in the 1970s these worlds overlapped and interlaced to the point where it became impossible to disentangle the scarlet threads that made up the tapestry of murder. The case of Howard Green and Carol Marron was only one example. The multiple victims of the Son of Sam cult were another, and, as Herman Slater moved the Warlock Shop to Manhattan, he unwittingly raised the stakes.

Magickal Childe became an even stronger magnet than the Warlock Shop, which was, after all, in Brooklyn; to this day there are still Manhattanites who have never ventured over the bridge into that borough. Being on West Nineteenth Street increased Herman Slater's business exponentially; it also brought a lot of new customers, from celebrities like John Lennon and Yoko Ono (who were interested in Egyptology and divination), to people like producer (and murder victim) Roy Radin and his entourage, all the way to Mafia runners and solitary Satanists. The cult Terry identifies as The Children was known to Slater, though not by that name. Although Slater himself was never involved (to my knowledge) in anything illegal or questionable, as one of polite society's "outcasts," he had access to levels of the New York City underworld that were normally closed to the rest of us. He would regale me with tales of organized crime and the operation of New York's gay bars, and how cult beliefs and behavior were prevalent there. He would talk about filmmakers and photographers and a cult that operated among the entourage of a famous Italian clothes designer who lived in a gorgeous apartment on the Upper West Side, in the "sister building to the Dakota" (the building where *Rosemary's Baby* was filmed and where John Lennon and Yoko Ono lived). The occult renaissance of the 1970s attracted the youth and the bourgeoisie. Meanwhile, another "renaissance" of a sorts was taking place among the monied and the powerful: real estate brokers, bankers, doctors, and attorneys on the one hand and fashion models, magazine photographers, designers, and decorators on the other. One of the unifying factors in these "super cults" was drugs; another was prostitution of a special variety, ranging from child pornography to sadomasochism to underage men and women.

When word began to leak out that Herman Slater had in his possession the manuscript of the *Necronomicon,* it became an additional thrill to these jaded thrill seekers. As a security precaution, all copies of our book proposal were removed from the bookstore and nothing was left behind to indicate who was involved in the project. My own identity and address was erased from any files Herman may have had in his possession. Although he'd been advertising the book's existence since at least 1974 in the pages of his *Earth Religion News,* we decided to keep a low profile from then on.

The book was still not complete—it would not be finished until October 1975—and we did not want to attract unwanted attention from cultists who were serious about getting their hands on the original manuscript.

Years later, sources close to Roman Polanski—the director of *Rosemary's Baby* and husband of the murdered actress Sharon Tate—would tell us the Polish director had learned of the story of the *Necronomicon,* including details not generally known to the public. This became the subject matter for the film *The Ninth Gate,* starring Johnny Depp as a rare book dealer who becomes involved with a mysterious volume of black magic that is concerned with "gates" to the underworld: a clear reference to the *Necronomicon.* Anyone who met me in those days in the 1970s would recognize the Johnny Depp character: glasses, beard, black clothes, black raincoat, bag over one shoulder. The intrigue that follows Depp throughout the movie parallels some of the events in the real story, including the references to wealthy individuals who sought the power of the book for themselves.

Another movie—*Ghostbusters* (1984)—would mock the ideas of the *Necronomicon* with the introduction of a Sumerian demon atop a miniature ziggurat in the refrigerator of a New York City apartment and the idea of a "Gatekeeper." Dan Aykroyd, one of the film's stars, is involved in studying the paranormal in real life and his brother is a genuine ghostbuster, so he is probably the avenue by which the *Necronomicon* references made the silver screen. Those of us who had been involved in the *Necronomicon* project took all of this in good humor, of course, and enjoyed the quiet celebrity . . . or notoriety.

Finally, in October 1975, the translation had been completed along with my Introduction. The manuscript was ready for publication, but it would be two long years before it would see print. Until then, the occult renaissance in New York would reach its highest and most intense phase. All the while, below the surface of the New Age boom that profited Herman Slater and the Warlock Shop/Magickal Childe bookstores, lurked another more palpable renaissance: the rebirth of pure evil.

The first murder attributed to the Son of Sam killer took place on July 29, 1976. Donna Lauria was shot in front of her house in Queens, along with her friend Jody Valente, who survived the attack. More attacks followed, all committed with a .44 caliber Bulldog revolver, and with increasing intensity. Soon the killer would begin sending letters to the newspapers, boasting of his prowess in cryptic, occult terminology. Eyewitnesses would describe what were clearly two different individuals, even though the authorities were satisfied when they finally arrested David Berkowitz in August 1977 and charged him as the sole gunman in the killings. Berkowitz pleaded guilty, so the nation was spared a murder trial. This turned out to be a mistake, since the police closed their books on the case and it would be several more years before an overwhelming amount of evidence that more than one killer was involved would force them to reopen it.

Berkowitz—who is now in prison with no possibility of ever getting out—has since admitted that he was part of a cult, and that the cult was responsible for the killings. He has not denied that he took part in some of the murders himself; he admits being a killer. However, he has offered the authorities—and Maury Terry, the investigator—much additional evidence to show that a renegade branch of the Process was involved. Terry's investigation went much further, and eventually the structure of an underground cult of assassins and drug dealers was made visible. This led him to connect the murder of Roy Radin—a Broadway producer—with the cult, with a hired killer known as "Manson II" and, indeed, with the original Charles Manson Family. This was the "satanic network" uncovered by Geraldo Rivera and others. While it was not nearly as widespread and insidious as television tabloid journalism made it appear, this network did exist and murders were committed in its name (along with a host of other crimes).

We knew this, and when the second edition of the *Necronomicon* was finally published—in December 1979—we said that the first edition had been published in "the middle of the killing spree of the .44 caliber killer, known to the press as the Son of Sam." Why did we say that, when Berkowitz had already been arrested in August 1977, four months earlier? How could it be "the middle of the killing spree"? Like so many other hints dropped in the various editions of the *Necronomicon,* this was a throwaway line, an invitation to greater research by the book's critics and the press: research that never took place. We stated that it was the "middle of the killing spree" because we knew that the killings had continued. Cult member and Berkowitz associate John Carr (the man who brought Berkowitz into the cult) was murdered in 1978. His brother, Scientologist and cult member Michael Carr—a suspected associate of William Prazsky, socialized with the "kinky" gay set in New York, and, like Prazsky, a lover of knighthoods and titles of nobility—was slain in October 1979. The murders of Howard Green and Carol Marron took place in December 1979—the same month that the second edition of the *Necronomicon* was published. This was all evidence that the cult was still operating with its usual vigor and cleaning up loose ends.

Something had to be done to counteract the sinister atmosphere that had been created by The Children. The first "Sam" killing had taken place in July 1976, the month of the

American Bicentennial celebrations. Watergate, the Ford pardon of Nixon, the coming election of Jimmy Carter . . . these were tumultuous times for America. Those of us involved in the occult decided to become more proactive, to promote a positive view of our beliefs and practices. The labor of translating and preparing the manuscript of the *Necronomicon* was behind me. Getting it published was up to Herman Slater. I focused my attention on other matters, and these included the formation of an ad hoc group of like-minded individuals who saw in the occult renaissance something vibrant and intellectually stimulating, something worthy of celebration.

This group became the short-lived but influential Star-Group One.

5: Magickal Childe

had completed the Introduction to the *Necronomi-con* on October 12, 1975. It was the centennial of Aleister Crowley's birth, and the dedication to the book indicates that. Occult calendars would weigh very heavily on my mind as the next few years progressed. As we shall see, the precise date of October 12, 1975, had another association, a link that none of us could have imagined or predicted.

Herman Slater had by then managed to move his successful Warlock Shop to Manhattan, where he had much more space, including a back area that would serve as a room for classes as well as a "temple" for the local Pagan Way chapter—a group of pagans and would-be witches—and eventually as the only site in New York where Gnostic Masses would be held.

The Gnostic Mass is the only public ceremony regularly held under the auspices of the Ordo Templi Orientis: the OTO. This organization, which was founded in Germany in the early years of the twentieth century, had become firmly identified with Aleister Crowley and his religious creed of Thelema, or "Will." The Gnostic Mass at first appears to be a blasphemous spoof of the Catholic Mass, for it contains an altar, a priest, a holy book, and a sacrament. However, there is also a priestess, a sacred lance that is stroked suggestively by the priestess, and the sacrament itself, which consists of flour mixed with bodily fluids: menstrual fluid as well as semen. Thus, observers could be forgiven for believing that the Gnostic Mass was in actuality a Black Mass.

Its purpose was not to present a travesty of the Catholic ritual, however, but to incorporate some essential themes of both Thelema and of various other occult concepts. Those who understand the original Mass—understand, that is, its mystical elements—can see some of the esoteric material of the Catholic Mass made more obvious in its Gnostic incarnation. For a cult that operates primarily in secret, the Gnostic Mass is a way of holding public ceremonies that can be attended by anyone and thus act as a draw for attracting new recruits (at least in theory).

The priesthood of the Gnostic Catholic Church—the agency of the OTO that was responsible for the Mass—was ordained by bishops who also claim apostolic succession and, in many cases, the *same* apostolic succession as that enjoyed by Walter Propheta of the American Orthodox Catholic Church and Andrew Prazsky of the Autocephalous Slavonic Orthodox Catholic Church. For a time the "quality" of the Gnostic succession was suspect, since there were too many broken lines between the French occultists who started the Gnostic Catholic Church a hundred years ago and the current crop of Gnostic bishops. Steps were taken to correct this irregularity in the last twenty years or so, but for the most part it would seem as if the Gnostic bishops are no longer in a line of valid succession. An exception may be the episcopacy of one Michel Bertiaux, a practitioner of both Thelema and of Haitian voudon, who obtained his succession through a series of consecrations that stretches back over many years. I don't expect the reader to be overly concerned about this subject, so I will leave it here except to say that the interest of hard-core Aleister Crowley cultists in the validity of their apostolic succession is both amusing and alarming . . . for only a validly ordained priest (that is, a priest with a valid line of apostolic succession) could, in theory, successfully perform a Black Mass.

Occultists—no matter what their stripe—value the spiritual efficacy of the rituals of the Catholic Church. That there is some form of spiritual power inherent in the performance of the Mass is a belief beyond any shadow of a doubt among magicians, sorcerers, witches, and occult practitioners generally. Therefore, if one is validly ordained within a valid succession of bishops going back in unbroken line from the present day to the very first bishop, Saint Peter, then it is believed that this power has been transferred down two thousand years from the hands of Jesus Christ himself, passed on and growing stronger through the ages. "What you seal on earth shall be sealed in heaven," Jesus told Peter, as quoted in the Gospels—in a remarkable reframing of the words of the Emerald Tablet of Hermes, "As above, so below"—thus effectively making the Church the oldest magical society in the world. Regardless of how any individual magician feels about the Church, the lure of such power is irresistible.

This same power is passed down through the line of apostolic succession enjoyed by the Orthodox bishops as well, since—at least until 1054 AD—they and the Catholics were part of the same Church. Thus, the occultist who was unable to obtain his succession through the Western Rite or Catholic side of the Church had another alternative: the Eastern Rite or Orthodox side. When I met with "bishops" of the Gnostic Catholic Church—such as Richard Guernon, or "Gurney" as he was known—during informal sessions and classes I gave for the OTO, I brought up this very point. Needless to say, the interest of the OTO was quite high in obtaining valid succession, because they wanted legitimacy in the eyes of the religious world on the one hand, and the power that such succession would give them on the other. In other words, they were not so different from any of the other groups of "wandering bishops" abroad in the land.

At the same time as the OTO was trying to regroup in New York, the witch covens were active and recruiting members through Magickal Childe and the local Pagan Way operation. Margot Adler has written about this period extensively in *Drawing Down the Moon,* so it is not necessary to go into detail here. Ms. Adler, a descendant of famed psychologist Alfred Adler, is a keen observer of the scene and can be relied upon for her characterizations of the people involved in the national pagan movement. One of the witch groups with which she was affiliated for a time in New York City also numbered science fiction and fantasy author Patricia Kennealy-Morrison among its members: Ms. Morrison was the wife of Jim Morrison, lead singer and poet laureate of the influential Sixties rock group The Doors, whom she wed in a pagan hand-fasting ceremony on June 24, 1970. (In 1990, Ms. Morrison was made a Dame of the Ordo Supremus Militaris Hierosolymitani, which dignity was bestowed on her in Rosslyn Chapel in Scotland, demonstrating once again the degree to which the worlds of noble titles, occultism, and the Church become intertwined and incestuous.)

Another major factor in the occult boom of the 1970s was the trilogy by Robert Anton Wilson and Robert Shea, *Illuminatus!* More than anything else, *Illuminatus!* gave a kind of social context for the occult renaissance, providing an identification that was quite different from the "New Age" atmosphere of yoga, Buddhism, and Tibetan bells. *Illuminatus!* devotees were interested in Aleister Crowley, Timothy Leary, radical politics, conspiracy theories, science fiction, and magic. This was a far cry from Maharishi Mahesh Yogi. This new movement was more intellectual, certainly more cerebral, and attracted Marvel Comics writers and illustrators as well as followers of Crowley, LSD enthusiasts, avant-garde musicians, disaffected Theosophists, and science fiction authors. In New York City, this crowd gravitated around a pub on West Thirteenth Street known as the Bells of Hell and its resident band, Turner & Kirwan of Wexford.

Turner & Kirwan would go on to greater glory, first as The Major Thinkers, and then, ultimately (and minus keyboardist Pierce Turner), Black 47, the Irish agit-rock band that has appeared in several Hollywood films and whose lead singer and songwriter, Larry Kirwan, had also made a name for himself as playwright and novelist. Magic—particularly of the Aleister Crowley variety—was the attraction, and Turner & Kirwan would write several songs about Crowley and his wife, Rose Kelly, as well as record Crowley's *Book of the Law* in a memorable rock-opera format.

Performances of the band at the Bells of Hell were heavily attended by this new crowd of occultists, certainly a bizarre enough phenomenon in a city of bizarre phenomena. It was probably the closest New York had come to realizing the strange little witch bistro of the film *Bell, Book and Candle*. Eventually, some members of this crowd—now known collectively as StarGroup One—would create the New York Tarot: a Tarot deck composed of iconic photographs of most of the principal players, including Larry Kirwan, Pierce Turner, Margot Adler, avant-garde poet Copernicus, Quentin Crisp, Philippe Petit, and so many others. Ms. Giani Siri, one of the group's most dedicated members, created the deck (from which I am most noticeably absent, except in the dedication, since I am loath to have my picture taken).

Classes at Magickal Childe were continuous, usually

taking place all weekend and often during the week as well. Many of the members of StarGroup One would attend, but there were also many others from all walks of life who were interested in the curricula, which ranged from Asian occultism to shamanism to ceremonial magic to divination. Separate classes were held on the Enochian system of Elizabethan magician John Dee, others on the Golden Dawn system of magic. Some of these classes were paid, others free.

At the same time, Magickal Childe attracted the interest of the news media (predictably around Halloween). In addition, we were asked to create an occult exhibit for the Museum of American Folk Art in Manhattan, an event that was covered by the *New York Times*.[1] (My contribution, of course, was the ceremonial magic exhibit.) Thus, while the more satanically oriented cults were initiating their followers through the sacrifice of dogs in Untermyer and Pelham Bay Parks and preparing their initiates for murder and crime, there was an entirely different movement that shared some of the same beliefs—such as a magical perspective of the world, with its system of correspondences, its "As Above, So Below" doctrine, and a general distrust of organized religion and of authority in general, a kind of spiritual paranoia—but the two camps expressed these beliefs in radically different ways, each side despising the other but acknowledging a common enemy in Church and State. Since groups like the Pagan Way, StarGroup One, and something called the Aquarian Anti-Defamation League were visible, they would receive the most investigation whenever an "occult crime" had occurred, even though they were the least likely groups to be so involved. The same was true of the OTO and other

---

[1] Rita Reif, "Blessed by Witches, an Occult Show Is Unveiled," *New York Times,* January 17, 1973, 34

more serious occult organizations, which, at that time were sharing in the general goodwill created by StarGroup One and its informal affiliates.

All of this activity, however, was not advancing the cause of the *Necronomicon*. By the middle of 1976 it had still not found a publisher.

And then, out of the clear blue sky, in walked one of the most talented of all the personalities involved with the project.

Larry Barnes.

Kosmo

Lawrence K. Barnes was born on May 10, 1952, to a family of printers. His grandfather had begun a printing and lithography business which was inherited by his father, Hugh Barnes. When I knew him, Larry himself ran Barnes Graphics, which was a subsidiary of the parent company (no pun intended).

Larry had a genius for painting. His art was mostly done in miniatures, like early American miniatures, except that his favorite—one could say, obsessive—topic was alien life and alien landscapes. He confided to me one day that he had seen a UFO floating around his backyard when he was a child growing up in New Jersey. This experience seems to have had a strong impact on his development both as an artist and as a personality.

He graduated from the University of Colorado at Denver in 1972, where he studied art. He became involved not only in watercolors and ink drawings, but also in some forms of sculpture. His most famous was that of an alien in a glass coffin, replete with dry ice smoke pouring out of its vents. It made the cover of a flying saucer magazine in the late

1970s, where the "journalist" claimed it had been discovered during an excavation in the basement of the Empire State Building!

Outer space, aliens, UFOs. These were important influences on Larry Barnes. There was another: comics.

Larry spoke in word bubbles, like a comic book character. His favorites seemed to be Marvel characters, but there were others, like those from *Tales from the Crypt* and *Weird Tales,* and still others of his own devising. One of his favorite words was "doomed," which he would pronounce with full melodramatic intensity, "Doooomed!" Another was "thetic" as an abbreviation for "pathetic," a favorite epithet. When something was not up to his standards, the verdict would be "thetic," as in, "What do you think of this drawing? Thetic, right? The artist is doooomed. Boorrrrrrrnnnn . . . to *lose,* baby, yeah!" Born to lose. A phrase repeated as often, or more, than thetic and doomed. A phrase that haunted Larry in odd moments during the day or the even odder nights. *Born.* Short for "born to lose." It would eventually take over from doomed. As in: "This drawing is totally born." Or, "What do you think, Simon? Is it born?"

When spotting a desirable young woman on a summer's day drive through the City in his silver-gray Lincoln Continental, he would stick his head out of the window and intone, not too loudly, "Come to me. *Come.* Larry won't hurt you. Not . . . *much.*" He was a walking, talking cartoon, and this manic intensity hid a soul that was struggling with profound personal problems for which it seemed there were no easy solutions.

He had an older brother who died as a result of heroin addiction sometime before I met him, and this affected Larry deeply. That, his UFO experience, and his unusual artistic ability, combined to make him a kind of existential comedian, but a comedian whose act was played on a very small stage and to a sometimes irritated, even desperate, audience: his friends, his family, his coworkers and business associates. Like most comedians, he was doing stand-up without a net. His "secret name"—the one only his true friends and family knew—was "Kosmo." It seems to have been an extension of another of Larry's favorite words, *cosmic.* He lived in a world surrounded by cosmic influences and patterns, like the repetition of certain number sequences he saw everywhere: on license plates, on invoices, checks, credit card receipts. He saw 13 and 333 and 666 and 555 (the Greek numerology of the word *Necronomicon* is 555) appear all the time, and those of us who traveled with him in his long rides in the Lincoln Continental had no choice but to notice the numbers too, and to conclude that there *was* something going on around Larry. Something . . . cosmic.

Like every secret name, it both reveals and conceals. In secret societies, one's secret name was known only to one's fellow initiates, who did not know one's birth name; at the same time, those who knew you by your birth name did not know your secret name, or even if you had one; that was the whole point of a secret society. That split in personalities, that gentle form of dissociation (as opposed to the traumatic dissociation brought about by physical or sexual abuse), is a core feature of all religions and cults. When one is confirmed Catholic, one chooses a saint's name; when one converts to Islam, one takes an Arab name (preferably one with an august Islamic heritage). It separates us from the rest of the world, and creates an insular one in which we are secure. In Larry's case, Kosmo was the repository of his alien personality, the one who had traveled—if only figuratively, or through the use of strange drugs—to other worlds and who was possessed of an appropriately otherworldly persona.

There was the Larry Barnes who worked at his father's company to earn money and create attractive corporate brochures and company profiles . . . and then there was Kosmo, whom we can't help but feel was his preferred personality, his "real" self.

And then came the *Necronomicon,* and, strangely, a purpose or at least a context to his life, one that managed to bridge both Larry Barnes *and* Kosmo. Even I did not understand the importance of the book to Larry until sometime later, and then I was shocked at what I discovered.

The story of how Larry came into the picture goes like this:

Larry's childhood friend, Bruce—whom I refer to as "B.A.K." in the preface to the second edition of the *Necronomicon*—brought him to Herman's store in Manhattan one day in 1976. Larry enjoyed the décor—proclaiming it "seriously distorted"—and casually, sneeringly, but with an inner tremble, asked Herman if he had a copy of the *Necronomicon* among all the other questionable literature on his shelves. Herman smiled, pulled the manuscript from beneath the counter and handed it to him. *Voilà!*

That story has been told so many times, to the point where it seems apocryphal, but that is what happened. By 1976, I had decided to let Herman hold a copy of the book to show potential publishers since it seemed that any interest at all had dwindled to next to nothing, and anyway, I was feeling a sense of hubris over the initial success of StarGroup One and its ability to present a charming and more sophisticated face of occultism to the world.

But the experience of finding the *Necronomicon* stunned Larry Barnes. Herman had been holding onto the book and looking for a publisher for quite some time. The members of the group that had midwifed the *Necronomicon* into respectable English had already begun to break up and seek greener pastures. Various publishers had already turned it down, and Herman was despairing of ever finding a home for it. Then in walked Larry Barnes, scion of a printing business and a man who nurtured a lifelong fascination for the works of H.P. Lovecraft.

He even *looked* like Lovecraft. With his long, narrow face and haunted eyes, he could have portrayed Lovecraft in a made-for-TV movie. I talked to Herman later that day on something totally unrelated when he cut me off and told me I had to talk to someone who had walked into his store that afternoon looking for the *Necronomicon*.

I met Larry that night at an apartment in Manhattan that was luxurious and tastefully decorated. This was a far cry from the usual places to which I was invited: studio bed-sits in dilapidated tenement buildings or huge lofts in which the inhabitants spent everything on the rent and had nothing left over for furniture or amenities. Larry Barnes represented taste, style, and not a little wealth. And he was passionate about the *Necronomicon*. He wanted to print it. Publish it. Promote it. Period.

He was younger, tanned, clean-shaven, healthy and fit (as opposed to my ashy pallor, crucifix-thin torso, dark beard, and black clothes). He looked like a California surfer flung onto the rocks of Manhattan Island and who had been searching in vain for his board ever since. All during the time I knew him, even when he was floundering in the grip of his various addictions, he never looked sick, and he was never without a tan. He wore shorts and sandals in the summer and even into the autumn, as long as possible. He was, ironically, the picture of health in a city that is normally dark, dreary, dusty, and dank. He was full of nervous energy, and occasionally had a hard time focusing on a single conversation or a single topic. In the midst of an important business discussion, he would break off and say, "Simon! Look at this? What do you think? Is it born? Is it . . . *twisted?*" handing me a toy alien or the photo of a UFO in flight, raising his eyebrows and staring, bug-eyed, into the distance. We looked like complete opposites: the wealthy, glowing, manic Beach Boy against the dark, threadbare ascetic; a kind of New York intellectual who looked more like a film-school dropout than Magic Man, against the Wild Child from New Jersey.

He brought in a number of other players. One of these was Jim Wasserman, an experienced book designer who worked for Samuel Weiser's, the occult bookseller located in Manhattan. Weiser's was the *sina qua non* of occult bookstores. I used to go to Weiser's when it was still a secondhand bookstore just below Fourteenth Street off Union Square; in those days it was huge, but the occult collection was in the basement, dimly lit, with a comfortable couch, and all the strangest people in the City as customers and browsers. The success of the occult department was such that eventually Weiser's dropped the secondhand business and devoted itself entirely to the occult and "Orientalia."

Wasserman's credentials, therefore, were impeccable. What I did not realize at the time was his membership in the OTO. Wasserman belonged to a branch that was run by one Marcelo Motta, a Brazilian occultist who claimed to be the legitimate head of the order. That would change the year the *Necronomicon* was published, when a kind of custody battle took place between Motta and an ex-Army captain by the name of Grady McMurtry for leadership of the Order. When the dust settled, Wasserman had defected and was working for the McMurtry gang, a situation in which he found himself referred to in print by Motta as "deceased"; but we are getting ahead of our story.

Others were brought in by Larry to handle various aspects of the book's design. This was in the days before computers were used for everything, so experienced professionals were called in to deal with the minutiae. Larry was a perfectionist, as anyone who ever worked with him knows. He had an eye for detail and an infuriating habit of never being satisfied with a result. He also tended to overdesign, and this is evident in the finished book's eldritch appearance. There were those of us who might have preferred a book that was starker, a simple black cover perhaps and the single world *Necronomicon* in small print in the center. That was too film noir for a man who preferred the Hammer film approach. In any event, it was not Larry's style for it did not allow him to create; it limited his input to one of financing and production management, and to anyone who knew Larry, that was not acceptable. The *Necronomicon* had to be as much *his* creation as it was the fruit of the labor of translators and the book's sole editor: me.

He also, perhaps, understood the potential market more than I did. The book's ultimate design may have had a lot to do with its initial success. Larry would take the book from the domain of a few occultist snobs and gothic horror aficionados and present it in the way it was embraced by the eventual paperback publisher, Avon: a book for the mass market; a book that was not only a grimoire, a serious occult book, but that was also in its own way entertainment. I look back on Larry's contribution now as a stroke of genius: the Marvelization, if you will, of ceremonial magic.

Many "serious occultists" criticized the book's mass market popularity, as if popular acceptance immediately devalues

a book's credibility. I have always had a hard time understanding that point of view: as if charging fifty dollars for a
copy of the book was somehow preferable, more solemn,
more . . . occult than charging five dollars. As if it raised the
stakes, separated the wheat from the chaff, when all it does
is separate the rich from the poor. People who profess to be
ceremonial magicians like to think of themselves as elitists,
possessed of a deep understanding of the workings of the
paranormal world. Most of the so-called magicians I have
encountered, however, are anything but. The world of ceremonial magic for them is an escape, a tailor-made environment in which they can claim to be powerful or wise . . . like
teenagers in a role-playing game. Dungeons and Dragons,
perhaps. Or the card game Magic.

But take that aura of "specialness" away from them and
give it to the masses, and they turn ugly. They don't want to
see the pearls of their inadequate education and imaginary
initiations squandered on the hoi polloi, the lumpen prole-
tariat, the petit bourgeoisie. They don't want to accept that a
person picking up a paperback book for less than ten dollars
is able to summon the same forces as someone who has
spent years (or, at least, weeks!) studying the arcane sci-
ences and mumbling a lot of half-understood gibberish for
which they themselves have no historical or social context,
no psychological or intellectual grounding.

Larry's popularization of the *Necronomicon* was a political act, and it had interesting consequences. More than the
self-conscious politics of the Dadaists or Surrealists, it was
an act played out on a grand scale and with considerable
aplomb. He began to market the book through such media as
Omni and *Psychology Today* . . . and *National Lampoon*.
The book became famous. Even as it was attacked by fundamentalist Christians for being "satanic," it was praised in fan

mail we received from all branches of the military as being "right on." It is still, at the time of this writing, a best seller at Fort Benning. They "got it"; the Christians did not.

But before the advertising, the printing.

Larry proposed that he buy all the rights to the book. This was problematic for me, for several reasons. In the first place, what would Herman's position be? At the very least I owed him first shot at selling the book in his store and to his mailing list. In the second place, I was reminded of all the problems respected occult author Israel Regardie—among others—had had with publishers and how signing away the rights for a small payment usually resulted in regrets later as the original owner saw book sales skyrocket while his own paltry fee disappeared after the first month's rent. Just as Regardie did not write the rituals that appear in his mammoth volume on the Golden Dawn, I did not write the rituals in the *Necronomicon;* nonetheless, I regarded the book as my property. I discovered it, I arranged for its translation, I edited the final draft, I wrote the Introduction. No one had more input to the final product than I did, and no one questioned my rights to it. Had I signed it away for five or ten thousand dollars, my sanity *would* have been questioned by everyone, from Herman Slater down to the least contributor.

And there was yet another problem. The book was stolen. Not the final draft, of course, but the original manuscript. No one knew if Chapo and Hubak had mentioned its existence to the FBI. Why would they? It was just another bundle of papers—useless to them, but of value to Prazsky, their erstwhile protector—in a collection with other bundles of papers. Yet, someone, somewhere, might lay claim to it; and if they did, I had no idea where the manuscript now rested. With Prazsky, still? Or had he gotten rid of it? I didn't dare contact him to find out, since we had parted on bad terms. I was also afraid, quite frankly, that his phone was tapped or his mail read. This was during the Watergate revelations, remember, and the MK-ULTRA hearings. Paranoia was the Demon of the Air at that time, and we were all possessed.

Thus was Schlangekraft Publishing formed.

Critics have mused over the name, wondering where it came from. They rightly understand *schlangekraft* to mean "serpent power," but they have no idea of its context. That's because the critics were not around during the most intense occult renaissance America had ever known. Had they been there, most of what they criticize about the *Necronomicon* would be irrelevant, most of the "mysteries" resolved.

As mentioned, in 1975 the authorial team of Robert Anton Wilson and Robert Shea had published a novel that would become an underground classic: *Illuminatus!*

Published as a trilogy, *Illuminatus!* was a kind of New Age *Ulysses*. It weaves together various threads of conspiracy theory, Aleister Crowley–brand occultism, Timothy Leary–brand drug mysticism, reincarnated Nazis, Asian martial arts, Libertarian politics and economics, and deranged sex, all in an intense and utterly compelling tale of cosmic intrigue and stream-of-consciousness illumination. It won over a huge population of younger readers that had become disaffected by organized religion and organized politics of any kind but were equally frustrated by New Age "mumbo jumbo" and radical, left-wing politics whose proponents seemed just as fanatic as the enemies they were trying to unseat. *Illuminatus!* became a home for *everyone else*.

The "eye in the pyramid" motif of *Illuminatus!* also became an obsessive concern of Larry Barnes, who began using it as an icon everywhere in his office and, later, in ads for the *Necronomicon* and in the book itself, on the title page. In the context of the *Illuminatus* trilogy, *schlangekraft* was used not only in the obvious sense of "serpent power" (a reference to Tantric yoga and the power of kundalini), but also in another, more obscene, sense as "penis power," *schlange* or *schlong* being a vulgar Yiddish term for the male member. It was an inside joke, and one that I adapted as the name of the new publishing company that would be responsible for the *Necronomicon*. In arrangements with friends who had worked on the book at various times, we created a new corporation, and this one would be responsible for the book's coming into print. Larry Barnes was not a member of this corporation. Instead, he entered into an arrangement with us that would split any profits from the sale of the book fifty-fifty. Our contribution to the deal was the book itself; Larry's contribution was the financing for the first, deluxe, limited edition. And, in the midst of all this, we ensured that Herman Slater's interests were also protected by giving him an exclusive first shot at retailing it.

This deal was worked out during an intense meeting at the headquarters of the Barnes conglomerate. Larry's father, Hugh Barnes, was opposed to any deal that did not give exclusive rights to his son; understandably so, for Hugh Barnes was a businessman and wanted the best possible deal. However, as the editor and as the spokesman for Schlangekraft, I resisted any attempt to sign away the book's future so cavalierly. Hugh walked into and out of the meeting room with counteroffers, while I worked out the details with Larry. Finally, we had a deal we could all live with: Larry got his fifty percent of all future profits, after his initial investment had been paid back through sales. It was done, and work began to proceed on the book.

Once Herman Slater knew the deal had been signed, he began to advertise the book at his store and in direct mailings to his by now considerable mailing list. At the same time, Larry tried to sell the paperback rights at once, hoping that a paperback sale would pay for his investment up front. We spent weeks negotiating with Simon & Schuster, but they eventually turned it down; it did not end in a complete failure, however, for the editor in charge of the proposal at Simon & Schuster was a very attractive, petite blonde who eventually became Larry's *enamorata.* (Whether that had begun before the approach to the publisher or after is not clear to me at this time; there is a possibility that Larry already knew her before the *Necronomicon* project was a reality.) As we worried about the paperback sale, however, another development was taking place that rendered the whole mission moot.

Advance sales for the *Necronomicon,* through Herman's store and mailing list, more than paid for the costs of printing and binding the book, even taking into account Herman's forty percent cut. The book had already paid for itself. We were in business.

The first printing consisted of 666 leatherbound, silver-stamped, beribboned special editions on heavy paper, and 1,275 clothbound copies. The leatherbound version retailed for fifty dollars, and the clothbound for thirty dollars. That meant a total retail value of $71,550 (1977). Of course, that was less $32,198 for Herman's discount as a reseller, leaving nearly $39,350 before costs. After subtracting printing and binding costs—which were considerable—and advertising costs, and a number of books that were given as gifts, whatever was left over was plowed back into a second edition in 1979–80, and then a third in 1981. While some profit-taking did take place, the bookkeeping became hopelessly muddled, with cartons of books flying around the City uninvoiced in the trunk of Larry's car to supply first Herman

Slater and then, after much protesting by Herman, other outlets around town who were clamoring for a chance to sell the dreaded *Necronomicon*.

None of this happened on time, though.

People had been sending in their advance orders—many of them *prepaid*—six to nine months before the book was actually available. That was one of the major reasons behind the rush to get the book into print, a rush that has been commented upon by various self-anointed judges of the book's merits. The popular misconception is that the rush was due to some sinister agenda; far from it, of course. Herman had taken cash up front and did not want to pay it back, and the natives were getting restless.

Just as importantly, from our point of view, was the occult calendar. We originally wanted the book to come out on October 12, 1977, for that would have been Crowley's birthday, a date commemorated in the dedication of the book. However, even with all the haste with which we were capable, that date was not going to happen.

Then I realized that December 1, 1977, was to be the thirtieth anniversary of Crowley's death. That seemed the perfect choice for the book's release: 1977 was also the fortieth anniversary of the death of H.P. Lovecraft. Larry agreed that it was all but certain we could make that date, so we announced it with great fanfare.

In fact, we threw a party.

In the months leading up to the book party—held, appropriately enough, at the Inferno Disco on Nineteenth Street—Larry seemed more preoccupied than usual. The book's design and printing was coming along well, and I accompanied him to the binders to check on the silver stamping and the leather. It was while we were driving back from New

Jersey to New York that he mentioned what was troubling him.

"Simon," he asked, "is it true? About the book?"

"What do you mean?"

One hand on the wheel, another rummaging through the galleys of the book, he flipped open the pages and pointed to the dedication.

"The date it was completed, October 12, 1975? That's Crowley's birthday?"

I remembered the date vividly.

"Yes, why?"

"Was that *really* the date you finished it?"

All the translation work had been completed, all the research done at the various libraries and universities. Everything was in a complete pile in my apartment, and I had been working through it, section by section, during the entire summer. At the same time, I had been holding classes on virtually every aspect of the occult. It was a very busy time, and I was feeling the pressure to complete the manuscript before the end of the year. Herman Slater was eager to have it in his hands, and I was just as eager to rid myself of what had become an onerous task.

The major sections had all been completed at various stages by the summer of 1975. What remained was the Introduction, a context within which to place the book and its message, if there was one. As the summer months cooled into autumn, a certain clarity of mind came over me and I saw my way through it. I had wrestled with the Introduction for a long time, for various reasons.

In the first place, I was very conscious of the seemingly anti-Christian nature of what I was doing. After all, no Christian denomination approves of magic or occultism, notwithstanding the many times to which occultism is resorted in the Old Testament, such as the episode of the Witch of Endor. Here I was, an Eastern Orthodox priest, writing an Introduction to the *Necronomicon!* In addition, I was a conflicted priest at that. The excesses of Roman Catholicism over the centuries—excesses that led to war, murder, and executions, even of my Eastern Orthodox brethren during the sack of Constantinople, for instance— bothered me greatly. In addition, I was at that stage of my life quite ambiguous in my feelings towards my own church. The politics, the infighting, the hypocrisy were poisoning me against my brothers.

Thus, if my Introduction was anti-Catholic, need it be also anti-Christian?

As I struggled with these issues, and as I realized that the intellect of Aleister Crowley and his no-nonsense approach to magic had informed my early education in the occult— even as his contempt for women and his native racism bothered me on other levels—I began to write what became the Introduction in a matter of days.

Christianity, as it is popularly understood, is a religion for the common person: for the person with no special training in theology or church history, who desires only to be led and to be told what to do. At one point the Catholic Church was even selling indulgences, allowing those with enough money to buy their way out of Purgatory (not a concept familiar to Eastern Orthodoxy, by the way) and into Heaven. It was this cynical manipulation of the faithful that brought about the Reformation and the famous ninety-five theses of Martin Luther. But it also brought about more wars, this time fought over religion and religious loyalties, as if this is what Christ had intended when he said, "I come to bring not peace but the sword."

Yet, there was a hidden side to Christianity; a Christianity of secrets, of signs and symbols, of a golden stairway to personal enlightenment. It had been all but forgotten, except in the pages of the grimoires where such ideas are implicit in everything the magician is told to do. Magic for me was not antagonistic to the idea of Christianity, but it *was* problematic.

I slowly drew my thoughts together, and what was to be the Introduction—my real contribution to the book—was finally finished in the late afternoon of October 12, 1975. It was only later that night that I realized I had completed it on Crowley's birthday. I signed the bottom of the Introduction with that date and thought no more about it.

But it had a more horrible significance, and one that cannot easily be discounted as "coincidence."

"Yes," I told Larry, mystified as to why he would bring up that bit of arcana. "I finished it on October 12, 1975. Why?"

As we drove across the George Washington Bridge and began to head downtown on the West Side Highway, he told me.

"That's the day my brother Wayne died of a drug overdose."

Of course, I did not know Larry then, and certainly didn't know his brother, Wayne. I met Larry Barnes for the first time a year later. Obviously, Larry had understood the significance of the book's dedication in ways that were totally unknown to me:

Dedication
On the One Hundredth Anniversary
Of the Nativity of the Poet
ALEISTER CROWLEY
1875–1975
Ad Meiorum Cthulhi Gloriam

Crowley, of course, was born on October 12, 1985. The book had been completed not only on his birthday, but on the centenary of his birth. On that very day, Wayne Barnes had died. The dedication finishes with the Latin phrase *Ad Meiorum Cthulhi Gloriam,* or "To the Greater Glory of Cthulhu." What explosion occurred in Larry's cortex when he saw that dedication and realized its significance? The correlation of Crowley, the *Necronomicon,* and Cthulhu with the death of his brother . . . no wonder the book became for him a personal quest, an obsession that occupied him to the end of his days as he struggled to understand its meaning, for he had been led—as if by the hand—to Magickal Childe bookstore and to Herman Slater, who lifted the final draft of the book from beneath the counter and handed it him, a manuscript that bore on its dedication page the date of his brother's death.

No other publisher had accepted the book. It looked as if it would have to wait until Herman made enough money from his other ventures to pay for the publication himself. Everyone else had turned it down. It sat there, waiting, for Larry Barnes to walk in one day and *ask* for it.

As the day of the book's publication loomed, it was decided to throw a book party to announce it, and also to provide a venue for what was fast becoming an occult rebirth in New York City. In the years starting with the opening of the Warlock Shop in June 1972 to the *Necronomicon* publication in December 1977, tremendous things were happening in the cultural environment of the City and the country at large. The publication of *Illuminatus!* in 1975 was one of those events, but 1977 also saw the release of important new directions in cinema history. *Close Encounters of the Third Kind* opened that year, as did *Star Wars.* Aliens were on everyone's mind, and Larry Barnes was in his element. In addition, the OTO was coming out of retirement.

A power struggle was taking place between the faction loyal to aging hippie and former Army captain Grady McMurtry, and an equally bizarre Brazilian named Marcelo Motta. Jim Wasserman, who was designing the *Necronomicon,* had switched loyalties from Motta to McMurtry on July 18, 1976. At the Magickal Childe bookstore, the OTO was conducting Gnostic Masses in the back room that had been reserved for group rituals, classes, and the like. A regulation size Gnostic altar was set up and the Masses were held with regularity, complete with "cakes of light."

Officiating at these ceremonies was a gentleman we shall call Sean, a member of the Order who eventually became disaffected when the McMurtry gang gained prominence in April 1977. This was when the "Caliphate" was formed, naming McMurtry as the Caliph, or successor, to Crowley ... something that the available documentation from Crowley did not unequivocally support. No matter. On October 12, 1977—the date originally planned for the release of the *Necronomicon*—the OTO "Grand Lodge" was declared, and the McMurtry faction was formally at war with the Motta faction over control of who would be considered the OHO, or "Outer Head of the Order." This situation eventually went to the American courts (!), which declared McMurtry the winner. This was, of course, a disaster in many ways, most especially concerning ownership of the Crowley copyrights, which the McMurtry OTO claimed for themselves, thirty years after Crowley's death.

Ironically, Sean later became an Eastern Orthodox priest in the Prazsky succession, based in Ohio, married to a former student of mine, and runs a small denomination, an amalgam of Eastern Orthodox Christianity and a brand of pre-Roman Catholic Celtic Catholicism. So, Sean essentially went in the opposite direction from me: from magician to Eastern Orthodox priest in the Prazsky line, while I went from Eastern Orthodox priest to magician. Both of us were touched by the episcopacy of William A. Prazsky, however, even though Sean probably never knew of the relationship between Prazsky, Chapo, Hubak, and the *Necronomicon*, which occurred before his time.

In December 1977, however, all of this steam was coming to a head. The Son of Sam murders had been taking place since 1974 (at least); the first known murder associated with the Sam cult had been at midnight on October 12, 1974, in California, at the Stanford Memorial Church: the bloody sacrifice of Arlis Perry, a Christian and student at Stanford University, on the day of Aleister Crowley's birthday, in a church, ritualistically, and a year to the day before the *Necronomicon* was completed. The killings then moved to New York City with the famous Son of Sam murders that had the City spellbound for months until the arrest of David Berkowitz on August 10, 1977.

Although Berkowitz had taken the fall for the Sam killings, those of us who were heavily involved in the occult scene at the time knew, as I said before, that Berkowitz had not acted alone and that the killings had continued. Andrew Prazsky himself was living in a world that straddled both the occult underground and the religious underground, surrounded by influences from both sides. His consecration of Andre Pennachio on October 12, 1969—once again, Crowley's birthday—was a nod to these factors; Pennachio was well-known in the same circles that included some of the Sam conspirators, such as producer and promoter Roy Radin, who, from his Long Island enclave, dabbled in the occult and once contacted me with a proposal to film a demonic conjuration, a proposal I turned down. Radin was later slain by a man identified as "Manson II," an episode covered exhaustively in Maury Terry's book on the Sam cult, *The Ultimate Evil.*

Further, the year 1977 saw some other dramatic developments. The Hillside Strangler murders began in California in October, possibly on the same day that the girlfriend of New Age activist and "social engineer" Ira Einhorn, Holly Maddux, was murdered and stuffed in a box in Einhorn's apartment in Philadelphia. The Gerald Stano serial murders—begun in Florida in 1973—were still taking place in the South. The Richard Chase "Dracula" murders would begin that December; the FBI raided Scientology offices in Los Angeles and Washington, D.C., and Scientology founder L. Ron Hubbard, his wife, and nine others burgled federal offices that same year; and President Jimmy Carter ordered a high level U.S. government review of Soviet psychic research capabilities.

Nineteen seventy-seven was also the year that Satan returned to Earth, according to the controversial best seller *Michelle Remembers,* allegedly a true story about a satanic cult survivor and the book that started the craze later memorialized by Geraldo Rivera in his famous television broadcast of October 24, 1988, "Devil Worship: Exposing Satan's Underground," one of the most-watched programs in television history. The broadcast included live interviews with former FBI agent Ted Gunderson and investigative journalist Maury Terry, who both insisted on the reality of murderous satanic cults in the United States. The year 1977 also saw the death of the first known AIDS patient, Margrethe P. Rask, in Denmark.

At the same time, those of us involved in the occult revival of the 1970s saw the period as one of spiritual liberation. Anyone reading the Introduction and the various prefaces to the *Necronomicon* cannot help but come away with that impression. It must have been the first—if not the only—grimoire to agitate for spiritual liberation and enlightenment, in terms that are at once political and religious. This is an aspect of the book that is conveniently ignored by its critics, even as it is embraced by the masses of people who have used the book: its significance as a product of the times, as well as in its textual material. While the book has been blamed for everything from serial murder to fraud, one cannot actually *read* it and still hold the opinion that it was somehow "designed" to foment murder and mayhem.

The party that was held for the book on December 1, 1977, was an exuberant expression of the belief in an ultimate and imminent spiritual renaissance. It was an event attended by hundreds of people, many of them culled from the various groups and subgroups that had developed around the Magickal Childe bookstore and the *Necronomicon.* As mentioned above, one of the two bands that performed that night—The Major Thinkers—would go on to greater glory as Black 47, the Irish agit-rock band that has provided soundtrack material for several films and deservedly gained an enviable reputation as "the Irish bar band that made good."

Beginning in various Blarney Stones in the Bronx, The Major Thinkers soon became a standard act at the Bells of Hell on West Thirteenth Street in the Village. As the movement spawned by *Illuminatus!,* Magickal Childe, and the *Necronomicon* exploded from the studio apartments and godfathered lofts into the streets, it was drawn to this strange little bar and its busy back room. The lead singer of The Major Thinkers, as mentioned, was Larry Kirwan, a native of Wexford, who had been a student of mine at Magickal Childe. He invited me to catch his act one day. After that memorable evening, an entire entourage began to form every Friday and Saturday night in the back room of the Bells, composed of my students, their friends, band groupies, and fellow travelers. We held specific concerts on days sacred to the occult calendar, such as Walpurgisnacht (April 30), Crowley's birthday (October 12), and the birthday of his first wife, Rose Kelly (who midwifed Crowley's *Book of the Law* during their honeymoon in Cairo in April 1904), which took place on July 23, the same day sacred to the rising of the Dog Star, Sirius, a star sacred to the ancient Egyptians.

As this grassroots movement gained momentum, it also attracted the Marvel Comics crowd, such as author Chris Claremont and his wife Bonnie—a talented jeweler and natural occultist—and Allyn Brodsky, among others, so that it became an amalgam of the fantasy and science fiction people on one side, the Marvel people on another, and the occultists on still another front. One could not tell the OTO from the witches or the sci-fi authors without a scorecard, and in its heyday there were even pot luck dinners that would have been the envy of any Unitarian congregation. We had created a *community* where it was believed none could be formed. And we had a mission: to bring occult knowledge and its weltanschauung to the world, to assist in its liberation from the stranglehold of venal politicians and abusive priests. It was New York City's own cultural revolution, and for several years its members could be found in all areas of city life, from music and the arts to medicine, business, banking, and the law.

The book party at the Inferno Disco brought all of these disparate elements together. It was a success, and lasted well into the night. The coordinating committee for the party was an ad hoc group of occultists known as StarGroup One. Composed of various members of the Magickal Childe crowd, it included personnel from the Wicca movement, the OTO, some unaffiliated fellow travelers, and myself. We arranged for the disco, the advertising, the brochures, the acts, the drinks and the food. It was the first such project of Star-Group One, and it went off without too many hitches.

Except one: the book wasn't ready yet.

Larry, as usual, had a few more final touches to make, and they took time. In the meantime, Elvis Presley had died that August, and Barnes was busy printing up an Elvis calendar and posters to make some quick cash, and that stalled the *Necronomicon* project for a while until he could focus on it again. While I had a mock-up of the book to show around that night, I couldn't actually fill any orders. The book would not be available for general consumption for another few weeks, until December 22, 1977 ... the Winter Solstice. They shipped in time for Christmas.

While the first edition had been a success, we spent 1978 basking in its glory and wondering what to do about a second edition. The leatherbound 666 deluxe copies had sold right out, and we were moving the clothbound editions quickly. Larry discovered a unique method for moving larger numbers faster. Barter space.

Barter space is a little-known strategy that magazine publishers use to fill up empty ad space in a hurry. If they have not filled an entire page with ads by deadline, or if an advertiser has pulled out at the last minute, they have empty space available right at crunch time. That space sometimes goes quite cheaply. Larry would take advantage of that to place ads for the *Necronomicon,* ads he designed himself, complete with elaborate moonscapes and eyes-in-pyramids. In addition, by using books as collateral for the ads and not actually paying for them in cash up front—bartering books for ads—he was able to place full-page, four-color ads in national magazines like *National Lampoon, Omni,* and *Psychology Today* with no money down. The magazines themselves took the orders for the books, sending us money only when the ad had been paid for by orders. We filled the orders, and everyone was happy. We never lost money that way, and usually had to hustle to fill the orders we received. Since Larry was generally disorganized, book orders usually wound up being filled in the middle of the night, which is one of the reasons why some autographed editions were signed not by me, but by Larry or one of his helpers. One of the stories current on the Internet is that I had "refused" to sign the books, which is patently untrue. I never refused to sign a *Necronomicon,* ever. I was not always informed when I had to sign books, however, since Larry would only decide he would fill orders long after good monks like me were asleep in their cells. He also did not feel comfortable around me when he was in the middle of his cocaine phase, and preferred people around him who shared his taste for drugs. Thus, the orders would be filled at two A.M. by Larry and any number of his associates and friends, and often this meant that someone else was signing "Simon" to the books, unknown to me until it was too late and the orders already had been filled.

Along with the orders came the fan mail.

It came from all over the country and from several foreign countries. The domestic mail could be broken down into two main categories: military fans and acned teenager fans. We knew they had acne, because they sent us pictures.

Larry had a great time posing as Simon during these exchanges, but only if women were involved. They would send photos of themselves in revealing poses, asking to communicate with me. I hardly ever saw this mail except on those rare occasions when Larry left his infamous "red file" lying around. This was a red file folder containing Larry's confidential communications on the *Necronomicon.* All the military fan mail and the female fan mail went into this folder, which he carried with him everywhere he went. I was a little annoyed that he kept this correspondence from me, but in the end I knew I would not be entering into long-term mail exchanges with the correspondents anyway, once I saw what they were writing.

The military men—and they were from every branch of the Armed Services—praised the book, without exception. (I was tempted to write "uniformly," but resisted.) One letter I remember in particular was on the stationery of the Strategic Air Command, informing us in a footnote that, by the way, arrangements for the Third World War were in preparation.

What can you say to that?

Another correspondent, however, did attract my interest.

At the time the book was being set in type—in other words, months before the book was available to the market—it was spotted by the Beat icon, William Burroughs.

Burroughs is probably best known for his quirky best seller, *Naked Lunch,* which was made into a film by David Cronenberg. Burroughs was part of the Beat network that heavily influenced American letters in the 1950s along with such other luminaries as Allen Ginsberg and Jack Kerouac. Having lived in North Africa for a while, he considered himself something of an authority on the magic and occultism of the local tribes. He was certainly an authority on their drugs, and was a self-acknowledged and unapologetic heroin addict. An heir to the Burroughs fortune, he had a small private income that allowed him to travel the world and indulge in his taste for drugs and young men. He had been married once, but killed his wife in an accidental shooting in Mexico. He had a son, who also became a writer. But his life was anything but middle class.

Fascinated by both guns and magic, Burroughs was a conspiracy theorist on a cosmic scale. His unique method of writing—which involved cutting and pasting material to create an arcane stream of consciousness, a variation on the Surrealists' "exquisite corpse"—was in its own way analogous to conspiracy theory: seeing meaning in what appears to be a random juxtaposition of events. Coincidence, synchronicity, call it what you will, Burroughs built a literary style structured on webs of connections that stream out into the universe. There was also something a little "comic book" about Burroughs's characters and plotting, especially in his later works, and he took enormous chances in his novels, which were at times banned for obscenity. Norman Mailer believes Burroughs was a true genius: an opinion shared by many, including Ken Kesey, Timothy Leary, and Allen Ginsberg. He left behind a legacy of over a dozen novels and collections of letters, essays, etc., and one note concerning the *Necronomicon*.

As the book was being set in type, Burroughs happened to be visiting the typesetters. He saw the galleys for the *Necronomicon* and sat down, there and then, to read the book through the night.

When Larry heard this from the typesetters the next day, he was enthusiastic. It seemed to indicate to him that the book might get the kind of critical attention that he craved but didn't know was possible. He asked Burroughs—who at that time was living in his "bunker" in lower Manhattan—to write something about the book, something that he could use in promotional material.

Burroughs responded with a two-page letter in which he spoke about magic and ceremonial magicians in general, men who were like Mafia dons safe inside their magic circles, sending demons to do their dirty work. It was a perceptive piece of writing on magic, however short it was. The final sentence was eventually used by the paperback publisher, Avon, as a blurb on the back cover:

"Let the secrets of the ages be revealed. The publication of the *Necronomicon* may well be a landmark in the history of spiritual liberation."

It echoed precisely the sentiment represented by the book's Introduction, and it showed that Burroughs—at least—understood what it was about and why it was being published. Critics have attacked the note Burroughs wrote in an attempt to downplay its significance, insisting that it was hardly a positive endorsement of the book. As it stands, the letter was received with unadulterated joy by Larry and myself. Larry, of course, would probably have prefered a review that less ambiguously praised the book to the heavens, but it was certainly an important document in and of itself. Burroughs had not written many such letters in his life, and the number of Burroughs's "endorsements" could probably be counted on the fingers of one hand. It was an important development, and raised the spirits of the *Necronomicon* crew, who believed it was a portent for success. It was also proof of the idea that publishing a grimoire could be evidence of "spiritual liberation" if someone with the profile of a Burroughs—who had made his reputation fighting for liberation, literary and sexual—could see that and accept it.

On the other side, though, were the critics who immediately—and predictably—cried "Foul." These were the people who decided at once that the book was a hoax, a cleverly contrived fabrication designed to bilk honest citizens out of their hard-earned cash. The problem with their arguments was that they were largely circular.

One argument was that Lovecraft himself said he invented the book, and thus the book did not exist.

Another argument said that the book did not accurately represent the fictional book created by Lovecraft, and therefore it was a hoax.

Quite often the same critics used both arguments.

Logically, then, if the book matched Lovecraft's invented fiction, then it was a good hoax; if it did not match Lovecraft's fictional *Necronomicon,* then it was a poor hoax. Any way you sliced it, then, the *Necronomicon* had to be a hoax.

I submit that if we had wanted to create a fictional *Necronomicon,* taking advantage of Lovecraft's fictional account of it, we would have done a much better job. As it stands, the *Necronomicon* contains testimony by an Arab and the title *Necronomicon* and not much else that could be immediately recognized from his tales. As we translated and edited the book from the Greek, we found words that were suggestive of the Cthulhu Mythos, that collection of stories by Lovecraft (and others) built around the existence of an extraterrestrial monster he called Cthulhu who lies waiting in the deepness of the world's oceans for the chance to rouse itself from its ageless slumber and wreak havoc on the world. The *Necronomicon*—according to Lovecraft—was an ancient book of magic that dealt with the mythology of the Cthulhu Mythos and contained rituals that could break open the gate between this world and the next, thus allowing Cthulhu and any manner of other monsters easy access to the Earth.

There is a similarity—a strong similarity—between the Cthulhu Mythos as described above and the actual *Necronomicon.* However, it would have been a much neater package if the book contained actual references to all of the Lovecraftian personae in scrupulous detail. That is not the case. I had identified the term *kutu-lu,* for instance, as a Sumerian word meaning "man of the underworld," and I believe that to be valid, as well as a number of other Sumerian and Akkadian words and phrases that I believe have counterparts in Lovecraft's work. But as a hoax, the *Necronomicon* is rather weak. One of the book's design staff—Khem Caigan—has complained in other places[2] that he offered to fix the book and make it more consistent with the Cthulhu Mythos, but that he was turned down flat. He seems miffed at this, but of course his offer was rejected. We had no intention of adulterating the book in any way, or of attempting to make it more "Lovecraft" than it was. We had a manuscript and we had a translation of that manuscript, and there was really no more to be done. To work over the existing text and make it more acceptable to Lovecraft scholars *would* have been a hoax, and we were not interested in that option at all. We wanted to present the book we had: a translation into English of an ancient Greek manuscript that called itself *Necronomicon.* Had we wanted to create a hoax, we would have enlisted Mr. Caigan's aid, I am sure.

The main question before us is, I think: is the *Necronomicon* we offered the *Necronomicon* mentioned by Lovecraft or invented by Lovecraft? There is no way to know the answer to this. I believe that Lovecraft heard the name from somewhere, because the coincidence is too startling otherwise. Yet, as we have shown, coincidence does make a regular and unsettling appearance around the persons and events connected to the book, such as the death of Larry Barnes's

---

[2] In a statement available widely on the Web entitled "The Simonomicon and Me"

brother on the very day that the final draft was completed, or the strange appearance of William Burroughs at the typesetters on the very day that the galleys were being completed.

The *Necronomicon* does offer a series of initiatory steps, called the Gates, which is similar to motifs in the Lovecraft stories. The near-hysterical ranting of the Arab's testimony is eerily similar to the type of deranged paranoia we find in Lovecraft's work. These things lead me to believe that this is the *Necronomicon* of Lovecraft's fiction.

Some things are missing, however.

The name of the Arab is never revealed in the text we have. There is no mention of "Abdul Alhazred," an impossible name in Arabic, by the way, since it violates Arab syntax. A more correct version might be "Abdul Hazred," if "Hazred," was a proper Arab noun, but even that does not appear in the text. (Had we wished to create a hoax, we probably would have included this name!) The Arabic title for *Necronomicon* was, according to Lovecraft, *Al 'Azif* which *is* genuine Arabic. It is mentioned in several old studies of Semitic magic and religion, such as William Robertson Smith's *Lectures on the Religion of the Semites* (1927), in which it is given as "the eerie sound of the *jinn*."[3] Lovecraft translates it as the nocturnal buzzing of insects. Close enough.

The Sumerian nature of the book is also attacked, or rather, my interpretation of it. That the book has Sumerian features is beyond question, and I was able to source much, but certainly not all, of the book's rituals and chants in other works on the Sumerian religion that were available at the time. Critics have used my bibliography as evidence that the

---

[3] W.R. Smith, *Lectures on the Religion of the Semites* (London: A&C Black, 1927), 566

book was compiled from those very sources! One marvels at
the logic behind this bit of sophistry. Instead of seeing my
research as supporting my contention that the book is basically a Sumerian grimoire, they see the grimoire as repre-
senting Sumerian research. In the desperate struggle to
prove the *Necronomicon* a fraud, the critics have resorted to
all sorts of mental gymnastics, even going so far as to con-
tradict themselves and each other if necessary.

While the critics attacked the book, however, the people
embraced it. Here was a workable collection of magical ritual that was pre-Christian in nature. There were no invocations of Jesus and the saints, such as may be found in more
European and medieval texts. There was no mention of Jehovah or Adonai. The entire structure of the book was pagan.
While some of the entities evoked were not Sumerian but
were of later Akkadian or Babylonian or even Coptic
nature—as I clearly define in the Introduction[4]—it was still
representative of an ancient approach to occult initiation. That
there may have been later glosses by centuries of magicians
who were brought up in non-Sumerian, non-Babylonian
contexts—as I also point out in the Introduction and the
Preface—does not dilute the book's basic structure, or its
power. Such degradations of pure Sumerian myth and ritual
were bound to take place over the millennia. It still remains
that the invocations in the *Necronomicon* are quite ancient
and are, in many cases, phonetic approximations of chants
in the Sumerian language. That makes it the oldest book of
magic in the Western world.

This bothered many people. The Wiccans were having a
hard enough time coming to grips with the fact that their
Books of Shadows were only about forty or fifty years old,

---

[4] *Necronomicon,* xix, xx, xxxii, xxxiii, etc.

rather than the four or five hundred years old they had believed them to be. That Gerald Gardner—with assistance from Aleister Crowley (or was it the other way around?)—created the Book of Shadows out of whole cloth is by now recognized and accepted by the majority of modern-day witches. That the *Necronomicon*—a usurper—should come along and profess to be the oldest pagan magic text in the world was yet another perceived blow to the witches and self-professed pagans. How could it be pagan? How could it fit in with the party line that paganism was all harmony and light, a New Age religion in the modern mold of political correctness? It was so . . . so . . . *evil*.

Really? Is it?

People who object to the *Necronomicon* object to its reputation rather than to its text. The *Necronomicon* has an aura of strangeness, of otherness, of which the occult revivalists are afraid. It doesn't send the right message. At least, it didn't in 1977.

While the *Illuminatus!* crowd in New York loved the *Necronomicon*, the people responsible for the reorganization taking place in the Wicca world were leery of it. It seemed to have a message of its own, and it wasn't about the nice horned god and the lubricious Moon goddess. It wasn't about sweetness and light and the love of Nature. It embodied a kind of *fear* of Nature, a fear of being abandoned by the gods, that could only be remedied by a proactive search for godhood, the domination of hordes of evil spirits and a relentless program of self-initiation and ascent up the Gates: to power, yes, and to safety.

Dangerous? Of course.

PART TWO

—◦—

The Sumerian Tradition
and the Hidden God

6: The Lost Gods of Sumer

Our work is therefore historically authentic;
the rediscovery of the Sumerian tradition.
> —ALEISTER CROWLEY, as quoted in Kenneth Grant,
> *The Magical Revival,* 52

The central issue of the *Necronomicon* that bedevils most of its critics is the fact that it is presented as a Sumerian grimoire. They point to inconsistences between what the *Necronomicon* states and the actual practices of ancient Sumer. This is a "straw man" argument, for nowhere do we insist that the book is itself a pristine copy of an ancient Sumerian cuneiform text; instead, we point out that it was a Greek manuscript that appeared to have been translated from an Arabic original. In fact, when it comes to specific recensions of Sumerian hymns—for instance, in the case of the *Enuma Elish* we admit that the version in the *Necronomicon* is "bastardized"[1]—we clearly state that the versions in the book are not identical to the originals but have suffered from many interpolations and glosses. Obviously, over thousands of years, much that was originally Sumerian would have been adulterated and distorted. What we do insist, however, is that the *Necronomicon* contains so many references to the religion and mythology of Sumer—and to the later Akkadian and Babylonian civilizations that displaced it—that what we have is a unique survival of an

---

[1] *Necronomicon,* xx

ancient belief system and occult technology, one that predates the medieval grimoires even as it shares some neo-Platonist elements (inevitable, since neo-Platonist philosophy was widespread and influential in the cities of the Mediterranean centuries before the *Necronomicon* was presumably being written in Arabic). That there would be Gnostic elements is also undeniable, such as the idea that the world is a battleground between opposing forces, since Gnosticism was so prevalent in the Middle East and constituted a kind of underground cult at the time Islam was gaining ascendancy in the region.

None of that takes away from the inescapable fact that the names of the principal gods of the *Necronomicon* are also the gods of ancient Sumer as well as some of later Babylon. What we seem to have is an attempt by a Middle Eastern occultist to syncretize the oral tradition of his cult, a Sumerian tradition, with the more literate Gnostic and neo-Platonist influences alive in his environment. Yet, it is this phenomenon that is fiercely attacked by the book's critics because, as we all know, Sumerian texts were not translated until the nineteenth century, when Sumerian-Akkadian tablets were uncovered in what is now Iraq. It is considered impossible that Sumerian mythology would have been preserved in some other, living form down through the millennia, in spite of the fact that we now know the Akkadians and Babylonians preserved the Sumerian language and much of Sumer's religion after their conquests of that territory, and in spite of the allusions to Sumer in the Old Testament as "Shinar." The historian's belief in the disappearance of all traces of Sumer has since been shown to be a false assumption, as we shall see.

I state in the Introduction that Sumerian civilization appeared from out of nowhere, full-blown. This has been sharply criticized as an error of fact. At the time the Introduction

was written, however (in 1975), not much was known about
the actual origins of the Sumerian peoples, and even such
scientific observers as Carl Sagan were forced to admit as
late as 1966 that "we do not know where the Sumerians
came from."[2] This was the general consensus of opinion at
the time; today, with additional archaeological discoveries
in the region, we entertain the theory that what we know as
the Sumerian civilization was the result of a gradual development of local Mesopotamian tribes from nomadic hunter-
gatherers to more sophisticated urban dwellers around 4000
BC, the so-called Ubaid period, with even the suggestion
that these local tribes were invaded by the peoples who
eventually became known as Sumerian. But where did they
come from? Explorer and archaeologist—and one of the
first discoverers of the ancient Sumerian city of Ur, C.
Leonard Woolley—wrote many years ago that the Sumerians arrived in Mesopotamia from the sea, and that elements
of their civilization could be traced as far east as Afghanistan
and Baluchistan, all the way to the Indus Valley[3] and *its*
equally mysterious civilization, to which Sumer is consistently linked, either by trade or by language. Sagan, though,
goes on to ponder whether the Sumerians were descended
from space people, since their own epics seem to point to an
astral origin as well as an ocean origin.

All of this was being considered at the time the *Necronomicon* was published. One should remember that there
was no Internet in those days, and that all research had to be
done by physically visiting libraries and universities and
talking to professors and grad students to get an idea of the

[2] Carl Sagan and I.S. Shklovskii, *Intelligent Life in the Universe,* 456

[3] C. Leonard Woolley, *The Sumerians* (New York: Norton, 1965), 8

current thinking on the subject. As such, the Introduction and the point of view of its editor is reflective of the common state of knowledge at the time, and of the fact that the only available *printed* information on Sumer were old books and academic articles published years, if not decades, earlier. It was in 1994 that historian Michael Baigent would write, "Archaeology, then, does not support the belief, *current earlier this century,* that the Sumerian civilization appeared suddenly and mysteriously, fully developed, upon the Mesopotamian plains . . ."[4] (emphasis added). He does admit, however, that one compelling mystery about the Sumerians does remain: the insistence in their literature that they were descended from a race that had existed before the Flood and had a list of their kings from before the Flood. The fact that the Sumerian language is totally unrelated to any others in the region—that is, it is not Semitic, as are the later Babylonian languages and, of course, Arabic and Hebrew—is another interesting and relevant point, perhaps evidence that the Sumerian people came from northeast of Mesopotamia, from present-day Iran (which is the site of an ancient, non-Semitic culture) or from even farther afield, since archaeological evidence points to contact between Sumer and what is now Afghanistan and Pakistan and the Indus Valley, and linguistic evidence points to contact between Sumer and India.

I also point to the idea that Sumer was the point of origin of all we know about the creation of the world and a war that took place in ancient prehistory between cosmic forces. Lately, such historians and commentators as the aforementioned Michael Baigent (one of the coauthors of *Holy Blood,*

---

[4] Michael Baigent, *From the Omens of Babylon: Astrology and Ancient Mesopotamia* (London: Arkana, 1994), 27

Holy Grail) have written books on the very same subject, linking the Sumerian and Babylonian religions and belief systems to later Gnosticism and Hermeticism (*From the Omens of Babylon: Astrology and Ancient Mesopotamia; Ancient Traces; The Elixir and the Stone;* etc.). Alan F. Alford has done the same in *The Phoenix Solution,* as has, of course, the irrepressible Zecharia Sitchin in a series of books on the subject, *The Earth Chronicles.* The Introduction to the *Necronomicon* was not written in an intellectual or academic vacuum, therefore; far from it. But the point of view I put forward was not acceptable to the book's critics: that it represents evidence for the survival of this ancient mythology thousands of years after it disappeared, and hundreds—if not a thousand—years *before* the rediscovery of Sumer in the middle of the nineteenth century.

Yet, Sumerian culture *did* survive into the twentieth century, albeit in an esoteric and virtually clandestine fashion, and along the supposed route of the Sumerians from East Asia to Mesopotamia. We are talking of the Toda people of India.

The Sumerians of the Nilgiri Hills

In the very southwestern part of India, in the state known as Tamil Nadu, there is a range of over seven thousand hills. At the very highest level of these Nilgiri Hills there dwells an exotic tribe with its own traditions and religion. In the past few hundred years—and especially since the time of the British Empire, which colonized India—these people, called the Toda, have been slowly integrating into Hindu society. At the time of this writing there are at most only a few thousand left. (Some estimates put the number of Toda at less than one thousand, or more optimistically 1,500.) They live in a region of stone circles and megaliths that archaeologists

believe were there before the Toda arrived, since the Toda
seem ignorant of their purpose. Yet the Toda are keepers of a
deeper secret—the secret of their own origins.

Genetically, they are different in many respects from the
surrounding tribes. They do not carry a marker for sickle-cell
anemia, for instance, even though neighboring tribes do. They
are predominantly fair-skinned, in contrast to the darker, more
Dravidian tribes of the Nilgiri Hills. They worship the buffalo,
and see in the horns of this beast a reference to the crescent
Moon, whose images they carve on stone tablets and on their
homes. They are strict vegetarians, yet they keep cattle for
their milk . . . and occasionally sacrifice them in barbaric and
savage rituals.

They observe several important deities, who are believed
to reside on their principal hills, but also acknowledge more
than one thousand others. Chief among the gods is the God
of the Underworld, a being known to them as On, who is
also credited for having created them and their buffaloes (according to some authorities; according to others, they were
created by a goddess).

For many years it was believed that the Toda are descendants of a group of Sumerians who fled eastward, possibly
during the time of the Akkadian or Babylonian invasions, for
in their prayers and incantations can be discerned the names
of Sumerian gods.

The most obvious, of course, is On, for who can that be
but the Sumerian An or Anu, also mentioned repeatedly in
the *Necronomicon?* (Another possibility is Nanna, the God
of the Moon, since the Toda worship the Moon god.) The
Toda believe that the land of death is in the west; that could
mean neighboring Kerala (according to some anthropologists), but it could as easily mean Mesopotamia, or even
the land of Magan mentioned in the *Necronomicon* and now

believed to be the region of Oman. They believe that the two
main rivers of the Nilgiri Hills are ruled by two other gods,
like a Tigris and Euphrates in miniature. The language they
speak today is considered a Dravidian dialect, but there is
evidence of a relationship between Dravidian and the Elamite
language of ancient Mesopotamia—a nation that bordered
Sumer—and, in fact, this proposed language group is called
Elamite-Dravidian. There is much controversy over the origins of the Toda dialect in particular, since the presence of
foreign words indicates at the very least some borrowing
from another culture. Early anthropologists were quick to
identify this culture as . . . Sumerian.

An examination of some of the stone monuments of the
Toda reveal amazing similarities to images found on Sumerian cylinder seals, such as seven-pointed stars and the crescent moon, and the relation of the crescent moon to the
horns of the buffalo. (Seven-pointed stars are believed to be
sacred to the Sumerian god Enlil, son of Anu, according to
Rawlinson and other authorities, and may also be a reference to a constellation of seven stars, either the Pleiades or
Ursa Major.) The Toda stones recall the *kudurru,* or bound-
ary stones, of the Kassites—an Iranian tribe that overran
Babylon about 1600 BCE until they were overrun in turn by
the Elamites four hundred years later. One such stone
shows—at the top—a lunar crescent, a sun disk, and an
eight-rayed star; below it is an altar with what appears to be
a pair of horns on top, believed to be an altar to Anu. In more
ranks below we find most of the more famous Sumerian
deities represented, with—at the very bottom—Ningizzida
and the Scorpion Man.[5] Circles, crescents and stars are typi-

---

[5] See, for instance, Carel J. Du Ry, *Art of the Ancient Near and Middle East*
(New York: Abrams, 1969), 92.

cal decorations of both Toda and Mesopotamian standing stones, as are the horns of the buffalo.

No less an occultist than Madame Helena Blavatsky—founder of the Theosophical Society and author of *The Secret Doctrine* and *Isis Unveiled*—became embroiled in the Toda controversy as early as March 24, 1878, in a letter published in the *London Spiritualist* concerning remarks she made concerning the Toda in *Isis Unveiled*. In this letter, she mentions another theory concerning the Toda: that they are descendants of one of the Lost Tribes of Israel, a theory also shared at the time by the anthropologist Prince Peter of Greece.

The Toda practice animal sacrifice in the form of the buffalo, which is considered sacred to the god of the Moon: a deity that is male to the Toda, as it was to the Sumerians. Oddly, they do not eat the buffalo after it is sacrificed, since, as noted, they were strict vegetarians, but leave the corpse within the stone circle—a "bull ring" of about thirty feet in diameter bordered by blocks of granite—in which it was sacrificed in accordance with a complicated ritual. Unfortunately, female infanticide was also practiced in this manner until recently, the doomed infant thrown into the bull ring and the bulls incited to trample her to death.

The sacrifice of the buffaloes is also a barbaric affair. Depending on the occasion, the number of bulls to be sacrificed varies. The manner of killing them, however, is with a heavy hammer blow between the horns. In a ritual similar to what one would expect from a Spanish bullfight, young men jump into the ring and each tries to kill as many as possible with their hammers. He who kills the most is considered a hero, blessed by the God of the Moon.

These ceremonies and practices are so unusual that it was natural for observers to assume that the Toda were not native

Mounted ad copy for the first edition of the *Necronomicon*. The lunar landscape with the Earth in the background was taken from a mural on the wall of Larry Barnes's office in Queens, New York.

Courtesy of the author

Larry Barnes and his father, Hugh.

Courtesy of Hugh Barnes

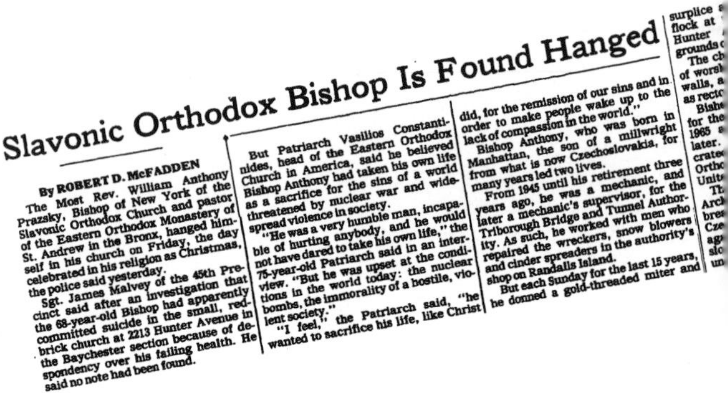

Slavonic Orthodox Bishop Is Found Hanged

By ROBERT D. McFADDEN

The Most Rev. William Anthony Prazsky, Bishop of New York of the Slavonic Orthodox Church and pastor of the Eastern Orthodox Monastery of St. Andrew in the Bronx, hanged himself in his church on Friday, the day celebrated in his religion as Christmas, the police said yesterday.

Sgt. James Malvey of the 45th Precinct said after an investigation that the 68-year-old Bishop had apparently committed suicide in the small, red-brick church at 2213 Hunter Avenue in the Baychester section because of despondency over his failing health. He said no note had been found.

But Patriarch Vasilios Constantinides, head of the Eastern Orthodox Church in America, said he believed Bishop Anthony had taken his own life as a sacrifice for the sins of a world threatened by nuclear war and widespread violence in society.

"He was a very humble man, incapable of hurting anybody, and he would not have dared to take his own life," the 75-year-old Patriarch said in an interview. "But he was upset at the conditions in the world today: the nuclear bombs, the immorality of a hostile, violent society."

"I feel," the Patriarch said, "he wanted to sacrifice his life, like Christ did, for the remission of our sins and in order to make people wake up to the lack of compassion in the world."

Bishop Anthony, who was born in Manhattan, the son of a millwright from what is now Czechoslovakia, for many years led two lives.

From 1945 until his retirement three years ago, he was a mechanic, and later a mechanic's supervisor, for the Triborough Bridge and Tunnel Authority. As such, he worked with men who repaired the wreckers, snow blowers and cinder spreaders in the authority's shop on Randalls Island.

But each Sunday for the last 15 years, he donned a gold-threaded miter and surplice ... flock at ... Hunter ... grounds ...

The first of the *Necronomicon*-related deaths, the suicide of Andrew Prazsky's father, as it was covered in *The New York Times.*

This story, from page one of *The New York Times*, made headlines all over the country. Michael Hubak and Steven Chapo were members of Andrew Prazsky's church and were not unfrocked at the time of their arrest but active members.

to his small
had built on
west of the
he Bronx.
75-seat house
n the altar and
uses that serve
parish hall.
ised night classes
dox ministry in
ted three years
1, he was conse-
the new Slavonic
archdiocese of the

headed by his son,
w Przasky, is a
tion founded by
icans in protest
invasion of Czecho-
the church remains
ction of Eastern Or-

thodoxy. The Slavonic Orthodox Church has a membership of about 2,000 in the New York area and several thousand members in a half-dozen other American cities.

The Bishop was the chancellor, or No. 2 figure, in the archdiocese, a baldish man with a long gray beard and a baritone voice that resounded from the choir as well as the pulpit.

"He looked like Santa Claus," Patriarch Vasilios said. "He had a hearty laugh and was always helping people in every way he could. When somebody had no heat, he'd fix the boiler. If somebody had a leak, he'd go up and fix the roof. He worked for people for nothing. He gave them money."

According to Sergeant Malvey, detectives who interviewed members of the family learned that the Bishop had been suffering from stomach ailments and had grown despondent recently. On Friday, after a day of solemn and joyous Christmas services, the Bishop left the rectory and went into the church.

"They thought he went into the chapel to pray," the sergeant said.

At about 7 P.M., Archbishop Andrew entered the church to call his father to dinner and found his body hanging from a rope that had been thrown over a rafter in the middle of the chapel in front of the altar.

"He was a prince of a man, deeply philosophic and compassionate," Patriarch Vasilios said. "He will be remembered because he left the imprint of his goodness: the sharing of his love."

2 Unfrocked 'Byzantine Priests' Held in Yale Rare-Book Thefts

By LAWRENCE FELLOWS
Special to The New York Times

NEW HAVEN, March 16—Two men who described themselves as unfrocked Byzantine priests were indicted today on charges that for years they stole ancient books, atlases and manuscripts from the Yale Library to sell to rare-book dealers in New York and Chicago.

The Federal Bureau of Investigation said it had found hundreds of valuable books at St. Stephen's Monastery, 144-32 Hillside Avenue, Queens, that served the men as a temporary home and chapel.

From markings in the books that have been found, they appeared to have come from the libraries at the University of Chicago, the University of Washington, Fordham University, Dartmouth College, Harvard University, Indiana University, the University of Notre Dame and Manhattan College, as well from Yale, authorities said.

Among the books are some of the rarest in the world, officials said. Some of the old atlases contained hand-painted maps, and some of them had been taken apart to be framed and sold separately. No estimate has been made of the damage to the books, or of the number of books that may still be missing, or of the value of all that were taken.

The accused are Steven Chapo, 24 years old, and Michael Huback, 46. Both identified themselves as members

Continued on Page 37, Column 1

UNITED STATES DEPARTMENT OF JUSTICE

FEDERAL BUREAU OF INVESTIGATION

REVIEWED BY FBI/JFK TASK FORCE

ON 9/24/96 dd

☒ RELEASE IN FULL
☐ RELEASE IN PART

WASHINGTON, D.C. 20535

March 2, 1967

In Reply, Please Refer to
File No.

ASSASSINATION OF PRESIDENT JOHN FITZGERALD KENNEDY
NOVEMBER 22, 1963, DALLAS, TEXAS

On February 23, 1967, Carl John Stanley of Louisville, Kentucky, furnished information to a Special Agent of the Louisville Office of the Federal Bureau of Investigation and to two detectives of the Louisville Police Department that he was acquainted with David William Ferrie and John Martin through church activities. Stanley calls himself "Most Reverend Christopher Maria Stanley" and refers to himself as "Archbishop of the Metropolitan Eastern Province, American Orthodox Catholic Church." John Martin is identical with Jack S. Martin, private investigator who has previously reported to us concerning his contacts with James Garrison, District Attorney of New Orleans, Louisiana, in connection with Garrison's investigation of the assassination of John F. Kennedy.

Stanley claimed that in July, 1961, on the recommendation of Bishop John Martin he and Martin consecrated David Ferrie as a bishop. He said Ferrie was deposed as a bishop in January, 1962, when it was learned that he had been discharged from his position with Eastern Airlines because of homosexual activity.

Stanley alleged that last year or the year before Martin was in Louisville from Thanksgiving Day until February 25th. He continued that Martin drinks a great deal and on one occasion while drinking Martin said that David Ferrie and Lee Harvey Oswald were "buddies" and that he, Martin, was connected with them. Martin allegedly made the statement that he would shoot Ferrie if he could get him in the right place and that "Ferrie was also in that plot to assassinate the President." Stanley also named Jerry De Pugh, address unknown, and George Augustine Hyde, a bishop in another church, as associates of Ferrie and Martin.

Later in the interview Stanley placed the date he received the information from Martin as January 3, 1966. In addition, he claimed that Martin said Ferrie, De Pugh, Hyde, Lee Harvey Oswald, and Martin lived together, worked together, were close friends, and were connected with a Cuban organization. When Stanley asked Martin further about Oswald, Martin "clammed up."

Democratic front!

A copy of an FBI summary of Archbishop Carl Stanley's testimony in 1967 in which Stanley told officials he had deposed Bishop David Ferrie when he learned of Ferrie's homosexuality. This testimony was made only weeks before Stanley's own death and shortly after he met with Archbishop Propheta in New York. The timing is suggestive.

Courtesy of National Archives

UNITED STATES GOVERNMENT

Memorandum

: Mr. W. C. Sullivan

: W. A. Branigan

CT: ASSASSINATION OF PRESIDENT
JOHN FITZGERALD KENNEDY
NOVEMBER 22, 1963
DALLAS, TEXAS

1 – Mr. Deloach
1 – Mr. Wick
DATE: 3/10/67
1 – Inspector Jensen
1 – Mr. Rosen
1 – Mr. Sullivan
1 – Mr. Branigan
1 – Mr. Lenihan

By teletype dated March 9, 1967, the Louisville Office reported that Carl John Stanley died of a heart attack in Louisville on the evening of March 8, 1967.

Carl John Stanley was a purported bishop of the "American Orthodox Catholic Church." In memorandum Mr. Branigan to Mr. Sullivan dated March 1, 1967, in captioned matter, it was reported that Stanley volunteered information to the Louisville Office on February 23, 1967, indicating he knew David William Ferrie and Jack Martin, both of whom have received considerable publicity in connection with the investigation being conducted by New Orleans District Attorney Garrison. Stanley claimed that approximately January, 1966, Martin was in Louisville and claimed that Lee Harvey Oswald and David William Ferrie were "buddies" and that Martin was also connected with them.

Stanley also informed our Agents that he had contacted New Orleans District Attorney Garrison "about a month ago" and had furnished Garrison the data he allegedly received from Martin.

Stanley had an arrest record for sending obscene letters through the mail, was convicted for automobile theft and had been arrested on burglary charges in San Francisco. Chief of Detectives at Louisville, Kentucky, regarded Stanley as crazy and a confidence man.

We have previously suggested that Stanley may have been the individual who touched off Garrison's investigation of the assassination and led to Garrison's contact with Jack Martin.

ACTION:

For information.

REL: kmg
(8)

A notice for the file of the death of Carl Stanley in March of 1967, barely one month after the mysterious death of fellow clergyman David Ferrie in New Orleans in February. Stanley died only weeks after his return from a visit to New York City to meet with Archishop Propheta, his superior.

Courtesy of National Archives

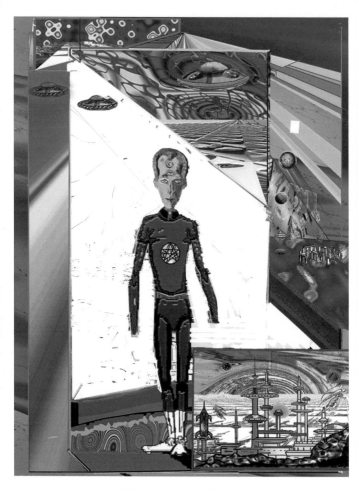

"Alien" by Larry Barnes.

This is a self-portrait of Larry—in his Kosmo Persona—with the seal of the *Necronomicon* on his chest.

Courtesy of Hugh Barnes

"Robotwife" by Larry Barnes.

This is a design that was to be used for a rock band that Larry was forming. The eye-in-the-pyramid motif makes its appearance, as well as three symbols from the *Necronomicon* and the "eldritch style" borders, recognizable from the hardcover edition of the *Necronomicon*.

Courtesy of Hugh Barnes

A Toda Monument:
Tamil Nadu, India.

This monument shows Babylonian influences and is thought to be related to the Sumerian *kudurru* stones with carvings of the Moon, a Star, and a Buffalo.

Courtesy of Chantal Boulanger-Maloney

Another Toda Monument: Tamil Nadu, India.

This shows a seven-rayed star and a number of crescents including those of the horns of a buffalo. The buffaloes are sacred to the Toda, who sacrifice them in savage rituals, but as the Toda are vegetarians, the meat isn't eaten.

Courtesy of Chantal Boulanger-Maloney

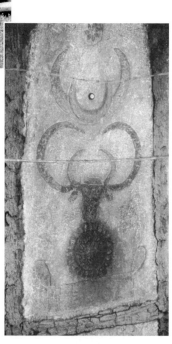

to India or, at least, that they adopted curious beliefs from somewhere outside the subcontinent. The tall stature of the men, their strange dress, their secretive religion with very little in common with Hinduism, and, most important, their language and the language of their rituals, all point to the Toda being survivors of another civilization. That this civilization was Mesopotamian is just one of the theories advanced, but as we can see from the evidence, it is a compelling case.

Part of the ongoing argument over the Sumerians is the origin of their language. It has been generally accepted among academics that Sumerian is a non-Semitic language, totally unrelated to any of the surrounding tongues or dialects of the time, and equally unrelated to Indo-European or "Aryan"; attempts are sometimes made to link Sumerian with Finno-Ugric or other anomalous European languages with no link to either Indo-European or Semitic. However, there is today a group of linguists who are impressed by the number of words that Sumerian has in common with Sanskrit and other Indo-European languages. When I stated this in the Introduction to the *Necronomicon* in 1975, it was a cause for some haughty disdain by the critics; however, even now, thirty years later, the controversy still rages over the precise origin of Sumerian and its relationship to other languages, principally Indo-European or what is known as Aryan. Further, the Toda people themselves are a linguistic and anthropological mystery, since their language, customs, dress, and religion are anomalous in the Indian province of Tamil Nadu. Even their physical appearance is at odds with their neighbors. Evidence for contact between Indian populations and those of Mesopotamia is taken for granted now. After all, the ancient civilization of Sumer abutted the Persian Gulf. It would have been a matter of a few months at

most for ancient oceangoing vessels to make the trip between Sumer and the southwest coast of India, where the
Nilgiri Hills and the Toda tribe can be found.

According to archaeologists, the higher the elevation of a
people, the longer they have lived in the region compared to
others in the same place. Newcomers arrive in the lowlands;
old-timers occupy the high ground, or flee to the hills to
avoid invaders. This is true of the Toda, who live at the highest elevations in the Nilgiri Hills, with their neighbors at
successively lower elevations down to the plains. In addition, Sumerian literature suggests that the Sumerians considered themselves to be originally a race of mountain
dwellers, as they believe the gods—and therefore the source
of their race—dwelt on the mountaintops. Their temples—
the ziggurats—were attempts to duplicate these sacred
mountains. (The nearest real mountains to Sumer were those
of the Zagros mountain range in what is now present-day
Iran. One theory has it that the Sumerians arrived in
Mesopotamia by crossing these mountains on their way
from the Indus Valley. Another theory, of course, is that they
made their way to Mesopotamia by sea from what is now
Pakistan or India.)

The proximity of the Nilgiri Hills to the southwest coast
of India and the Laccadive Sea, coupled with the fair-
skinned Toda, their "Old Testament" appearance, and their
unique language with its suspected Sumerian loan words—
as well as their strange mythology with its god, On—has
given rise to much speculation that the Toda are descended
from Sumerians, or at least from a people who lived in
Sumer or Babylon and were subject to their linguistic and religious influences. They would be living evidence of the survival into modern times of the Sumerian tradition, evidence
that goes hand in hand with that found in the *Necronomicon*.

Further analysis of the Indo-European language and Sumerian vocabulary has shown many suggestive links between the two languages. This may mean nothing more than that the Aryan invaders had either trade or other connections with the Sumerians; but that alone is important for our thesis that the Toda were Sumerian refugees, for we know the Aryans were in India at least as early as 2000 BCE, when Sumer was in its death struggles with the Babylonian invaders. Did some Sumerians flee in boats or on land along the Persian Gulf to the Arabian Sea, going in the same general direction to India taken by the Aryan invaders on horseback, and preserving what they could of their culture along the way?

What is more, did other Sumerians flee northward or westward?

The Yezidi Sect and the Worship of Shaitan

One of the most controversial sects of modern times is the Yezidi. A curious group that can be found in the northern part of Iraq in the region known as Kurdistan and not far from Mosul, they are secretive and mysterious. While sharing many beliefs in common with Islam, they have their own strange mythology and an important book that is never shown to outsiders.

The Yezidis captured the attention and imagination of G.I. Gurdjieff during his youth in the Transcaucasus region of southern Russia,[6] of Aleister Crowley on his travels through the region, and were further popularized in our time by Church of Satan founder Anton LaVey: and all for

---

[6] See G.I. Gurdjieff, *Meetings With Remarkable Men* (London: Arkana, 1985 edition), chapter IV.

the very simple reason that the Yezidis appear to worship . . . Satan.

The Yezidis consider themselves the oldest tribe of Kurds, and their religion combines elements of Islam, Christianity, Judaism, and even Manicheanism. They observe the rites of baptism, for instance, and revere Jesus as a prophet (as do all devout Muslims), but have a creation story that is far different from anything one might find in either the Torah or the Quran.

An edition of the *Mashaf Resh,* or *Black Book,* of the Yezidis was made available to a traveler in the region a hundred years ago and was published in English around 1909. As the Yezidis never show this book to outsiders—and nearly every one is an outsider who was not born into the Yezidi tribe—its provenance is questionable, but it is representative of what we know about the cult and what they have admitted themselves.[7]

Their creation epic has God—called Yazdan, from which it is assumed the Yezidi take their collective name—creating seven angels. The first among these is Melek Azazel, who became Taus Melek, the chief angel. Anyone who is familiar with ancient Judaism—or who has simply seen the 1998 film *Fallen,* starring Denzel Washington—knows that Azazel is a demon.

Most familiar as the goat mentioned in Leviticus, upon whose head the sins of the people were burdened during the Day of Atonement, this "scapegoat" was led out into the desert to die (or, as is stated in the Mishnah, pushed over a cliff). It is interesting to note that a bull was also sacrificed on that day as part of the ancient ritual of Atonement, and that, according to Exodus 24:5, young men were selected to

---

[7] I highly recommend the Web site www.sacred-texts.com for this and other valuable and difficult to find online texts.

perform the sacrifices of the covenant between God and man in the Sinai desert, which included the slaughter of calves: an odd parallel to the Toda sacrificial ritual.

The name Azazel is obscure, and has been translated different ways by different commentators. In some cases it is thought to mean "the goat that departs," hence the scapegoat. To others, Azazel means "Strong One of God." Other commentators place the name of Azazel firmly in the forefront of a group of demons or jinn known as *se'irim,* goat-demons or perhaps the Goat God. Descriptions of Azazel in an apocryphal work, the *Apocalypse of Abraham,* have him assume the form of an unclean bird that tries to steal part of a sacrifice of Abraham, and later that of a dragon with human hands and feet and six wings to each side. In Islamic theology, Azazel is Iblis, the Lord of Demons, a dweller in the wastes and the vast empty spaces of the desert. Another name for Azazel is *Asiz,* a god worshipped by the Canaanites. One cannot help but notice a similarity between *Asiz* and *Azif,* the "nocturnal howling of the *jinn*" that is the *Necronomicon*'s Arabic title.

Azazel, in any catalogue of spiritual forces, is an evil spirit, and was judged to be so by virtually every commentator. Somehow, this demon became an angel to the Yezidis. The name "Shaitan"—or Satan—also comes up as a term of honor for this angel, and the Yezidi consciously avoid using words that begin with the same letter, out of either deference or fear. They never refer to Shaitan by name, but only by such terms as "Exalted Chief " or even "Prince of Darkness," names that were also used for Azazel. Their philosophy is simple, if we are to believe the reports that have come down to us: that Yazdan (God) is remote and relatively unaffected by what happens on earth; the angels, however, are rulers of this world and one day will be received back into heaven. Although Taus Melek—or Azazel, or Shaitan—is a fallen angel, he still strives to return to heaven and to take the Yezidi with him. This event is supposed to take place in about four thousand more years. Until then they worship their founder—Sheikh Adi ben Musafir—at his shrine not far from the ancient site of Nineveh, a shrine whose entrance is adorned with occult symbols, including a vertically rising black snake. *(Schlangekraft?)* In addition, their official symbol shows the peacock—a symbol of Taus Melek (which means "peacock angel")—and a crescent moon, as well as numerous cuneiform symbols including *the eight-rayed cuneiform star known as a sign of divinity in Sumer.*[8] In fact, the image of the peacock has twelve wings, which is reminiscent of the twelve wings of Azazel.

It is interesting to note that at the time Sheikh Adi died, in 1155 AD, there was current in the region around Mosul—and thus in the neighborhood where Yezidism was born—a belief in the King of the Jinn. In 1064 AD it was believed that the King of the Jinn had died, and that whoever did not mourn his passing would perish. In 1204 AD, during a serious epidemic, a "woman of the Jinn" was reputed to have lost her son and placed a curse that whoever did not mourn his death would perish.[9] To devout Muslims, the Jinn—from where we get our word "genie"—*do* exist, since we know they are mentioned many times in the Quran. They are spiritual forces and may be either bad or good, or even Muslim. They possess supernatural powers, and most owe their allegiance to Shaitan. Thus, one can see why the Muslims may have considered the Yezidi to be dangerous devil worshippers, even though the latter conduct themselves with honor

---

[8] See the Web site www.yezidi.org for this fascinating emblem.

[9] W.R. Smith, op. cit., 412

and dignity, and practice their secret and syncretistic faith in remote areas.

Indeed, by all accounts, the Yezidis are a remarkably honest and decent people. They behave according to a strict code of moral conduct, and were persecuted terribly under their Islamic rulers, in particular Saddam Hussein, who decimated their population (along with the other Kurdish tribes he massacred), and there are some now living in Europe and the United States who simply wish to be left alone to live their lives in peace.

The lunar crescent, the cuneiform star, the belief in creation caused by seven angels, an eventual return to a forgetful God, and their historic home in Mesopotamia may all link the Yezidi to a survival of Sumerian or at least Babylonian religion among the Kurdish peoples from which they evolved. Their esoteric practices, their respect for demonic forces, and their mysterious *Black Book* all point to another possible survival: that of the beliefs and rites preserved in the *Necronomicon*.

Cutha, Kutu, and the Underworld

But we are not finished with this small history lesson on ancient Sumer and Babylon and their possible survival among the Toda and the Yezidis. There is one more destination on our itinerary, and it is equally as mysterious and—considering the events of the current time frame in which this is being written—possibly even dangerous. I speak of the realm of Cutha, the Underworld.

There has been as much controversy over the term "Cutha" as over the origins of the Sumerians, Yezidis, and Todas. I put forward my thesis that the Lovecraftian entity known as Cthulhu may be a form of KUTULU, a Sumerian

word meaning "Man of Kutu" or "Man of the Underworld." This has been attacked, naturally, by those who
see in my Sumerian phraseology as well as my Sumerian
history errors reflecting poor scholarship. However, as we
will see, the facts instead support the case I made in 1975
and which I make again today. What I did not know at the
time was the extent of the idea of the Sumerian city of
Cutha and its deep significance to chthonic, or underworld,
deities.

Cutha was located in the north of the Kingdom of Sumer
and Akkad, and was a city sacred to Nergal, the God of
Mars, whose temple there was called *E-shidlam,* or the
"House of Shadow." It was also the site of a great necropolis, a city of the dead. As described by that great historian
of Babylon, A.H. Sayce, in a series of lectures published in
1898:

> Nergal occupies a peculiar position. He was the local deity
> of the town called Gudua, "the resting-place," by the
> Accadians—a name changed by the Semites into Kutu or
> Cutha—which is now represented by the mounds of Tel-
> Ibrahim. For reasons unknown to us, the necropolis of Cutha
> became famous at an early time; and though the Babylonian
> kings, like the kings of Assyria and Judah, were buried in
> their own palaces, it is probable that many of their subjects
> preferred a sepulchre in the neighbourhood of Cutha.[10]

In speaking of Nergal, he goes on to describe him as a god
whose "throne was placed in Hades" and was "in fact, the
personification of death":

---

[10] A.H. Sayce, *Lectures on the Origin and Growth of Religion as Illustrated
by the Religion of the Ancient Babylonians* (Oxford: Williams & Norgate,
1898), 195

Hence his title of "the strong one," the invincible god who overpowers the mightiest of mortal things. The realm over which he ruled was "the great city" *(uru-gal);* great, indeed, it must have been, for it contained all the multitudes of men who had passed away from the earth. . . . But he was also "king of Cutha," as well as of "the desert" on whose borders Cutha stood and where its necropolis was probably situated . . . [11]

Alert readers will see immediately that "the strong one" was also the epithet of Azazel, and that both Nergal and Azazel were gods of the desert. A rather unsettling reference to Nergal is as the sacrificer of men, of the humans who are "the cattle of the god" Nergal; perhaps a natural enough extrapolation by a culture of cattle herders but disconcerting nevertheless.

A.H. Sayce, in the same series of lectures mentioned above, also cites a tablet written for the temple of Nergal at Cutha. He describes it this way:

The words of the text are put in the mouth of Nergal, the destroyer, who is represented as sending out the hosts of the ancient brood of chaos to their destruction. Nergal is identified with Nerra, the plague-god who smites them with pestilence, or rather with Ner, the terrible "king who gives not peace to his country, the shepherd who grants no favour to his people."[12]

The tablet goes on to describe "how the armies of chaos came into existence," referring to Tiamat, the "dragon of

[11] Ibid, 195–96

[12] Ibid, 372

chaos" who suckled them. Sayce goes on to equate Tiamat with the Hebrew *t'hom,* or "deep," which is also known in Assyrian as *tamtu,* the "deep sea." This source of chaos was also referred to as *abzu, apzu, apshu,* or other variants, depending on whether the source is Semitic, Sumerian, Akkadian, etc. The mythology concerning the *absu* also depends on which tradition you are reading. According to Woolley, this was also the term used for a drain in the temple of the ziggurat "down which were poured the libations to the god."[13] In Sayce, the association of *absu* with Tiamat—the dragon of chaos—is quite clear. Later myths have ascribed to *absu* a seemingly more benign significance, as the abode where Ea (or Enki)—the god of wisdom—dwells, based on a pun between *apzu,* "the deep," and *ab-zu,* "the house of knowledge." It is a common understanding in the modern Western world to associate wisdom and knowledge with all good things; however, the Sumerians had a keener understanding of the relationship between chaos and destruction on the one hand and "wisdom" and "knowledge" on the other.[14] Further, this "deep" was considered not only to be the watery abyss below or around the earth, but also the heavens: deep space.

In one of the Inanna legends—recounted by Kramer[15]—the goddess goes to visit Ea in the Absu in order to charm out of him the divine decrees that are necessary to form any civilization. She gets Enki drunk, and he agrees to give her the decrees, which she quickly spirits away on her boat.

---

[13] Woolley, *The Sumerians,* 150

[14] For a modern study that questions the assumption that all knowledge is good, see Roger Shattuck, *Forbidden Knowledge: From Prometheus to Pornography* (New York: St. Martin's Press, 1996).

[15] Samuel Noah Kramer, *The Sumerians: Their History, Culture and Character* (Chicago: University of Chicago Press, 1971), 160–62

Enki, upon regaining consciousness, becomes angry and sends sea monsters after her to reclaim the missing decrees, ordering them to stop her at any one of the seven "stages" she must pass on her way back to her home city. (Inanna takes several of these "seven stage" or "seven gate" journeys from the Underworld in her religious tradition.) Thus, one is forced to wonder what kind of benign place the Absu must be if its king must be tricked into giving up the laws of civilization and then finds it proper to send sea monsters after the goddess to get them back. The vision of the ancient Sumerians concerning the Absu was not of a peaceful, benign, and benevolent place from which all good things come, but a kingdom ruled by a despot and populated by sea monsters, among other creatures. Ask Inanna, who, on her flight from the Absu, must ask her vizier, Ninshubur, again and again for help as Enki attacks her boat repeatedly with his sea monsters until she finally returns safely home with the stolen goods.

Cutha is mentioned in the Bible, particularly in a phrase to be found in 4 Kings 17:24 (Douay Rheims), where it states, "And the king of the Assyrians brought people from Babylon, and from Cutha, and from Avah, and from Emath, and from Sepharvaim: and placed them in the cities of Samaria instead of the children of Israel." And in 17:29-30: "And every nation made gods of their own, and put them in the temples of the high places, which the Samaritans had made: every nation in their cities where they dwelt. For the men of Babylon made Sochothbenoth: and the Cuthites made Nergel: and the men of Emath made Asima." Thus, when we speak of the Cuthites in Biblical terms, clearly we are speaking of the men of Cutha and of the worship of Nergal. Later, the Jewish term *"Cuthim"* is used synonymously with Samaritan in the Talmud. This is an important point, for the identity of Cuthites with Samaritans—with the worshippers of the Lord of the Necropolis and the Underworld, the Strong One, the God of the Desert—will bring us to some startling (and controversial) discoveries.

It has long been known that the Samaritans were enemies of the Jews, even as they were nominally Jews themselves, for they valued the first five books of the Old Testament, the Torah, while ignoring the rest, including the rabbinical writings and commentators (such as Ezra) that came later and formed the Septaugint. You might imagine the Samaritans as Jewish "fundamentalists" in that sense. Indeed, they still exist as a small ethnic group in Israel, and still practice animal sacrifice according to the old traditions. The Jews looked down on the Samaritans as being hardly better than the Gentiles; the testimony in the Fourth Book of Kings, previously cited, gave the Jews ample reason for despising and fearing the Samaritans,[16] who were obviously composed of people descended from a long line of pagans and idolators for whom the Torah was but an extension of their own heretical practices.

The Samaritans, however, were present and very active in Saudi Arabia in the centuries after the destruction of the Second Temple. In the seventh century AD we find them in Mecca, where the Prophet Mohammed would make their acquaintance. In fact, there has been a lot of disputed scholarship on this point, for Mohammed was a member of a priestly Arab tribe called Quraysh, Quraish, or Koreish, who were in charge of the Black Stone of Mecca, what is called the Ka'aba (or "Cube") and in which direction all devout

---

[16] The most famous Western magician of all, Simon Magus, was himself a Samaritan. His system was described as a combination of Babylonian and Samaritan elements, and he was, of course, a Magus, which is a Zoroastrian term. Simon Magus is considered one of the early fathers of Gnosticism.

Muslims pray five times every day. In Mohammed's youth, however, the Black Stone was a pagan shrine that held 360 idols and was erected and maintained by Mohammed's tribe, the Quraysh.

Mohammed knew that there was animosity between the Samaritans and the Jews, since the Samaritans rejected the scriptural additions of the famous scribe Ezra, and he sought to exploit that animosity, especially as he was attempting to win over the Jews of Mecca and Medina so they might convert to his new religion, and getting the cold shoulder in response. In fact, Mohammed may have referred to this animosity obliquely, in Surah 9 ("Repentance") verse 30:

> And the Jews say: Ezra is the son of Allah, and the Christians say: The Messiah is the son of Allah. That is their saying with their mouths.

The Jews never said that Ezra was the son of Allah, not according to any other scriptural or Talmudic reference I can find, but it would not have been beyond the ability of the Samaritans to plant that malicious seed of doubt in Mohammed's mind. Mohammed, after all, had approached the (non-Samaritan) Jews of Medina in an effort to get them to recognize that he was the Messiah they were awaiting, and there was a slight possibility for a while that they would, a possibility that dissolved after a short time. Did Mohammed, in rancor, use this idea of Ezra's "corruption" of the scriptures—an idea that could only have come from the Samaritans—as an excuse to attack the Jews? After all, Mohammed also believed that the Samaritans themselves were the worshippers of the golden calf, the idol that caused Moses to lose his temper on Mount Sinai (Quran, Surah 20:85-97).

But there might have been another reason.

According to an old *Encyclopedia Britannica* and other sources, the Quraysh tribe of Mecca *were believed to have originated in ancient Cutha itself.*[17]

That there would be a relationship between the founder of Islam, the Prophet Mohammed, and the militant worshippers of Nergal of Cutha, the Lord of the Underworld, is a startling possibility. The Quraysh were a priestly class, which is why they were in charge of Mecca's holiest shrine, the Black Stone. In a rare, pre-Islamic poem written by the poet Zuhair, and actually hung in the Ka'aba before it was seized by Mohammed, it is written:

> There I swear by the temple, round which walk the men who built it from the tribes of Quraish and Jurhum . . .

This indicates that the circummabulation of the Ka'aba was a ritual performed long before the advent of Islam, and encouraged by Mohammed's tribe, the Quraysh.

And in an Ismaili text, untitled but dating from a time after the death of the Prophet, a text dealing with some of the esoteric philosophy of the Ismailis, it is written:

> These things, O my lords and brethren, are the verity of my knowledge, and the philosophy of my essence and my quality, and my circuit of my Ka'beh . . . and my prostration to the Muhammedan Kibleh and the Kureishite Ka'beh . . .

Thus, these ancient priests (known as *al-kahinan* in Arabic and as *kohenim* in Hebrew) were known to have erected the Black Stone of the Ka'aba themselves, and to oversee the

---

[17] *Encyclopedia Britannica*, 1911 edition, volume 17, 409

pilgrimmage of pagan Arabs from every corner of the land to "walk round" the sacred temple. The number of idols in the Ka'aba is invariably given as 360, which is suggestive of a Gnostic influence at the very least, if not a Sumerian and Babylonian influence, for 360 is a number derived from Sumerian mythology which originated the idea of a 360-degree circle in the first place, as "60" was the basis of their number system, and six times sixty was a number of perfection. The very name of the Quraysh is said to mean "Cyrus," the name of the first Persian king who restored the pagan worship of the Cuthites and other Mesopotamian tribes and reestablished the priestly orders. The symbol of Islam, the crescent and the star, is an echo of the same motif we find on the Sumerian and Akkadian cylinder seals, the symbols of the Yezidi, and the stone monuments of the Toda. And the devout Muslim must circumambulate the Ka'aba seven times, an echo of the seven-stepped ziggurats and the seven Gates of the *Necronomicon,* in a mystical journey that begins in his homeland, stretches across miles of desert, and involves the bloody sacrifice of goats and sheep along the way. That the seven circuits around the Ka'aba are representative of the seven Gates and the seven stages of the Sumerian ziggurats is confirmed by the simple fact that all of these result in communion with ineffable forces and bring the aspirant into contact with the Divine. Even Mohammed himself was sometimes referred to as a "Sabaean," a term that has come down to us as meaning a race of ancient astrologers but which also had a negative connotation, meaning a diviner or fortune-teller.[18]

Indeed, once the armies of Islam had marched on Mesopotamia and conquered it, they called Chaldea (the Biblical

---

[18] See the Pickthall translation of the Quran for this reference, in his opening remarks to Surah 20.

name for the region of southern Mesopotamia that used to be called Sumer) the "Garden of Quraysh," a title that aggravated many of the other Arab tribes who had fought long and hard to win Mesopotamia for Islam. Mohammed himself was frequently at odds with the Quraysh, and it was only with difficulty that he managed to win their obedience to his faith and their support for his military campaigns, campaigns that were enormously successful and continued long after his death, campaigns worthy of the blessings of Nergal, the God of Mars, the God of War, Chaos and Destruction.

Were the Quraysh—a priestly pagan tribe that were the builders and caretakers of the sacred shrine of the Black Stone of Mecca, the tribe that gave birth to its most famous son, the Prophet Mohammed—really Cuthites, "men of KUTU"? Was the invasion of Mesopotamia by the Arab armies a way for the Quraysh to return to their ancestral home in triumph?

According to an historian of the Arab penninsula, Philip K. Hitti, there was considerable influence on the Quraysh tribe and its practices from Mesopotamia. Even the chief deity of the Quraysh shrine, the Ka'aba, was Hubal:

> The tradition in ibn-Hisham, which makes 'Amr ibn-Luhayy the importer of this idol from Moab or Mesopotamia, may have a kernel of truth in so far as it retains a memory of the Aramaic origin of the deity.[19]

Part of the problem in understanding early Arab history is the fact that there was very little written down by the tribes in Arabia before the advent of Islam. Arab historians were

---

[19] Philip K. Hitti, *History of the Arabs,* 10th edition (New York: St. Martin's Press, 1985), 100

writing in the centuries *after* the Hegira, and often the actual
data was scarce and colored with a predictably Islamic bias.
What we do know is that Arab tradition places the Quraysh
at some point in their history in al-Hirah, a region located
near what had been Babylon and had once (about 200 AD)
been the capital of "Persian Arabia."[20]

> According to traditions preserved in ibn-Rustah it was from
> al-Hirah that the Quraysh acquired the art of writing and the
> system of false belief.[21]

The "system of false belief" is further clarified by Hitti
in a footnote to this passage wherein he describes this belief
as the practices of the Persian *zandik,* or Magian. Thus,
with the Quraysh came both writing and the Magian practices of ancient Persia. This was the tribe that would gain
control of the Ka'aba and introduce the idols of Hubal and
the goddess of Venus, al 'Uzza ". . . the most venerated idol
among the Quraysh, and Mohammed as a young man offered her a sacrifice."[22]

That Mesopotamian religion and magic—including
specifically the God of Cutha/KUTU, Nergal—was known
throughout Arabia as late as the first century AD is clear
from the writing of Robert G. Hoyland[23] and others.

In his notes to the *Lectures on the Religion of the Semites*
by William Robertson Smith, Stanley A. Cook writes:

---

[20] Ibid, 81

[21] Ibid

[22] Ibid, 99

[23] Robert G. Hoyland, *Arabia and the Arabs: From the Bronze Age to the Coming of Islam* (New York: Routledge, 2002), 139–45

W.R.S. compares the Arabic *'azif,* the eerie sound of the
jinn. Among special chthonic deities are Nergal, Molek
(Milk), and Kronos . . . [24]

It is interesting that Smith's remarks on *'azif* should be
followed immediately by Cook's references to chthonic
deities, such as Nergal, Lord of Kutha or KUTU, for the
mythical Lovecraftian university, Miskatonic, is a very
clever play on words that has gone unnoticed—or denied—
by Lovecraft scholars and critics of the *Necronomicon* alike.

Mis-Chthonic Mythos

The word "chthonic" is pronounced in America as
"thawnik," which is probably why the wordplay has gone unnoticed in this country. In England, however, it is pronounced
"ka-thonic"—as witness the *Oxford English Dictionary*—in
imitation of how the word is pronounced in the original
Greek. (For instance, the Greeks pronounce the initial *p* in
psyche—*p-syche*—just as the Spanish do, for example, although English-speakers pronounce the word as if it were
written "syche.") I submit that Lovecraft, the inveterate
scholar of arcane utterings, would have known this and used
it as the basis for his "Miskatonic University." Critics point
out that "miskatonic" is simply an imaginary American Indian word, but they miss the point. It is *certainly* an imaginary Indian word, since Lovecraft lived in Rhode Island,
which is a state full of towns and rivers with similar-
sounding names; but it is also a play on the word "chthonic,"
with the negative prefix *mis* (as in *mis*take, *mis*perception)

---

resulting in "Miskatonic," which can only mean an evil, chthonic force, like—for instance—Cthulhu. Thus, Miskatonic was a clever and meaningful pun that has sadly gone unnoticed by Lovecraft's own defenders.

With his strong interest in the Underworld—a land not always necessarily under the earth but also in the heavens, "out of space" to use his phrase—it is inevitable that Lovecraft's writings reflect a preoccupation with all sorts of chthonic and potentially chthonic deities and demons, of which Cthulhu is perhaps the most prominent, a denizen of KUTU, of Kutha: the necropolis that gave us the *Necronomicon*.

The centerpiece of the consensus opinion that Lovecraft invented the idea of the *Necronomicon* and Cthulhu out of whole cloth has been nudged—if not outright attacked—by a specialist in medieval grimoires, Joseph H. Peterson, who located a name virtually identical to Cthulhu in a Hebrew manuscript of the early eighteenth century, the *Mafteah Shelomoh,* or "Key of Solomon." Not to be confused with the *Greater Key of Solomon,* that was translated by S. L. MacGregor Mathers, the *Mafteah Shelomoh* remained undiscovered for years until after Mathers's edition, although Mathers himself knew it existed but assumed it had been lost.

What is startling about this document is that the name and seal of Cthulhu—spelled in Hebrew letters KThULH—is followed immediately by that of *Mazkim*!

Anyone who has read the *Necronomicon* knows that the Mazkim are a class of demon appearing in the Testimony of the Mad Arab (and in the Maklu Text) as *masqim xul,* an "ambusher, lier-in-wait." The citation comes from the Gollancz edition of this text, and I have seen a bound volume containing photocopies of the entire manuscript, which is also available as jpeg files in the collection published by Esoterica

Archives[25] as a CD-ROM. Other editions also exist, such as the one in the British Library, Oriental collection, according to Peterson, referenced in the *British Library Journal* of 1995. It seems like more than just coincidence to find both these entities side by side in a manuscript that predates the *Necronomicon* by more than two hundred years.

That is not to say that the *Mafteah Shelomoh* is a version of the *Necronomicon*; far from it. But it does imply that the name Cthulhu was known to a Jewish magician of the eighteenth century, which suggests that the chthonic monster would have been known to other magicians both before and after the *Mafteah Shelomoh* was written. This provides a precedent for the *Necronomicon* and a pre-Lovecraft occurrence of the name.

And then we have the *Necronomicon* itself, *Al-Azif*, written by an Arab who was privy to this information, this esoteric background to the religious and political turmoil of the Middle East, yesterday and today; an Arab who had access to the ancient traditions of Cutha, the Underworld, and its insane god of chaos and destruction, Nergal.

An Arab gone mad.

---

[25] At www.esotericarchives.com

7: The Hidden God

The birthplace of Western occultism, as of Western religion, is the Middle East. We can speak of Celtic and Teutonic pagan practices, of barbaric neolithic sacrifices in the shadow of Stonehenge or the caves of Lascaux, of the ecstatic Eleusinian mysteries, but in the end the most dramatic influence on modern occultism derives from the Qabala of the Jews, the astrology of the Babylonians, and the syncretistic mass of supernatural beliefs and practices inherited from the ancient Egyptians, the Gnostics, the Arabs, the Manicheans, and others that have come down to us in such esoteric traditions as alchemy, Rosicrucianism, Templarism, and Freemasonry. Even the modern-day cult known as Wicca owes the rituals in its Book of Shadows largely to the Qabalistic practices of the Golden Dawn and of Aleister Crowley, who received *his* revelation in a hotel room in Cairo.

Secrecy was, and is, the background of these practices. Not only the secrecy of the cults, but the very secrecy inherent in nature itself: the hidden laws that govern gravity, magnetic attraction, electricity, health and sickness, life after death, and many others. Secrecy is also inherent in the vast and complex system of correspondences that links all phenomena, all creatures, all events, in apparent violation of the law of cause and effect. Behind this veil of secrecy dwells an equally invisible power, a force whose true nature is perhaps unknowable but which has been the subject of intense study by generations of wise men, sages, and shamans. To know this power is to be able to manipulate the machinery of connections from which the world, and the experience of the world, arises: to operate in secret, and to reap secret rewards.

To the ancient people, as well as to the occultists of the present day, whatever is secret—whatever is out of sight, hidden, obscured—is somehow related to that ultimate power, that potent hidden God. History is viewed as the story of an ongoing conspiracy among esoteric groups for power over the planet. The sex act is viewed as the repository of a secret power hidden in nature itself. Wars, revolutions, assassinations are all considered to be the exoteric evidence of esoteric events, and behind these events are shadowy groups who are able to summon dark forces to their aid. This has been the case since the time of the Bible, when it was believed there were cults abroad in the land who were "skillful to rouse Leviathan" (Job, 3:8).

Once a god becomes known, visible, tangible, the object of veneration by the masses, it loses its appeal to the cultist. In a sense, it has lost spiritual power while gaining social prominence. This "antisocial" stance of the occultist is reflected also in other areas, such as madness and sanity. Sanity is the mental state approved by consensus; madness is a mental state, but it is not approved. Instead, it is considered to be a sickness in modern society, and evidence of demonic possession—that is, possession by a spiritual force not the god of society—by older civilizations.

Which brings us to the Mad Arab of the *Necronomicon*.

* * *

H.P. Lovecraft, in his short stories about the *Necronomicon,* mentions that it was written by the "Mad Arab Abdul Alhazred." As noted earlier, Abdul Alhazred is not a proper name in Arabic. Fortunately for us, there is no such name appearing anywhere in the manuscript of the *Necronomicon* we translated and published. The author of the manuscript is unknown, and indeed the manuscript actually breaks off toward the end, so we do not know who signed it, if anyone did.

Was the manuscript originally in Arabic in the first place?

As we had it in the Greek recension, there is every possibility that it was written originally in that language and not in Arabic, except for internal evidence that disproves this thesis.

The narrator is definitely an Arab, for he refers to Arab locations and events in the first chapter we entitled, appropriately, "The Testimony of the Mad Arab." It is in this chapter that we first come across the name KUTULU, which I identified in the book and in the previous chapter as a word referring to Cutha, the ancient city associated with a famous necropolis and—by extension—to the Underworld. More important, however, it is also a word in Arabic, and in fact one which appears in the Quran.

This fact was not known to us when we researched and translated the book, since what we had was in Greek, and KUTULU, while not Greek, seemed to refer to Sumer and Babylon in the context of the other prayers and chants, and not to the later Arab tribes or language. The "Mad Arab" appearance was not investigated by us, simply because it did not seem relevant to the compelling Sumerian connections, which were potentially much more explosive. However, in the years since the publication of the *Necronomicon,* I was made aware of the legitimacy of the Arab references.

In the Quran, in Sura 25, verse 29, we read:

لَّقَدْ أَضَلَّنِى عَنِ ٱلذِّكْرِ بَعْدَ إِذْ جَآءَنِى ۗ وَكَانَ ٱلشَّيْطَٰنُ لِلْإِنسَٰنِ خَذُولًا

This was translated by Pickthall as, "He verily led me astray from the Reminder after it had reached me. Satan was ever man's deserter in the hour of need." In one form of Arabic transliteration, the above verse would be pronounced as:

Laqad adallanee AAani alththikri baAAda ith jaanee wakana alshshaytanu lil-insani khathoolan

It is the last word that interests us, for it is variously spelled (in Roman letters) *khathoolu, khadhulu,* or *qdhadhulu.* It means "deserter" or "abandoner," and is another epithet for Satan (*al shshaytanu*) in the Quran, even as it has other, more mystical meanings among the Sufis and the magicians of pre-Islamic Arabia. For us, though, *khathoolu* is, simply, Cthulhu.

I am indebted to a nameless associate who pointed me in the direction of an old Internet posting by one Parker Ryan from 1994 where this relationship is discussed sensibly and at length[1] His posting—which has been preserved on a few other Internet sites since then—is worth reading for a more in-depth study of Arab magic and its relationship to the stories of H.P. Lovecraft and the *Necronomicon* in particular, for there are so many points of similarity that Ryan is forced to ask if Lovecraft had access to unpublished Arab material or if this is all just a matter of "coincidence."

---

[1] Found on the alt.discordia.net site in 2004.

Who, or what, is Cthulhu or *qhadhulu?*

In the first place, the concept of *qhadhulu* as a "deserter" or "abandoner" is interesting in the context of Sumero-Babylonian religion, since in those days the gods were understood to have forgotten or abandoned the people. We are moved by the couplet that ends so many Sumerian prayers, "Spirit of the Sky, remember! Spirit of the Earth, remember!" To the Sumerians, the gods had forsaken them, forgotten them, abandoned them. They have to be constantly reminded that we are here, awaiting their return. It is a poignant concept, and one that has resonance for the West even today as Christian fundamentalists and other sects wait impatiently for the return of Jesus, the "Second Coming." While Christians will not assert that Jesus has "forgotten" them or "abandoned" them—since one can communicate with Jesus through prayer and be filled with the power of Jesus on earth—Jesus has not yet returned to "judge the living and the dead." The Last Days may be upon us, but they have not yet arrived in full force.

The *qhadhulu* of the pre-Islamic Arabs, however, was a force to be reckoned with, a manifestation of the power of the Jinn: the mysterious ancient race that predated Adam and that was made to bow down before Adam. Satan—or Ibliss, as he is also known to the Arabs—refused to bow down, since he belonged to the earlier race and saw Adam as a newcomer not worthy of worship. To the Arabs, Satan or Ibliss is the king of the Jinn, and more importantly *the Jinn are a race of beings and are not fallen angels.* According to Islamic law and tradition, the Jinn procreate, eat and drink, and die, and have the power of choice. The angels—again, according to Islamic tradition—do not have choice or free will. The Jinn, as the first created race on earth, do.

The Jinn are at times visible and invisible, depending on

their desire and upon the ability of the faithful to see them. They have supernatural powers and abilities, can travel immediately to any place on earth, and can find lost treasure, etc. Some of the Jinn have even converted to Islam, but others are loyal to Shaitan or Ibliss, the Satan of the Judeo-Christian tradition.[2]

We become aware of the Jinn most powerfully through the phenomenon of demonic possession. As the Jinn are believed to be souls without bodies, they are eager to inhabit a body if at all possible. While the Jinn are said to reside in desert places, in wastelands like the famous *Rub al-Khali,* or "Empty Quarter" of southern Saudi Arabia (the site of Lovecraft's Irem, or City of Pillars), they are also known to appear without warning in the cities and towns of Arabia, and to take possession of hapless individuals much in the way familiar to us through books and movies like *The Exorcist.* In fact, *The Exorcist* begins in the deserts of Iraq, in an archaeological dig in what was once Babylon, and the possessing spirit is the Mesopotamian demon, Pazuzu.

But possession by the Jinn can be both positive and negative. According to Sufi tradition, poets and mystics—as well as madmen—are often thought to be possessed by spirits. The Prophet Mohammed himself was accused of being *jinn*-possessed before his new religion became official in Arabia. Nasruddin, the famous Sufi sage, behaved in a fashion that could only be considered "mad." That a book of mysticism and magic should be penned by a "mad Arab" is actually rather appropriate for the culture. As mentioned, Mohammed

---

[2] See, for instance, Ahmad H. Sakr, *Al-Jinn* (Lombard, Illinois: Foundation for Islamic Knowledge, 1994) for a list of Quranic references and some traditional background, as well as Al-Haj Khan Bahadur Altaf Admad Kherie, *Index-Cum Concordance for the Holy Quran* (Singapore: Omar Brothers, 1991) for a comprehensive concordance.

himself—the author of the Quran—was considered a "mad Arab." The Sufi mystics were "mad." Madness was practically a job requirement. Madness, and a gift for language.

Arabists claim that the poetry of the Quran is what gives the book its emotive power; its language is flowing, compelling, and powerful in the original Arabic, similar to a type of rhythmic utterance called "diviner's speech." In fact, at first the Arabs of Mecca thought of Mohammed as a kind of diviner based on his recitation of what would soon become the Surahs of the Quran, undertaken in front of the Ka'aba. There is a long tradition of Arab poetry that predates the Islamic period; unfortunately, most of what was composed in the centuries before Mohammed was born has been lost, since it was an oral tradition and very little was written down. It is just this element of Arab literary history that provides us with another clue as to the true nature of the *Necronomicon,* for our claim is that the Sumerian tradition survived for thousands of years not only in cuneiform writing on clay tablets in Babylon, but in the oral tradition of people like the Toda of India or others, such as the mad Arabs who cultivated and maintained their native tradition secretly among the nations of the Middle East.

The date given by Lovecraft for the first appearance of the *Necronomicon* is 730 AD, in Damascus. If we take that date at face value, it means the book would have been written almost exactly one hundred years after the death of the Prophet Mohammed in 632 AD, and thus at the height of Islamic militarism in the Middle East and Europe. One can imagine the stress being put on the pagan Arab priests and magicians of the invaded territories, and the reluctant committing to paper of the traditions that had survived orally for millennia, for Islam did not spread only by spiritual conversion and "gentle persuasion," but by fire and sword, and the resulting executions of idolators and "demon worshippers." We know, for instance, that a composite tribe of Arabs of Yemeni origin who migrated to Bahrain and later to al-Hirah were the Tanukh. The beliefs of the pagan Tanukh mingled with those of local Christians, Jews, and Magians (Zoroastrians), so that by the time of the Islamic conquest of Iraq one large contingent of Tanukh were Christian and were forced to convert to Islam on pain of death. (These Tanukh are believed to be the ancestors of the modern Druze.) The distress of our mad Arab, said by Lovecraft to have been a Yemeni by birth, is evident in every word he writes, and one wonders if the horrible, impending doom to which he refers has its source not only in the dread monsters of the chthonic temples of the Rub al-Khali—the ancient, and real, City of the Pillars, Irem (or, as it was sometimes called, Ubar, the "Atlantis of the Sands")—but in the ferocious zeal of the Caliphs, for whom heresy and treason were one and the same, and conversion a matter of politics as much as of religion.

The last chapter of the book is the second part of the "Testimony of the Mad Arab," and it contains so many references that it has taken years to understand them, and even now there are still gaps in our comprehension. He prays, "May the heart of the Unknown God return to its place for me!" This could be an allusion to the same Hidden God mentioned at the beginning of this chapter.

I am not the only one to have noticed a profound connection between the themes of the *Necronomicon* and those of the Western occult tradition in general, connections I could never have anticipated when the book was first published in 1977 but which have become clearer with time.

In succeeding years, other occultists of various persuasions have worked with the book and examined it carefully. One of these, and certainly the most well-known, was Kenneth Grant.

Grant was a protégé of Crowley and is considered by many to be his natural successor and interpreter. The head of an OTO organization in England, he has published startling analyses of Crowley's writings with a degree of profundity that is otherwise lacking in serious modern occult literature. In his series of books on Western—and particularly Crowleyan or Thelemic—occultism, he has cause to reference the *Necronomicon* (which he terms the Schlangekraft recension, after the first company to publish it) many times. His *Nightside of Eden,* published in 1977 (the same year as the *Necronomicon*) has a few references to the fictional version mentioned by Lovecraft, but by 1980, when *Outside the Circles of Time* is published, he begins to refer to the "supposedly fictional *Necronomicon*"[3] and mentions it numerous times anyway. By the time of *Hecate's Fountain* in 1992, however, he begins to refer to the "Schlangekraft recension," and by the publication of *Outer Gateways* (in 1994) there are no less than forty references to it specifically and it becomes obvious that the *Necronomicon* has become an important influence on Grant's understanding of magic and Thelema.

To try to give an overview of Grant's ongoing exegesis of magical, occult, and Thelemic texts would be far beyond the scope of this, or possibly any, book. Grant's work stands on its own, and needs a careful and motivated reader and one who has the necessary background in qabalistic terminology, mythology, ancient history, comparative religion, etc. There are few such individuals abroad in the land today, so we will restrict ourselves to saying that Grant is fascinated—or obsessed—with the dark side of magic and occultism, a

---

[3] Kenneth Grant, *Outside the Circles of Time* (London: Frederick Muller, 1980), 35

side that is also linked inextricably with alien intelligence and interstellar visitors.

Grant understands that the practices and beliefs we casually refer to as demonic, or evil, or satanic, actually refers to an ancient religious philosophy that was understood by civilizations that existed before the Flood. The "Hidden God" of the ancients could be said to refer to the Egyptian god Set, the brother and enemy of Osiris, a god generally thought to be evil but who could have just as easily been the god of the land that was defeated. As an old adage tells us, "The demons of today were the gods of yesterday." Rather than simply state this, however, Grant attempts to *prove* it, and after having proved it, to describe how to regain contact with these Dark Lords. In Grant's world, the knowledge of these ancient gods was retained, secretly, by underground groups of magicians and occultists down through the ages and codified in their grimoires and even in their tales of fantasy. They are evidence of the origins of the human race, as well as of the race of the Jinn and other monstrous creations: origins for which space and time travelers from other dimensions are responsible, travelers whom we refer to as gods . . . or demons. To Grant, Lovecraft was unconsciously channeling these forces, for the textual evidence in his stories—once analyzed by Grant—reveal startling correspondences to the forbidden practices of the worshippers of Set and other "evil" gods.

It was Grant who understood that Sumer and the Sumerian tradition was at the root of the modern occult revival, and he knew this years before the *Necronomicon* was translated and published, having discussed Aleister Crowley's insistence on the importance of Sumer in his *The Magical Revival,* published in 1972; and it was Crowley and, later, his devotee Jack Parsons—the American rocket scientist who became a sincere Thelemite and magician, and who proclaimed himself the Anti-Christ—who realized the importance of Sumer to their own occult tradition years before Herman Slater, L.K. Barnes, and the rest of us who were involved with the *Necronomicon* project.

The mysterious posting by Parker Ryan, mentioned above, indicates that possibly Lovecraft had access to the real *Necronomicon,* otherwise his knowledge of arcane Arab occult lore has no ready explanation. It is, of course, our contention as well. We raised the possibility that Lovecraft's information might have been related to a book on Arab mysticism in the possession of the Golden Dawn as early as 1915, an eighth century AD (or earlier) manuscript called *The Veils of Negative Existence,* mentioned by occult historian, Francis King.[4]

Grant goes further in his research by drawing inferences from the myths of the Yezidi as well as the books written by Crowley to prove that the Yezidi are worshipping what is essentially a Sumerian deity; he understands their Shaitan to be a survival of the gods of the Underworld, of Kutha or KUTU, and that their myths echo the tales told by Lovecraft of the existence of two distinct races who vie for control of our planet. The Yezidi believe that they were born of Adam, but not of Eve. The rest of humanity was born of Adam *and* Eve. In much the same way, the Arabs believe that the *jinn* are actual beings who live, invisibly, among us and are not the sons of Adam. When they die, it is believed, their bodies become corporeal and visible. This idea of distinct races of beings—almost, one might say, engineered races—is more common among the peoples of the Middle East than we might imagine, going back to the Sumerian tales of Tiamat,

---

4 Francis King, *Modern Ritual Magic* (Dorset, England: Prism Press, 1989), 136

the Ancient One, who fought with the younger gods under Marduk, and from whose body humans were created.

As scholars and historians such as De Santillana in *Hamlet's Mill,* Temple in *The Sirius Mystery,* and Zecharia Sitchin in his Earth Chronicles series have been pointing out for the last forty years or more, there is a stellar or astral component to the world's myths, hence the erection of the ziggurats, the "mountains of God," in Mesopotamia—some of which were designed around a seven-stepped planetary ladder to the stars, a "seven story mountain"—at whose summits contact with the Divine would take place at rites performed at special times of the year, between the high priest or king and a priestess whose sacred intercourse formed the template for the more modern *hierogamos,* or "sacred wedding," such as that found in the *Chymical Wedding of Christian Rosenkreutz,* one of the core documents of the Rosicrucian Order . . . an order supposedly founded by a seeker after esoteric knowledge who spent considerable time in the Middle East, according to the legend. In fact, many of the ancient legends may be poetic reconstructions of actual events that took place before written history, events that occurred in space and on Earth many millennia ago. The idea that what we call demons and gods may be screen memories for something more unsettling—memories of alien beings interfering with, or creating, human evolution—has been steadily gaining ground in the literature of the occult as well as in the paranoid press.

Is magic a technology?

The Necronomicon and Thelema

At least one of the people involved in the *Necronomicon* project was a self-avowed Thelemite: a follower of Aleister Crowley and his revelations, as recorded in the *Book of the*

Law. He accepted Crowley's *Book of the Law* as the Bible of the New Age, and had been initiated into the OTO prior to Grady McMurtry's seizure of the Order beginning in the 1960s. His beliefs, however, were more avant-garde than mainstream, and he never maintained his status within the order once he saw which way the wind was blowing.

We will call him Mister X.

Mister X was a devotee of Jack Parsons and of the Babalon Working, Parsons's attempt at ritually communicating with the Biblical Whore of Babylon. Some of the Crowleyan references in the Introduction to the *Necronomicon* can safely be attributed to his influence. He introduced us all to the ideas of Kenneth Grant, in whom we saw a kindred spirit and guiding light. In fact, if it was not for Mister X, I might not have understood the value of the *Necronomicon* beyond that of a mere curiosity. It was due to X, Jack Parsons, and Kenneth Grant that I gradually came to realize that the *Necronomicon* was truly an exceptional and unique grimoire.

Critics have attacked my equation of Aiwaz—the spiritual being who communicated the *Book of the Law* to Crowley in Cairo in 1904—to Lovecraft's "blind idiot god of chaos." As usual, a little knowledge can be a dangerous thing. Had the critics looked a little deeper into the Grant and Parsons works, they would have found many references supporting just this point of view.

For instance, in Jack Parsons's own words, from *The Book of Babalon*:

The present age is under the influence of the force called, in magical terminology, Horus. This force relates to fire, Mars, and the sun, that is, to power, violence, and energy. It also relates to a child, being innocent (i.e., undifferentiated). Its manifestations may be noted in the destruction of old institutions and ideas, the discovery and liberation of new energies, and the trend towards power governments, war, homosexuality, infantilism, and schizophrenia.

This force is completely blind . . .

Mars, of course, is the planet assigned to the Sumerian god Nergal, ruler of Cutha or KUTU, and Parsons's description sounds like equal parts of Nergal and Lovecraft's "blind idiot god of chaos"; and it was Aiwaz who alerted Crowley to the Age of Horus. It is interesting to note Parsons's association of this "blind force" to children, as the last thirty years have shown us an increasing importance of the spiritual lives of children as they affect our culture and our security. We began to fear our children in such novels (and films) as *Rosemary's Baby, The Exorcist, The Omen,* and so many others. Then the children took up arms against us and against each other, in such tragedies as the Columbine massacre. Children are now recruited as soldiers in Africa and Asia, made to bear arms and commit hideous atrocities, including suicide bombings in the Middle East. This is the downside of the Age of Horus: the Massacre of the Innocents, by the Innocents. It is perhaps no wonder that the Son of Sam cult investigated by Maury Terry was called The Children.

This is a controversial point of view but I suggest that all the efforts of Church and State in the West to control, cultivate, and elevate our children have come to nothing. The emperor has no clothes, and the children have seen this. The contempt and disgust of the current generation for anything created or offered by their parents is an example of this kind of clear-sightedness; the problem is that there is nothing to take the place of what they see as the chaos around them. There seems to be no spiritual way out, no Gate.

The *Necronomicon* does not deny feelings of despair, anger, and rage, but *acknowledges* them and provides a means for channeling these emotions into spiritual liberation. It is the path of sorcery, of shamanism. The very Gates themselves represent a system that has been in use among shamans all over Asia, from Siberia to China. It is a technology, and an escape mechanism.

That Aleister Crowley and his occult system has connections with Sumeria and the gods of chaos is proven by the evidence. The letters of Jack Parsons to his disciple and soulmate Marjorie Cameron can be considered one piece of this evidence

His letter, dated January 25, 1950:

> The voice is of course disembodied . . . the formula, it would seem, is that of Inanna descending (or the Pistis Sophia). At the first stage she takes off her clothes, her soul, and so on until she stands completely naked before Anunnaki, the eyes of death . . .
>
> It is all a matter of devotion—of willed inversion. The Bornless One (Liber Samekh) is a Sumerian ritual of the same period.

He is referring to an invocation that is quite popular among magicians, the Bornless One (which can be found in some editions of *Goetia: the Lesser Key of Solomon the King*). Crowley had translated this invocation into Enochian, to give it even more power. Here, Parsons associates the Bornless One ritual with Sumeria and specifically with the Goddess Inanna and her trial before the Anunnaki. One is compelled to wonder if Parsons had access to another copy of the *Necronomicon,* for the provenance of this invocation is generally believed to be a Greco-Egyptian magical papyrus from about the time of Christ, as we learn from Budge in a work originally published in 1901.[5]

But Parsons was not alone in believing there was an important link between Sumeria and Thelema. Here, in Crowley's own words:

> Aiwaz is not a mere formula, like many Angelic names, but it is the true, most ancient name of the God of the Yezidi, and thus returns to the highest antiquity. *Our work is therefore historically authentic; the rediscovery of the Sumerian tradition.*[6]

This quotation comes from Kenneth Grant's seminal work, *The Magical Revival,* published in 1972, years before the *Necronomicon* was published. He goes on to state:

> I have italicized the last dozen words because they form the crux of Crowley's system, without which it is both incomprehensible and unfathomable; incomprehensible in its magical significance for the present magical revival, and unfathomable without the key supplied by the Sumerian tradition which involved the worship of Shaitan, the astronomical vehicle of which was Sirius.[7]

Thus, it would seem that the "rediscovery of the Sumerian tradition" is *central* to the whole concept of Thelema and the New Age, the "crux of Crowley's system." There are those who would complain that the *Necronomicon* is not an accurate representative of this tradition and that one should instead

---

[5] E.A. Wallis Budge, *Egyptian Magic* (New York: Dover, 1971), 176–77

[6] Kenneth Grant, *The Magical Revival* (London: Skoob, 1991 edition), 52

[7] Ibid

refer to the works by Samuel Noah Kramer and others on the subject. Kramer is indeed a good place to begin in order to understand something about Sumerian civilization; but the works of academics like Kramer are wholly lacking in the deeper concepts that underlie the Sumerian tradition because they exclude much of the magical and occult practices of the Sumerians in favor of the more philosophical and religious works so far translated. When Crowley writes of the Yezidi, we are on more fertile ground; we can follow that furrow all the way to India and the Toda people, who actually reference Sumerian deities in their invocations . . . something about which they could not have known from written tradition, since Sumeria was largely unknown until the archaeological discoveries of the nineteenth century.

As stated previously, it is my belief that the *Necronomicon* is a survival of the same tradition that informed both the Yezidi and the Toda: a Sumerian tradition that, however bowdlerized in the telling and retelling, carried within it an energy and power that was impossible to ignore or surpress. The *Necronomicon* may be an imperfect guide to the rituals and beliefs of ancient Sumer, but it is a cable for that current, a cable plugged directly into the rites of ancient Ur and Cutha. Over distance, some of the message may become garbled, and the effect of more recent Arab and East Asian civilizations may have contributed to a kind of "crosstalk," but the essential elements of the mystery remain. The work of Grant and Parsons and others has helped to "clean up" the signal and present us with a working and workable system for self-initiation, one that is appropriate for this Age if not for the previous one.

The Yezidi are an oppressed people, as are all the Kurdish tribes. They have borne the brunt of Islamic defamation and racism for centuries, and their villages have been the target of chemical weapons and automatic-rifle fire in the past fifty years. They are considered heretics by the Muslims, and yet they may not be Muslim at all but some kind of amalgamation of Judaism, Christianity, and Islam where the connecting tissue is not only Moses and Abraham, but Satan as well. Yet, in their *Black Book* and their cult of the Peacock Angel, Melek Ta'us, they stubbornly hold onto a set of beliefs that—while strange to many of us—they feel are certainly worth fighting and dying for. For the Yezidi—as for so many others around the world—spiritual liberation and political liberation are linked. They are part of the same struggle, and are a lesson to us of the dedication and force of will required for both. Modern occultists such as Crowley, Parsons, and Grant hear in the rites of the Yezidi a sympathetic chord that was once struck in ancient Sumer. Their followers agree.

Belief systems that stray from the normal are dangerous engines of enlightenment. Once a belief has been enshrined in the tabernacle of mainstream society, it loses its edge. Occultism is designed to force an individual to think outside "the box," but in this case we mean the black box of consciousness, of consensus reality. By forcing the brain to acknowledge other ways of looking at the world, occultism enlightens . . . but it does so at the peril of the occultist. If psychological safeguards are not in place, the experience of the occult can lead to madness and death. Many noble minds have suffered from too much knowledge, too deep an understanding of the world . . . and yet, too little knowledge and too shallow an understanding to save them. To survive the occult journey, one must be prepared to abandon one's ego; unfortunately for most occultists, their ego is the very last thing they are prepared to give up.

Self-initiation is at once the safest and the most dangerous method of saving oneself from the chaos and destruction that rages all around us. It is safest, for it avoids obedience to a guru who may or may not have one's best interests at heart; who may or may not be a genuine enlightened master, but a venal exploiter of human weakness. It is dangerous, because there is no one to provide a reality check or to guide the seeker when the path becomes dark. Occultism is not for the emotionally unstable or unbalanced, for one needs a clear head and a keen mind to negotiate its treacherous waters. It is a science of the heart and the soul as well as of the mind, so a certain degree of emotional sensitivity is required. Balancing sensitivity and stability is the greatest challenge the beginning occultist will face. One tends to shut off one's sensitivity once instability is suspected, and no amount of intellectual prodding will bring it back. But if one remains too sensitive, too "open" to the occult environment, then instability is almost a given and one begins to rationalize the most outrageous deeds, putting the intellect at the mercy of a deranged heart.

Occultism—particularly of the *Necronomicon* variety— demands a great degree of self-control, of what Crowley calls "Love under will." Imagine a convict attempting a prison break. Everything must be perfectly planned. The goal must be kept firmly in mind. The dangers are from people as well as from objects such as alarms, prison bars, concrete walls, barbed wire. It requires not only the understanding of a mechanic and an engineer, but the social sensitivity of a psychologist or a priest. Freedom is the goal, even if that means crawling in a sewer or digging a tunnel with a teaspoon.

In the mystical environment of the *Necronomicon,* it is just that. The gods have forgotten us. We are trapped in a prison we did not make, sentenced like a Kafkaesque hero for mysterious charges that were never explained to us, the "original sin"of the Catholic Church. Breaking out and breaking free requires a great degree of willpower, of self-control, of technical knowledge, of tremendous daring and courage. There are seven Gates to pass through on our way out of prison and to that ultimate freedom: spiritual liberation. It is the same type of spiritual liberation spoken of by the Hindus and the Buddhists, but the path taken is different and more proactive, as in all ceremonial magic systems. Again, William Burroughs wrote that "the publication of the *Necronomicon* may well be a landmark in the history of spiritual liberation."

We could not have said it better; but not all prison breaks are successful, and as we shall see in Chapter Nine, sometimes the prisoners are caught.

8: The Magic of the Black Book

The notoriety of the *Necronomicon* is based in large part on its function as a grimoire: a book of instructions for summoning spiritual forces. This is the core feature of ceremonial magic, and is represented in many medieval and later grimoires. It is also a core feature of many modern secret societies, such as the Golden Dawn of nineteenth century England and the twentieth century occult order of Aleister Crowley, the A∴A∴ or *Argentum Astrum* ("Silver Star"). The ability to make contact with angels, demons, or spirits of the dead is considered the *sina qua non* of occult power, and this ability had to be demonstrated before other initiates (for instance, in the Golden Dawn) in order that the candidate be allowed to progress further along the initiatory path. That means that the spiritual force—whatever it was—had to be summoned to *visible appearance,* appearance that could be seen and verified by other observers. While that sounds like fantasy today, it was taken quite seriously by the members of these orders, and indeed there is an entire literature of magic that has developed over the centuries concerning just this phenomenon.

While most grimoires address the summoning of angelic or demonic forces, planetary intelligences, etc., it is usually done in a purely Judeo-Christian medium filled with prayers to God and conjurations that invoke the name of God as a means to threaten the spirits to come forth. These systems, relics of more ancient practices, were developed alongside the religions of the time and, like the Qabala itself, were understood as a means of using secret formulae hidden within the Scriptures to manipulate Creation, from material things such as the elements to invisible beings such as the angels and the demons.

This idea that reciting a few prayers from a book enables one to master the unseen world is very attractive to the disenfranchised elements of our society. Those who are powerless in any other way—politically, economically, socially—can seek solace in these forbidden books and a means to self-empowerment. That is why troubled and disturbed teenagers find the occult so fascinating, for they are suffering from two forms of stress: the normal stress of being adolescent in a world full of stimulation and excess, and the stress that comes from psychological imbalance and disorder. In effect, these troubled youths are potential shamans for they fit many of the requirements of shamanism as described in works by Mircea Eliade, for instance: mental disorders, confusion over sexual identity, creative sensitivity, social ostracism. In the case of the shamans, the initiate returns to the tribe empowered by the spirits to fulfill a necessary role as healer and seer. In our case—in modern Western, scientifically oriented society—the "initiate" has no social function to fulfill, no "redeeming social value," and no cultural framework in which to understand the changes that are taking place within his soul or the strange desires that motivate him. He either outgrows this fascination with the occult as he forces himself into some semblance of balance or conformity, or he turns into a Roderick Ferrell and looks for sacrificial victims. There is rarely a desire to turn to organized religion for comfort or understanding, since the whole point of the occult quest is to seek out an alternative form of spiritual expression, one that provides a venue for the deep conflicts one is experiencing as well as an outlet for the antisocial acts he feels driven to commit. Organized religion is ill-equipped to deal in a constructive way with feelings of anger, rage, lust, and the other, baser human emotions and instincts. Its approach has always been to control or to exorcise those feelings, to rein them in or banish them entirely. The occultist—especially the young, adolescent occultist—distrusts that approach to what he believes are his natural inclinations. He does not want to be told that his feelings have no value or that they are evil. In fact, his idols tell him otherwise: the metal bands and the youth-oriented television and cinema offerings all tell him that his mental and emotional state is a logical consequence of the world in which he lives, and that he can trust no one, that is, no establishment figure. He sees the Church and the government hand in hand in hypocrisy; he still has spiritual longings, but knows that they cannot be assuaged in a temple or a cathedral. He finds himself increasingly drawn to the "dark side," where he realizes that there lurk forbidden gods and a forbidden faith dwelling in an abyss beneath the surface of his culture, and that there exists a secret mechanism for controlling the forces of nature that does not require heavy financing, a college degree, or a letter from Mom. He realizes that there is a real world of magicians and sorcerers and witches—or people who claim to be, at any rate—which indicates that maybe, just maybe, these powers are real. If you are willing to do the work.

If you are willing to go all the way.

If we mock these feelings and beliefs, we are in danger of mocking the root of every major world religion. Among Christians in the Charismatic movement, we have the spiritual gift of "discernment," in which one has the power to tell if a spiritual being is good or evil. We have exorcism, which is on the rise in the United States. We have stigmata and apparitions of saints and of the Virgin Mother all over the world. Among Hindus, we have the powers attributed to holy men who meditate on mandalas, recite mantras, and basically do everything a Western magician would do to obtain spiritual favors and abilities. We have mystical sects of Jews, Muslims, Buddhists, and many other religions. Thus, the beliefs of these new occultists are neither new nor outside the religious mainstream. What are they, then? They are—from the point of view of organized religion—dangerous. They require contact with dark forces instead of slavish, devotional prayer to God. They require the magician to be "proactive" in his relationship to the Underworld.

Where the famous grimoires such as the *Greater and Lesser Keys of Solomon,* or the *Grimoire of Pope Honorious,* or any of the others mentioned by Arthur Edward Waite in his *Book of Ceremonial Magic,* insist on hiding behind the Names of God when dealing with the Devil, the *Necronomicon* breaks away and states quite clearly that the magician is more or less on his own. He can pray to the gods, but he must remember that they are forgetful and may not hear, or listen, or pay attention to his pleas. Some occultists have found this approach rather more refreshing and honest, for it reflects what they have experienced already. Others find this approach to be more muscular, if seemingly more dangerous, than the other occult systems. Others still are frightened out of their wits when confronted with it, or dismiss it as a hoax, or forgery, or prank, or as simply not a very good grimoire.

A deeper look at the *Necronomicon,* therefore, seems in order.

There are two basic elements to an understanding of the magic of the *Necronomicon.* The first is the fact that it was written by an Arab who may or may not have been a devout Muslim. Since Islam proscribes the practice of magic of any kind, it would seem at first glance that the author was a heretic or apostate. In fact, magic is still practiced in many Muslim countries, from North Africa to Southeast Asia, where it is tolerated as long as Allah is somehow invoked in the process and the *jinn* are not worshipped. In the context of the eighth century AD the author of *Al 'Azif* could easily have been a Muslim, a member of one of the Kurdish tribes, one of the Yezidi, perhaps one of the Quraysh or Tanukh tribes, or even a Muslim mystic of some kind, perhaps an Ismaili or a follower of one of the Shi'ite sects that embraced mystical and Gnostic-type teachings (such as the cult of the Assassins a few centuries later). He would have seen similarities between the Sumerian occultism he put down in writing and some of the more purely Arab pagan practices and beliefs. In fact, to him they may have been one and the same. The sevenfold circumambulation of the Ka'aba—a shrine built by pagan priests from the town of Cutha, the City of the Underworld, the Land of KUTULU and the satanic *qhadhulu*—and the seven Gates of the *Necronomicon* would have been a relationship he understood.

The second element is that of Sumer—and later Akkad and Babylon—itself; a mystery he and his kind alone possessed, a

memory of an ancient kingdom that knew their kings from
before the Flood and understood how to summon dark
forces from the Underworld and from beyond the farthest
reaches of space as he understood it. The *Necronomicon* is a
blatant plea to the gods for help; it is blunt, naked, honest in
its appeal to the gods and in its characterization of them as
those who *abandoned (qhadhulu)* the human race and who
had to be reminded we were still here. Nowhere else in
Western magic or occultism is this acknowledgment made
so openly and with such a sense of desperate vulnerability
as it is in this book. Like the Christians, the author of the
Necronomicon is waiting for a Second Coming . . . but of
what?

At the same time, the book is full of dire warnings about
opening the Gates and letting in other forces: beings not of
the gods but of some other, terrible race. In its original Arabic we would have come across the term *jinn* in its pages, for
according to Arab tradition, this race is older than man and
yet is not of the angels, a race whose lord—Azazel—is the
god of the Yezidis and king of the evil spirits of Arab and Islamic legend, a legend inherited from the dying priesthood
of Sumer.

To assist humanity in its defense against this evil horde of
demonic creatures there is the black book of the *Necronomicon*. The initiatory structure in its pages is designed to create
a different type of initiate: a kind of black bodhisattva, a
spiritually enlightened and empowered sage whose task it is
to defend the race against these creatures before he or she
can make their own escape—an occult general, a master of
the mystic arts of offense and defense, a human being set
apart from the rest who must monitor the Gates and the in-

flux of evil influences that threatens to destroy the planet and enslave its inhabitants.

In order to do this, the candidate must be ritually clean so that the *jinn* do not attach themselves to the impurities of body and soul and thereby gain entrance to this world and to the inner defenses of the magician. The candidate must put himself through the sevenfold test of the Gates, becoming more and more powerful—and simultaneously more and more sensitive, more aware—with each step in the process.

Even the protector needs a protector, however, and this is where the Watcher comes in.

The Greek original for the word "watcher" is *egregore*. In the context of the "black book," the Watcher comes from a race of beings whose only purpose seems to be to function as bodyguards, a species of hired mercenary. As long as the rituals are properly observed and the appropriate sacrifices made, the Watcher will continue to protect the candidate during his lifetime. This is very possibly an echo of the Aryan belief concerning sacrifice that we find in the Vedas, for example. In this holy tradition of ancient India, as long as the sacrifices are properly performed the gods are forced to comply with the wishes of the sacrificers regardless of who makes the sacrifice or what they desire.[1] (As we have seen, there is a good possibility that the ancient race of Sumerians had Indo-European—"Aryan"—connections, as evidenced not only by their language, but by the survival of their beliefs among the Toda of Tamil Nadu.)

The controversy among occultists, pagans, and "cult cops" over the subject of blood sacrifice and the Watcher of the *Necronomicon* is only comprehensible to a modern-day

---

[1] See, for instance, the authoritative *Hindu Mysticism* by S.N. Dasgupta.

Westerner. To a Muslim, the idea of bloody sacrifice is a common one, and indeed, it is mandated during the performance of the *hajj,* the sacred pilgrimage to Mecca (and the obligatory circuit of the Ka'aba) every healthy and able Muslim is expected to take at least once in his or her lifetime. Therefore, to find it included as a requirement for the invocation of the Watcher in a book penned by an Arab of the eighth century is neither unexpected nor somehow sinister. To those whose modern sensitivities are offended by the idea of sacrifice, I can only apologize for our bad taste in translating that portion into English (rather than have it appear in Latin in the manner of Victorian historians writing about the sexual practices of the ancient Romans!). The bloody sacrifice has always been a symbol of the covenant between human beings and gods; in the days of Solomon's Temple, the blood from the sacrificial victims was actually splattered on the altar. Blood from slain lambs was painted on the doorways of the Jews during the time of the ten plagues in Pharaonic Egypt. The Samaritans still practice this sacrifice in this exact manner to this day. While we may pride ourselves in having somehow outgrown the need for bloody sacrifices, in the days of the *Necronomicon* this was a natural expression of ritual significance. Indeed, in the medieval grimoires one still finds the odd requirement for pigeon's blood or the sacrifice of some animal to procure a specific type of parchment from its skin, and no one has chastised the editors or publishers of those books for their reference to animal sacrifice.

The term *egregore* has been used by occultists of the last hundred years or so to refer to concepts like "group mind" or "group identity," claiming that it is a kind of thought-form created by the conscious or unconscious will of the group. The *Necronomicon,* however, sees in the Watcher an independent entity that exists outside the conscious creation of any one magician, and it is for this reason that we translated the Greek *egregore* as "Watcher," so as not to confuse the one with the other and also because the text insists that the "Watcher cares not what it watches," thus emphasizing its active role.

The initiatory framework of the *Necronomicon,* however, is where the true importance of this book is contained. While others may debate its origins and the degree to which its rituals were influenced by the rites of Sumer, Babylon, or even later Arab occult practices, the simple yet elegant arrangement of the Gates is what holds the greatest potential for spiritual power and enlightenment.

After the first installment of the Testimony, we proceed directly to the chapter entitled "Of the Zonei and Their Attributes." The Zonei—a word meaning "zoned" or "zoned ones"—in this case refers to the Lords of the seven philosophical planets, that is, the Moon, Mercury, Venus, the Sun, Mars, Jupiter, and Saturn. These were the only planets visible to the naked eye until comparatively recently, and as they appeared to travel against the backdrop of the fixed stars—the Zodiac—they were believed to move in their own "zones" or circuits through the heavens. In this instance, both the Moon and the Sun were considered "planets" for the simple reason that they appeared to move in zones just as the other five.

Each of the seven Lords is given a name in Sumerian or Babylonian, a number, a color, and a seal, including some instructions as to how to manufacture the seal and what powers or attributes the Lord has. These instructions are reminiscent of many found in later grimoires, and also echo similar instructions I've come across in old Middle Eastern and North African texts.

You will also find that the symbol of the eight-rayed star appears in many of the seals. This same symbol can be found on Sumerian cylinder seals and is an indication of divinity as it was the hieroglyphic for "God," AN, which eventually developed into cuneiform for the same word. (Some commentators have claimed that the eight-rayed star is a symbol of Inanna or Ishtar specifically, but since it is found on seals where this goddess is *not* mentioned, and since it provides the root for words meaning "god" or "divinity," I must differ with those who insist that it can only refer to Inanna.) The eight-rayed star later became the sacred symbol of Islam, as can be seen in their magnificent artwork and architecture, from the delicate lattices of the Dome of the Rock to the more modern steel and glass design of the twin towers of the Kuala Lumpur City Center in Malaysia. As mentioned before, it also appears on Yezidi artwork as the cuneiform original. Thus, the eight-rayed star has a long pedigree as a symbol for the Divine in the Middle East.

This association of the seven planets with seven deities and a complex of colors, numbers, etc., was not unknown to ancient Sumer and Babylon. As Rawlinson—an early archaeologist working in Iraq in the middle of the nineteenth century—points out in his work on the temple of Nebo at Borsippa (south of Babylon on the Euphrates River), the seven-staged ziggurat found there had been covered in different colors, one for each stage and one for each planet, in the same order as the planets are given in the *Necronomicon*.[2] In fact, the level of the ziggurat associated with Nebo was covered in blue pigment, and blue is the color given to Nebo in the *Necronomicon*. It should be noted that this asso-

---

[2] Michael Baigent, *From the Omens of Babylon: Astrology and Ancient Mesopotamia* (London: Arkana, 1994), 154–55

ciation of blue with Nebo (or Mercury) is unique to this system; in the Qabalistic system of the Golden Dawn and of Crowley's own A∴A∴, the color most often associated with Mercury is orange.[3] Thus, this is another interesting piece of evidence demonstrating that the occult system of the *Necronomicon* is more consistent with ancient Sumerian and Babylonian templates than it is with modern European systems. It provides an early matrix of correspondences—between planets, gods, colors, metals, numbers, etc.—that will eventually influence the creation of later occult systems, such as the Qabala, the memory systems of Giordano Bruno and others, and the alchemy of Paracelsus.

This basic system is the format of the next chapter, "The Book of Entrance, and of the Walking." The "Walking" is a means of self-initiation, a progressive ritual in which one travels from one zone to the next through a series of seven Gates—metaphorically speaking, from one step of the ziggurat to the next—until one reaches the top and final step, that of Saturn. At each step along the way, a name is revealed to the initiate: a kind of password that will allow entrance to the next Gate, and so on. These are written as a series of conjurations familiar in structure to anyone who has studied the medieval grimoires, except that the grimoires do not ordinarily insist that one conjure each of its spirits in precise order, or even each of them at all. Thus, we have a grimoire of spirit conjuration which is also a manual of self-initiation, making this system unique among the texts of ceremonial magic.

Those who find this system bizarre or incomprehensible should know that it is not at all unusual among the shamanic

---

[3] According to *777:* in the King Scale, Mercury is purple; in the Queen Scale, it's orange; in the Emperor Scale, it's red-russet; and in the Empress Scale, it's a yellowish-brown, flecked with white.

systems of North and Central Asia. Among the shamans of Siberia, for instance, initiation is obtained through a series of rituals that takes the initiate on a road through the heavens to the Pole Star. Among the Taoist magicians of ancient China, this same process was referred to as the Pace of Yu, and included a seven-stage initiatory system in which the seven planets were mirrored in the seven stars of the Great Bear constellation (a subject covered more extensively in *The Gates of the Necronomicon*).

In modern magic, the system of Golden Dawn initiation is somewhat similar in that initiation proceeds up the Qabalistic Tree of Life from the Sphere of the Earth to the Sphere of Jupiter, stopping at the Abyss, for a total of seven stages. (Aleister Crowley would later add the three remaining stages in his occult order, the A∴A∴, for a total of ten.) In the *Necronomicon*, this initiatory path extends to the level associated with Saturn, which in the Qabalistic Tree of Life is the Sphere of Binah, on the other side of the Abyss—the sphere associated with the initiatory grade of Master of the Temple— and may be thought of as a more ambitious framework for self-initiation.

We find in the "Book of Entrance" a set of drawings, one for each Gate, that must be drawn on the ground in the manner of a magic circle. It has been brought to my attention that the design for the Gate of the Moon is eerily similar to the "First Pentacle of the Moon" as shown in the *Greater Key of Solomon,* even to the small glyph on the lower right-hand side of the pentacle. Reference to the Hebrew writing in the Pentacle of the Moon is even more startling, as it contains a verse from the Psalms (107:16): "He hath broken the Gates of brass, and smitten the bars of iron asunder," certainly a suggestive verse in this context! The realization that these two diagrams were so similar led me to study the

Greater Key (and its origins) in even more detail, and perhaps at some future date I will make my findings known; suffice it to say here that I believe the diagram in the *Greater Key of Solomon* is a version of that found in the *Necronomicon* and an indication that the "black book" was known to later, Judeo-Christian magicians.

The chapter after the "Book of the Entrance" is entitled "The Incantations of the Gates" and is a set of seven incantations appropriate to the ritual of the Walking. After this, we find the "Conjuration of the Fire God" followed by the "Conjuration of the Watcher." It was normal among the tribes that inhabited the Middle East to consecrate or bless the fire, especially when the fire was being used to burn a sacrifice or to purify some implement. The Zoroastrians elevated this primitive practice to a central rite of their religion, and rituals for the invocation of fire are common in India among the Hindus as well.[4] Thus, the Fire Conjuration is not unusual in and of itself. In the *Necronomicon* the fire is considered to be a manifestation of a spiritual force that can destroy the spells of hostile magicians, and so the conjuration is quite fierce. One finds in most of the medieval grimoires instructions for the exorcism and blessing of fire, incense, paper, etc. (This is also common in the Roman Ritual of the Catholic Church.) As for the Watcher, we have already discussed it at length.

These chapters are followed by "The Maklu Text," which is a set of exorcisms that have a firm basis in Sumerian religion. The idea of exorcism is at least as old as Sumer, which means that the ancients believed in evil forces that could

---

[4] See, for instance, Tachikawa, Bahulkar, and Kolhatkar, *Indian Fire Ritual* (Delhi, India: Motilal Banarsidass, 2001), or the Sixth and Seventh *Kandas* of the *Satapatha-Brahmana* of the Madhyandina School.

possess or attack objects and persons, and that ritual formulae existed that could defend against these forces. If it is true that the gods of one religion become the demons of the one that replaces it, one has to wonder what gods these first-recorded demons once were and who worshipped them. The Maklu Text speaks of witches, which we must interpret in this case as persons who worked magic against others. From where did this occult technology originate? Were the witches of Sumer the priests and priestesses of the Old Gods, the Gods of the Sumerian creation epic, *Enuma Elish?* Did they worship the serpent Tiamat? Did they meet at night in the necropolis of Kutu, breathing in the odor of death and decay that is the atmosphere of the Underworld?

The next chapter, "The Book of Calling," is the more familiar type of magical text containing lists of names of power and occult symbols, but it is one in which the magician must first invoke "the four gates from the world between the spheres." These four gates refer to the four cardinal directions, but the text specifically mentions the "world between the spheres," which indicates that these four directions are not identical to the ones with which we are most familiar—north, south, east, and west—but pertain to directions in space from a point of reference not in this world. They are designed to orient the magician in a parallel dimension, which is to say to "dis-orient" him in *this* world so he may perceive reality from a different perspective. The ritual of the Walking takes the magician into space from which it can be said there are no cardinal directions since there is no stationary point of reference. He ascends the stars and becomes aware of the rarefied atmosphere of the quantum world where nonlocality suspends the ordinary understanding of the magic circle and extends it into multiple dimensions, where common concepts like space and time are modified to the point that they are no longer recognizable. In the Calling, one begins from this advanced state of enlightenment to create a "circle" from where the normal "directions" could only be drawn with the super-strings of modern theoretical physics. The manipulation of reality that lies at the heart of all magic technology employs methods that are only now being discovered in the laboratory and in the electronic entrails of the supercomputer. The high-speed networks that power our phone systems and provide the platform for the Internet are only crude symbols of the vast matrix of interconnectedness the ancient occult philosophers described in their "doctrine of correspondences," of which the seven-stepped ziggurat with its associations to planets, colors, and numbers is but another example.

Many commentators on the *Necronomicon* have stated that it is full of traps for the unwary, and therefore dangerous whether or not it is a hoax or a forgery. I must agree that the book is full of traps, but they are traps that the book uses to defend itself—to defend its technology—from misuse by the casual reader. One cannot really abuse the system until one understands it. The simple invocation of the four gates is one example. The *Necronomicon* is dangerous the way any book of ceremonial magic is dangerous: it not only questions consensus reality, it is written from the point of view of one who has already walked the path through alternate worlds and provides methods for doing the same. And while other books, other systems, seem safe—seem "escapable" or "reversible"—the *Necronomicon* makes no such promises. There is no way to reverse the psychological changes one experiences during the Walking. Frankly, there is no way to reverse the changes one experiences in *any* form of ceremonial magic, which is something the other grimoires don't tell you.

Once these changes begin to take place, one develops not only altered states of consciousness, but also abilities one did not have before. These abilities—somewhat akin to what the popular mind conceives of as "psychic powers"—may be of greater or lesser duration or power, may come and go, may change over time. Among the shamans, these powers are considered essential in order to serve the tribe, so they are cultivated and enhanced wherever possible, usually during séances where contact is made with spiritual forces, forces that—to us—may appear demonic.

In the rituals of the Calling, the magician is also expected to make contact with these forces and they are given names and capabilities. These are taken from the fifty names of the god Marduk—the chapter that follows the Calling—Marduk being the god who defeated the serpent Tiamat in the cosmic battle that resulted in the creation of humanity. Each of these fifty names has its own symbol as well as a brief summary of its powers. In addition, designs are given for the various implements and articles of clothing to be used and worn during the ceremonies. This includes a kind of crown on which is drawn the eight-pointed star that is the symbol of AN, the Sumerian sky-god and the origin of the cuneiform symbol for divinity. The copper dagger of INANNA also bears this symbol, as does one of the "mandals of calling."

After the chapter of the "Fifty Names of Marduk," we come to the "Magan Text," which is a form of the ancient epic in which INANNA descends to the Underworld, passing through seven Gates, where she is finally killed by being hung upon a stake at the very depths of the Land of the Dead. She is rescued, however, and rises back through the seven Gates, this time bringing a horde of demons with her who have been released through her resurrection. One is not certain what the Magan Text is doing in the *Necronomicon*, unless it is as a history of how these demonic forces came to be loosed upon the Earth in order to educate the magician and inform him of certain secret formulae that can be gleaned from a careful reading of the text. That this may be so is indicated by the next chapter of the book, which is entitled "The Urilia Text," or "The Book of the Worm." This text contains incantations to various abominable beings, and are to serve as a guide to the magician as to what kind of horrors his enemies evoke and the means they use to evoke them. The positioning of this chapter after the Magan Text is probably meant to warn the magician that the awful creatures worshipped and evoked by the evil magicians are those that were set loose upon the world when INANNA returned from the House of Death.

One should always keep in mind that the *Necronomicon* magician is a unique type of occultist. Whereas most modern magicians see their quest as a deeply personal one, related to individual spiritual goals of enlightenment or individuation, the *Necronomicon* magician has a broader social purpose, and that is to defend the planet against the hostile forces that lie in wait both in the Underworld and in the vast reaches of outer space (if, indeed, these are two different locales). The spiritual advancement of the *Necronomicon* magician is only valuable insofar as it serves to aid humanity, a humanity that is itself grossly unconcerned about its own spiritual advancement. Like homicide detectives who must wallow through the worst that humans can do to each other at every crime scene, the *Necronomicon* magician must be aware and informed of the worst spiritual forces that exist and plague humanity from every corner of space and time. It is no wonder, then, that the book itself has been blamed for so much evil, since it focuses on evil. It is a misguided approach, however; a little like blaming the Nuremberg Trials for the Holocaust.

The book finally ends with the last part of the "Testimony of the Mad Arab," a hurried statement in which the Arab warns of all sorts of dangers to humanity and tries to insert as many defensive measures as possible before the manuscript itself breaks off. The effect is chilling, and elevates the *Necronomicon* above the usual sorcerer's spellbook and into a realm where the grimoire has been written by a practicing magician who finds himself in terrible trouble before he is able to finish the book; a fact that acts as a warning to anyone who reads it and contemplates using its rituals.

Thus, critics of the book claim that it is dangerous and should not be offered to all and sundry. That this is evidence of their basic complaint that the book is actually too inexpensive and too readily available has already been discussed, but let's take their charge at face value.

We live in a world—and, if you are an American, in a country—where access to firearms is easy and inexpensive. Access to poisons of various descriptions and potencies can be had at any hardware store, grocery store, or pharmacy. Instructions for mixing chemicals with lethal intent can be found in books, magazines, and on the Internet. Ilicit drugs are widely available, especially in the poorer sections of our cities and towns. The possibilities for self-immolation or mass murder are legion. I would feel much safer if every handgun in America were replaced by a copy of the *Necronomicon;* any idiot can pull a trigger, but it takes someone with courage, will, intelligence, and determination to work with the occult in any form, and especially with the *Necronomicon*. Even then, the damage one can do to others with the *Necronomicon* is far, far less than the damage one can do to onself by misusing its system. Those who claim that publishing the *Necronomicon* makes us culpable of all sorts of violent crimes allegedly perpetrated in its name—a claim that has nowhere been proven—probably believe that most people would stick their finger in an electrical socket if they thought it could fit. As mentioned previously, those who have harmed themselves and others by using the Bible as their inspiration have been far more numerous, far more deadly, and committed far more horrific crimes than anyone associated with the *Necronomicon*. The Mad Arab would have been better off warning us about the horrors perpetrated by traditional monotheists than about those evoking Tiamat in the Babylonian desert.

One of the more important aspects of Sumerian religion and occultism is the interface between what is a religious or spiritual tradition and an astral belief system. By the time of the Torah, much of the astronomical tradition had either been lost, forgotten, or discarded; but during the age of Sumer and Babylon, the idea that the gods lived in the heavens and descended to the Earth from the stars was very real. The gods were identified with specific planets, a concept that does not appear in the Torah or in later Biblical writings with any degree of consistency. Thus, for the Sumerians and the later Babylonians, religious ritual was also astral ritual. If we study the grimoires of medieval ceremonial magic, we can see elements of this belief scattered here and there among the pages; in the *Necronomicon*, however, this linkage is made quite strongly. To invoke the gods is to make contact with denizens of outer space.

Kenneth Grant, the major interpreter of the works of magician Aleister Crowley, sees in occult practices the same evidence for interstellar contact through ritual. Grant also links this concept with the *Necronomicon* mythos, and sees in its magical system a method for communicating with extraterrestrial beings, beings we believe are angels, demons, or other spiritual forces. If we look at the system of the Golden Dawn—the British occult society that exerted so much influence on twentieth century magic—we see only faint echos of this point of view, burdened as it is by references to ancient Egyptian gods and Qabalistic and Masonic terminology. The magical groups that have sprung up around the *Necronomicon,* however, are consciously aware of this aspect to their practice and realize that the entities whose presences are made known during the course of their rituals may be described as either spiritual or extraterrestrial forces . . . or both.

It is entirely possible that the Sumerian religious experience—and, hence, all religious experience in the world that derives from it—is based on what could only be the most important and most profound psychic event in the history of humanity: contact with beings from another planet or star.

The Sumerians lived in a world that was forgotten by the gods, and which was infested all about with evil spirits. It was a dangerous place; they remembered the Flood and the civilization that existed before it, so they knew that cataclysmic forces could erupt at any moment and destroy the material things of life in an instant. So they built towers and temples that reached to the sky, and burned fires atop them to remind the gods of the heavens that they were still there, still waiting for the day when the gods would return. In the meantime, they had to keep an eye out for the demonic forces, the *jinn,* that lurked everywhere in the shadows, the *maskim* "liers-in-wait" who ambushed the lonely, the unwary, the unclean.

Blood Sacrifice

This element of the *Necronomicon* has been the source of the most contrived angst among its critics. As we will see, authors Harms and Gonce have actually laid a series of murders at its door, accusing the *Necronomicon* of being responsible for inciting teenage magicians to homicide. This kind of dubious double standard is to be expected from pious and morally myopic Christians who do not see that the Bible is full of murder and bloodshed; that the admonition "thou shalt not suffer a witch to live," for instance, was responsible for the horrors of the Inquisition and of the poor damned souls of Salem, Massachusetts, who were executed in order to fulfill this Old Testament law. Coming in particular from self-proclaimed occultists and "ceremonial magicians," as Gonce professes to be, it smacks of pure sensationalism of the grossest tabloid type. We can pick many important works of literature, as a matter of fact, and find that great crimes were committed due to their "inspiration": serial killer Leonard Lake, for example, was moved to commit his crimes after reading *The Collector* by John Fowles, but no one is accusing Fowles of incitement to homicide.

In the first place, animal sacrifice—a concept abhorrent to our tender, Western ears—is still widely practiced in the world today, and by a large segment of the world's population. Muslims practice animal sacrifice during the *hajj* to Mecca, when hundreds of thousands of goats are ritually slaughtered each year. Hindus practice animal sacrifice with regularity, particularly within the cult of Kali, throughout India and Southeast Asia. And, of course, the Afro-Caribbean religions of Santeria, Voudon, Macombe, Candomble, and Palo Mayombe all practice animal sacrifice, as do many animist religions of Africa. Thus, to hundreds of millions of people (at least one billion), the idea of animal sacrifice is an accepted part of their religion.

Aleister Crowley understood this, and wrote about it (in his *Magick in Theory and Practice,* Chapter XII, "Of the Bloody Sacrifice: And Matters Cognate"). While discussing the concept of animal sacrifice and describing its role in magic in some detail, he also touches on the subject of human sacrifice. In fact, a footnote to this chapter has caused much consternation among those who do not get either the joke or the sentiment: "It appears from the Magickal Records of Frater Perdurabo that He made this particular sacrifice on an average about 150 times every year between 1912 e.v. and 1928 e.v." People like Gonce would have been left, mouth agape, at this admission of massive human homicide, but it is assumed that Gonce knows better. For Crowley, the idea of human sacrifice was a metaphor for something else; his sense of humor, however, did not permit him to spell everything out cleanly for those who were muddling through his *Magick* and at the same time too stupid to understand it.

The human sacrifice to which Crowley refers is the sacrifice of seminal fluid. This is not so strange as it may appear, for it has an honorable pedigree. We find, for instance, in Danielou, "There are references to sacrifices of semen as an alternative to human sacrifices."[5] This idea of the sacrifice of bodily fluids in place of violent human sacrifice is very common to Thelema, where it is written in their Holy Book:

---

[5] *The Gods of India Hindu Polytheism* (New York: Inner Traditions, 1985), 66

"The best blood is of the moon, monthly," a clear reference to menstrual blood. To some alchemists, the Red Dragon and the White Eagle are references to menstrual blood and semen, respectively; and the "cakes of light" of the Gnostic Mass are composed of both substances.

However, no one has accused Thelema of promoting human sacrifice. The accusations against Crowley's alleged human sacrifices died down (no pun intended) when it was realized he was speaking allegorically.

But is the *Necronomicon* speaking in veiled terms as well?

Listen to this comment from an old grimoire, the *Fourth Book of Cornelius Agrippa,* in the section entitled "Necromancy":

> *From hence it is, that the Souls of the dead are not to be called up without blood . . .*

The souls of the dead. The Book of the Dead. The deeper consistency of these concepts is not to be denied. From necromancy to *Necronomicon,* it is understood that blood plays an important part in the rituals. However, as Crowley has pointed out—and as Danielou has confirmed—other substances may replace the blood of sacrifice and still be as efficacious, and this concept is as ancient as the rites themselves. If there are moral imbeciles who take the human sacrifice concept literally, then they will do so whatever the book: whether the *Necronomicon,* or *The Queen of the Damned,* or the Bible, or the Torah, or *Gunga Din.* That secret cults employ human sacrifice, in this day and age, and in the United States of America, cannot be denied. That they have been doing this long before the publication of the *Necronomicon* also cannot be denied. Happily they are in a minority; they are ill-equipped to handle the forces they have unleashed, and they will perish by the same sword they use in their rites. That is the Covenant that has existed since time immemorial, and its law is inescapable.

9: Dead Names

As the *Necronomicon* became notorious among occultists and Lovecraft scholars, it also came to the
attention of police departments around the country. In the
1970s and 1980s a new breed of law enforcement officer appeared in the land: the cult cop. These were police officers or
police department consultants who specialized in identifying and prosecuting crimes seemingly committed by occult
groups. They would analyze crime scenes where occult graf-
fiti was found, or evidence of blood sacrifice, or cases where
a body appeared to have been murdered as part of a ritual or
a victim was known to belong to an occult group.

Prompted in part by the hysteria surrounding the revelations of Maury Terry concerning the Process and the Son
of Sam murders, and the appearance of Terry and others on
a controversial Geraldo Rivera television program, these
cult cops found themselves with their hands full. Like the
witchcraft mania that gripped Salem at the end of the sev-
enteenth century, America was in the throes of "satanic
cult survivor syndrome": a new psychological category
defined by victims coming forward and claiming they
had been sexually and physically abused by members of a
cult. Often, these claims were accompanied by lurid tales

of generational cult activity and the bloody sacrifice of infants and children committed far from the prying eyes of the authorities. At one point it was claimed that tens of thousands of children went missing every year as a result of the insatiable thirst of satanic cults for fresh, virginal victims.

Eventually it was discovered that the statistics didn't quite match the claims of the "survivors." There simply could not have been that many sacrificial victims; some young women who claimed they had been used as "breeders" for the cults—carrying babies to term that would be sacrificed in obscene rituals, without any official record of their birth—were found never to have been pregnant at all. In fact, the FBI was having a hard time coming up with even a single solitary case of the ritual murder of an infant carried out by a cult. No bodies, no evidence, no crime scenes, no crime.

On October 24, 1988, Geraldo Rivera aired "Devil Worship: Exposing Satan's Underground," one of the most-watched shows in television history. Appearing on the program was Maury Terry, author of *The Ultimate Evil*, as well as former FBI special agent Ted Gunderson. The show concentrated on the claims of cult survivors concerning murdered infants and cult leaders who were well-respected members of their communities but kept a dangerous secret: the existence and survival of satanic cults in America going back for generations. The usual references to Manson and the Son of Sam case were made, and in the midst of this shocking material there was film footage shown of a "satanic" ritual site in which the *Necronomicon* was prominently displayed.

In 1989, and on the heels of the Geraldo broadcast, radio talk-show host Bob Larson published *Satanism: The Seduction of America's Youth*, with its fundamentalist Christian

approach to all things New Age. The book attacked virtually
everything remotely connected to the "New Age": astrology,
fortune telling, Wicca, the *I Ching,* the Ouija board, Eliphas
Levi, Aleister Crowley, the *Satanic Bible,* and of course the
Necronomicon. Larson erroneously attributes authorship of
the *Necronomicon* to H.P. Lovecraft, and otherwise demonstrates a lot of confusion where satanism, witchcraft, and
magic are concerned, but the real issue is not his lack of eru-
dition, but his condescending attitude toward anything that
does not reflect his brand of Christianity. For one thing, he
views merely having a copy of the *Necronomicon* as one of
the warning signs that your teenager may be involved with
the occult, along with listening to heavy metal music and
dressing in black.

But by far the most outrageous attacks on the *Necronomicon* have come not from the Christian fundamentalists or the
cult cops, but from those involved with occultism themselves.

With the arrival of the Internet and the BBS—or bulletin
board systems—in the 1980s, there was a steady growl of
disapproval concerning the *Necronomicon* by self-appointed
critics and judges of occult and pagan societies. Of course,
the book had many supporters as well, but they tended not to
show their faces or their Internet addresses lest they be
laughed out of the electronic occultist hall of fame, for the
consensus was that the *Necronomicon* was a hoax and anyone who believed otherwise was a hopeless dupe. After all,
one such typical posting read, "How could an Avon paperback be a real grimoire?"

In 1980 a paperback deal for the *Necronomicon* with Avon
Books—a large, New York publishing house—was signed.
Lea Braff was the agent who negotiated the deal, and she

found the hyperkinetic Larry Barnes somewhat intimidating. One day, after visiting the offices of Barnes Graphics for a business meeting, Ms. Braff was mugged. She phoned us in some distress, and we went to the rescue, calling 911 and summoning police assistance, as Larry muttered about the "curse of the *Necronomicon*," not completely without a soupçon of manic glee. Of course, it being New York City, we *would* get a detective who had some book ideas of his own, and once he knew that Braff was a literary agent, it was love at first sight. At least for the detective. As for the mugging, I don't believe they ever found the perpetrator.

Ms. Braff would eventually convert to Judaism and leave New York and the New York publishing world behind, but not before cutting the deal that would make the *Necronomicon* a name to conjure with.

Barnes had already created a stir with his barter ads in many major magazines. The hardcover edition of the book was doing well, and it was already typeset and designed, so it was an easy sell. All Avon had to do was reprint it, which they did, from a copy that included Larry Barnes's signature (and not mine), thus ensuring that Larry's immortal handwriting would go down in history. It may be too much to say that the *Necronomicon* was a best seller, but it has sold steadily in paperback since May 1980—more than 800,000 copies by the time this is being written—and has been translated into numerous languages, most of them illegally.

It was the paperback version of the book that earned the most notoriety, since it was inexpensive and easy to obtain, unlike the costly hardcover edition, which was available only in two or three stores at the most, and otherwise had to be ordered by mail. As the book moved out into mainstream America, it attracted a great many bad reviews from occultists of one description or another, in a tiff over the success of an occult book they themselves had not written.

By and large, serious occult books sell to a very small audience. There are a few exceptions, of course, depending on what you call "occult." The autobiographical books by Shirley MacLaine about her spiritual awakening hardly fit into that category, but the *Satanic Bible* does. Astrology books sell well, as do books about Nostradamus and his prophecies (especially during times of national anxiety; after the 9/11 attack, sales of Nostradamus-related titles skyrocketed all over the world). Yet, hard-core occult works such as those by Kenneth Grant or Aleister Crowley are not automatic best sellers, because they are written for a specialist audience. The *Necronomicon,* however, crossed over between the hard-core occult market and the popular occult market. Heavy metal bands found the sentiments in the book to be to their liking, and they have even copied some of the chants as lyrics. (Marilyn Manson admits he was influenced by the book as an adolescent.) The more the popular crowd bought and raved over the book, the more the "hard-core" elements found themselves sidelined and made irrelevant.

They struck back.

There are many Internet postings attacking the veracity or usefulness of the *Necronomicon,* but the team of Daniel Harms and John Wisdom Gonce III turned it into a cottage industry. Their Web site became a kind of clearinghouse for *Necronomicon*-related gossip and innuendo as well as criticism of the book based on some shaky scholarship. Gonce, in particular, fancies himself a magician and thus entitled to pronounce judgment on the book from the point of view of a magician. Of course, there is no universal standard for what constitutes a magician, so the claim is an easy one to make.

(Even easier than that of the wandering bishops; at least they have documents signed by other wandering bishops!)

All of the usual criticisms of the book were leveled over the course of several years of postings, which even included a brief exchange of e-mails between Harms and Peter Levenda, which were eventually turned into a book, *The Necronomicon Files,* first published in 1998, and again in 2003 by Samuel Weiser. While many of the book's claims have already been refuted in one way or another during the course of this history, the final chapter will address some of the other issues, since the charges made by Harms and Gonce are serious, if ill-founded and misleading.

The most pertinent charge in this context, however, is the one they make concerning the responsibility of the publishers and the editor in several "cult-related" murders. This should be addressed here.

The most well-documented case concerns that of the famous "vampire teens" of Kentucky who made national headlines in 1996. Rod Ferrell, a sixteen-year-old from Murray, Kentucky, was the self-proclaimed head of a vampiric cult that operated between Kentucky and Lake County, Florida. Ferrell was addicted to a Hollywood image of the occult and satanism, attracted by gothic role-playing games, and generally abusive to authority figures, including his own mother. He fit the image characterized by Christian fundamentalist Bob Larson as a heavy metal playing, black clothes wearing, rebellious teenager who read occult literature such as the *Satanic Bible* and the *Necronomicon* and who tried to figure out how to make the magic work.

In late November 1996 he and his band of four "vampires" murdered the father and mother of one of its members in a small town north of Orlando, Florida, by beating them to death. Investigations conducted after the capture of the group a week later indicated that their ringleader, Ferrell, had a copy of the *Necronomicon* in his possession and often discussed it with his friends. When their vehicle—a stolen Ford Explorer, taken from the crime scene—was searched, it was found to contain Anne Rice's novel, *Queen of the Damned,* and *The Ultimate Dracula,* along with the *Necronomicon* and some Disney films. (One wonders what influence *The Lion King* and *Aladdin* had over the obviously suggestible teens.)

The story of the Wendorf case—as it became known from the name of its victims—is told in a book by Clifford L. Linedecker entitled *The Vampire Killers.* There we learn that Rod Ferrell was a disturbed youth with a history of social and psychological disorders. Harms and Gonce, however, feel comfortable in blaming the *Necronomicon* for the mania of Ferrell and his associates and the subsequent murder of the Wendorfs, even though there is nothing in the *Necronomicon* to fuel a vampire feeding-frenzy. If one had to blame a book for the crimes, it seems obvious that the novels of Anne Rice would be higher on the list of contenders, but Harms and Gonce in their zeal to accuse the *Necronomicon* of *something* (even if they have to take the side of Bob Larson to do so) rush to imply that the blame for the murders should be placed squarely on the shoulders of the publishers and editor of the *Necronomicon.* They go on to cite another murder in which one of the perpetrators—a man named Glen Mason, who wanted to steal souls and was believed to be a Satanist who summoned demons from within a pentagram drawn with blood—had read the *Necronomicon,* and then Gonce goes on to state:

Whether Roderick Ferrell and Glen Mason's involvement with the Simon book was a cause or an effect of their murderous insanity is hard to say. Perhaps it was both. Much of this is admittedly speculation on my part, but it is at least highly educated speculation based on information from reliable news services, on my own experience as a magician and as a religious counselor, and on years of study of magickal texts, including, of course, the *Necronomicon*.[1]

I can only say that I have access to the same news services as Gonce, have experience as a magician and a religious counselor, and have studied magickal texts since the 1960s, and do not come to the same conclusion. It is a very dangerous road to go down, to begin blaming books for the commission of a crime. Gonce focuses on the *Necronomicon* because it supports his thesis. He could have easily focused on *The Witches Bible, The Satanic Bible,* or even *Queen of the Damned* in the Ferrell case, and any one of a dozen satanic volumes available to Glen Mason, as books that contributed to the killers' "murderous insanity." The fact that both Mason and Ferrell were disturbed youths from broken homes with a history of antisocial acting out is ignored in favor of the more sensationalistic claim that somehow the *Necronomicon* was responsible for their crimes. That the killers ignored the general themes of *all* of these books and instead ransacked them for anything that would fuel their own perverse delusions is mirrored in Gonce's own approach when he singles out the *Necronomicon* when it comes time to point fingers and utter pious condemnations.

As I write these lines in December 2004, I am informed that Dena Schlosser in McKinney, Texas, has just admitted to dismembering and killing her infant daughter due to ad-

---

[1] Daniel Harms and John Wisdom Gonce III, *The Necronomicon Files* (York Beach, Maine: Red Wheel/Weiser, 2003), 207

vice found in the Bible, for it states (in the book of Matthew): "If thy right hand offend thee, cut it off." These are the words of Jesus used as motivation for a hideous crime by a woman with a history of mental illness. In Rochester, New Hampshire, Nicole Mancini and John Thurber were arrested the previous month for attempting to sacrifice Nicole's three small boys on the altar of St. Mary's Church. Her reasoning was that since Jesus had sacrificed himself for her, she was going to return the favor. Why? To save her soul.

This is the same Bible that advises us, "Thou shalt not suffer a witch to live." Shall we hold the Bible responsible for the savage acts of the Inquisition, as well as for the madness of Dena Schlosser, Nicole Mancini, and John Thurber? According to Gonce's rationale, maybe we should.

He further cites a line out of context from the *Necronomicon*'s Magan Text in which it is stated that in order to summon the Queen of Ghouls it is necessary to spill blood upon a stone and to strike that stone with a sword that has slain eleven men. What Gonce does not mention is that the Magan Text is prefaced by the narrator with the words:

> The verses here following come from the secret text of some of the priests of a cult which is all that is left of the Old Faith that existed before Babylon was built, and it was originally in their tongue . . . And the horrors and ugliness that the Priest will encounter in his Rites are herein described, and their reasons, and their natures, and Essences.[2]

This is not, as Gonce claims, a book that "speaks approvingly of sacrifice—possibly even human sacrifice and/or suicide."[3]

---

[2] *Necronmicon* (New York: Schlangekraft, 1977), 153

[3] Harms and Gonce, op.cit., 207

It speaks of the "horrors and ugliness" of these practices, and the hideousness of the cult that endorses them, just as the book by Bob Larson speaks of the same issues, albeit in more modern language, and never in any manner speaks of suicide (approvingly or not). But it is also not a book that avoids discussing the topic of sacrifice, a fact of religious life for thousands of years and for many millions of people even today, as it certainly was at the time the book was written. Gonce—and many others like him—perhaps have unwittingly become possessed by the demons they fear most.

He later states that one should not "be allowed to market a spellbook you wrote last week as an ancient Sumerian text."[4] I wholeheartedly agree. However, a careful reading of the introduction to the *Necronomicon* makes it clear that we did not market an ancient Sumerian text that we "wrote last week," but a Greek translation of an Arab text that is a survival of Sumerian—as well as Akkadian and Babylonian—occult practices. That is what it is. That is what we offered—however ill-advisedly, in Gonce's view—to the general public who already had access to *The Satanic Bible, Magick in Theory and Practice, The Magus, The Book of Black Magic and of Pacts*, and many others too loathesome to mention.

I believe his bias becomes obvious when he refers to the *Necronomicon* as the "poor man's *Keys of Solomon*."[5] This is, of course, the general attitude of some occultists toward the Avon paperback who cannot accept that an inexpensive grimoire could actually be a genuine grimoire, an attitude made even more risable when one discovers that inexpen-

---

[4] Ibid, 210

[5] Ibid, 203

sive editions of the *Keys of Solomon* are equally available
in all of America's chain bookstores, from Borders to Barnes
& Noble, and even online. When these dollar elitists get
past the list price of the *Necronomicon*, it is possible that
even *they* may do some good and productive work in this
field.

However, as all this controversy over the *Necronomicon*
began to reach epic proportions, I was well out of the New
York City occult scene, having left it in 1984 when I began
traveling abroad after the tragic suicide of Bishop Anthony
Prazsky earlier that year.

The Book of the Dead

> *When I was seven years gone from my family,*
> *I learned that they had all died of their own hand . . .*
> "Testimony of the Mad Arab," *Necronomicon*

Bishop Anthony was a decent, hardworking, and frugal
man. I always found him to be upbeat and sociable, and was
constantly amazed at his ability to create marvelous iron and
steel ornamental pieces at his workshop, pieces that adorned
the Prazsky home on Hunter Avenue in the Bronx and, later,
the small church next door. He had come into the church
largely at the insistence of his son, Andrew Prazsky, and
never had any theological training or inclination. The story
published by the *New York Times* after his death[6]—stating
that he had studied for the priesthood in 1965—is a fabrication promoted by his son. Anthony Prazsky was nowhere
near a church in 1965, and only became involved in later

---

[6] Robert D. McFadden, "Slavonic Orthodox Bishop Is Found Hanged," *New
York Times*, January 8, 1984, 31

years when his son needed additional bishops to bolster the rolls of his tiny operation.

From all the evidence available to me, I would say that Anthony had become officially involved with the church in late 1969 after the informal resignation of Peter Levenda during the Andre Pennachio affair that spring and just before the reincorporation of the church as the Autocephalous Slavonic Orthodox Catholic Church in April 1970. Prior to that, he would wear the cassock and veiled hat of the Orthodox priest in order to accompany his son to various ecclesiastical functions, but he had not been ordained or in any other way under holy orders in those days. Quite simply, he did it as a lark.

In another article, *New York Times* on January 21, 1976—almost exactly eight years to the day before he committed suicide—Anthony Prazsky was described as a "gnomelike figure" who looked "more like a character out of Snow White than a bishop or an auto mechanic."[7] This is a reference to his full white beard and his short but stocky stature, a startling contrast to his tall, thin son. In the article, of course, he is referred to as Bill Prazsky, an assistant supervisor in the automotive shop, a man who began working for the Tribrio Bridge and Tunnel Authority in 1945 at the age of twenty-nine. Prior to that, he worked as a common laborer during the Depression. One interesting bit of information in the article is the claim that he was donating his salary to the church; this might, in fact, be true as part of a ploy to avoid taxation . . . at least, that is what his son, Bill Prazsky Jr.—or Archbishop Andrew, as he preferred to be known—would have told the reporter, a lie with tragic consequences.

---

[7] John D. Burns, "Bishop Works as a Mechanic," *New York Times,* January 21, 1976, 39

Andrew Prazsky, his only child, had ambivalent feelings about his parents. They had been separated since he was very young, his mother living in a rent-controlled apartment on the Lower East Side in Manhattan. Divorce laws being what they were in New York in the 1950s, when the cultural life of the city was in the stranglehold of the Roman Catholic Church under Cardinal Spellman, the Prazskys were never officially divorced. Regardless, young Andrew had learned to play one parent against the other in a never-ending game of spite and malice. He would eventually manage to persuade his parents to move back in together at the church residence on Hunter Avenue, from which post he was able to observe their every move and to increase his psychological pressure on both of them. One can only guess at the disturbing thoughts he nurtured in the dead of night against his parents and, by extension, against the rest of the world. He was known to all of us as someone who would stay up late, drinking endless amounts of sweet and milky coffee from a chipped enamel cup, smoking cigarettes, and plotting pointless plots against people whom he felt had slighted him or insulted him in some way.

"His ass will suck wind!" he would proclaim of the targeted and unsuspecting victim, using his favorite pejorative. And then he would play "Heart and Soul" on the family's upright piano, or a simplified form of Chopin's "Polonaise Militaire." As an alternative, he would crank up the ancient record player and spin some Gregorian chants or Slavonic liturgical music. If in a good mood, he would play an old hit single by Mary Hopkin, "Those Were the Days," or perhaps Donovan's "Mellow Yellow," a perennial favorite of Andrew Prazsky and his old friend Stanley Dubinsky.

And, if one were extremely unfortunate, young Andrew would sing along.

This type of mean streak was extended to his co-religionists, and part of Prazsky's problems later on stemmed from the fact that he was constantly plotting against *someone* for some imagined slight or to gain some minor advantage. He was a talented individual with a flair for languages—he managed to teach himself fairly fluent Greek—and an artistic ability as a craftsman in gold-leafing, gilding, and designing and sewing vestments, which would have earned him a decent reputation in the ecclesiastical world, but it wasn't enough for him.

He surrounded himself with antiques, some of which were quite costly, such as the ornate, enameled coal stoves that were everywhere in evidence on Hunter Avenue. He was a throwback to an earlier age, one in which he imagined his character, talents, and proclivities would have met with a more appreciative audience. He was an alien on Hunter Avenue. He was an alien in New York City, which has always opened its arms to the strange, the renegade, the outcast.

And, he was a thief.

When his two monks were arrested for the theft of the rare books discussed earlier, Prazsky panicked. He was afraid that some of the swag would be traced to him so he did the unthinkable: he burned the books and manuscripts he had, fearful that his fingerprints would be traced to them and that he would get sent up as the accessory he was. One has to realize the level of paranoia we were all sharing at that time in order to understand why the physical manuscript of the *Necronomicon* is not available for viewing. Prazsky, in a fit of blind panic at the thought of being arrested and possibly going to prison, could not have anything like that around and could not give the books and manuscripts to anyone else for safekeeping, afraid that his fingerprints on the pages would do him in. I do not know for certain that the *Necronomicon* was destroyed in the book-burning holocaust that took place only hours after news of the arrests came down because I was not present at the time; but I do know that it has not been discovered among his effects or, at least, that news of it has not been reported.

The lamentable destruction of Prazsky's occult collection notwithstanding, he was not deterred from other acts of unethical behavior toward those closest to him.

His father had worked hard his entire life—demanding, manual labor in every kind of weather out on the bridges and deep within the tunnels of the city—and after almost forty years in the city's employ had earned a sizable pension. He was counting on that pension to see him through his retirement years. In fact, he spent very little and counted every penny he did spend in an effort to ensure that this nest egg would remain fat and healthy when he was finally able to leave work for good. It was a dream he mentioned to me when I knew him, as he sat eating warm fruit cocktail out of a can and laughing at some situation comedy on television, and it's what kept him going—night after freezing winter night—back to the bridges and tunnels to work all kinds of shifts to put his salary and his overtime in the bank. That, and his pension, would have enabled him to live the kind of life he dreamed about when he finally retired.

His son, however, had other ideas.

It is important to realize that the younger Prazsky had never actually held down a job in his life. When he was pretending to go to college, his income came from the money supposedly being sent for his tuition. With that cash, he would buy his beloved antique stoves and clocks, and subsidize his sacerdotal finery. After a time, however, he couldn't keep that "income" flowing, especially when it became obvious that he wasn't actually attending university. His church had no income of any kind, aside from the occasional home-made miter he would sell to another bishop, so he fell back on one of the lessons he learned during his sojourn at the American Orthodox Catholic Church and at Archbishop Propheta's knee: begging.

Dressed in his complete Orthodox costume of flowing black robes and veiled hat, along with an ebony cane and a *panagia* hanging on a gold chain around his neck, he would wander the streets of Manhattan, going from door to door, literally begging for money for his church. He did not do this all the time, but when he did, he was able to clear more than a thousand dollars in a week; sometimes, depending on the season, more than a thousand dollars in a single day. It was a little dangerous, since he was unlicensed and, it is claimed, forged begging licenses for his associates to carry in case they were stopped and questioned by the authorities.

But even this was not enough to keep Prazsky in the style to which he was becoming accustomed. He needed more money to fund his various adventures, and there was a pile of it sitting very close by.

His father's pension.

The precise details are not known to me, except for one inescapable fact: by 1983, Anthony Prazsky's pension and life savings—on which he had pinned all his hopes for the future—were looted. It is said that a financial statement that came into his possession at the end of 1983 was the final, damning revelation that opened his eyes to his son's true nature and to his own, doomed future as a penniless old man living at the whim of his deceitful, dishonest son. It was too much.

On Christmas night—Russian Christmas, January 6, 1984—Anthony Prazsky went into the little church he had built with his own two hands (the church that he had built in a naive, hopeful gesture of love to his only child) and, on the night that Orthodox faithful celebrate the birth of the infant Jesus, he tied a rope around his neck in the freezing cold.

His son found him a little while later, hanging from the rafters, motionless. He had performed the one sin for which there is no redemption in the Church: suicide.

It had all come down on him at once. The stolen books and the federal investigation that followed led right to the door of the Slavonic Orthodox Church. The arrest and indictment of Hubak and Chapo. The burning of the books. The return of Michael Hubak as Father and then "Bishop Raphael" upon his release from federal prison at Danbury, when he became Andrew Prazsky's virtual servant. The crooked deals. The shafting of other churches. The looted bank accounts.

And the stories planted in the newspapers that "Bishop Anthony" had studied in a seminary in 1965 and was consecrated a bishop in 1969. Bill Prazsky's own coworkers had to know better than that. It was one thing to live a lie; it was quite another to be deceived by your own flesh and blood, and to be robbed of what you had worked for all your life. The son. The father. And the church that had united them, and then just as easily destroyed them.

No doubt it suddenly became easier to take your life than it was to go on living. But Bill Prazsky had the last laugh. For the day, he chose Christmas, the day of Jesus' birth; and for the place, he chose the church he built himself. He hung himself from a beam in front of the iconostasis, the icon screen on which are painted the faces of the saints, most notable among them in this case that of Saint Andrew, patron of the church he built and his son's chosen namesake.

The funeral began more than an hour late. Thirty-three-year-old Archbishop Metropolitan Andrew Prazsky was drunk, almost incoherent, but insisted on performing the service himself. Several of Anthony's coworkers were there, and a handful of people from the neighborhood. It was a sad sendoff to a man who died in despair, but at least he was surrounded by his friends, people who knew him before he was a "bishop," who knew him only as Bill Prazsky, assistant supervisor, and not as "Anthony" of the Slavonic Orthodox Church, the church that was the dream of his high-school-age son in 1968 in a working-class neighborhood in the Bronx.

The next to die was Andrew Prazsky himself.

From 1969 to 1990, Prazsky had worked very hard to ingratiate himself with the Ukrainian Autocephalous Orthodox Church (UAOC). Archbishop Hryhorij reconsecrated Prazsky and brought him into the Ukrainian communion, thus giving the nineteen-year-old kid from the Bronx a degree of legitimacy to which he was not, perhaps, entitled. But Hryhorij was rather old at that time, and having problems of his own.

Hryhorij was consecrated a bishop in Poland in 1942. There is a photograph on the church's Web site showing him at a *sobor*—or conference of bishops—in 1947. Alert readers will realize that 1942—the year Hryhorij was consecrated— is in the middle of the Second World War, and Hryhorij was in *Nazi-occupied Poland*. Most Catholics and Orthodox in Poland and the Ukraine were anti-Soviet because, quite simply, they were anti-Communist. The efforts of the Polish church in consecrating Ukrainian bishops was to set up a Ukrainian Orthodox Church in diaspora, as against the Ukrainian Orthodox, who were forced to owe their allegiance to Moscow. Further, the Soviets had done all they could to eradicate the Ukrainian language and culture in order to make the country more transparently Russian. In order to defend Ukraine and oppose godless communism, elements of the Ukrainian Orthodox Church decided to throw in their lot with the Nazis.

By the end of the war there was an entire division of Waffen SS that was totally composed of Ukrainian officers and men. This division managed to escape any kind of postwar tribunal—and to escape Europe entirely—by fleeing to the United States, South America, and Australia under the protection of the Western intelligence agencies. The leader of that SS division, General Pavlo Shandruk, wound up being buried with hero's honors at the headquarters of the UAOC in Bound Brook, New Jersey, and now rests in the church's cemetery there. To be fair, Ukrainians view Shandruk and his division as "freedom fighters" for Ukraine independence from the Soviets; but to many others, his SS division represented nothing less than allegiance with the rabid anti-Semitism and murderous pogroms of the Nazis.

If you look at the history of this church on its various—American and Ukrainian—Web sites, you will see a conspicuous blank where the war years are concerned. There is no mention of what the Ukrainian bishops were doing, where they were located, or what forces they supported during that time. That is because the truth is more horrible than they can easily admit.

By the 1980s, however, things were changing. Due to the thaw in U.S.-Soviet relations, the tearing down of the Berlin Wall, and the ongoing collapse of Soviet communism, the Eastern Orthodox world was facing new challenges and opportunities. The Russian Orthodox Church was seeking to consolidate its power and influence in North America, and opposed UAOC efforts to remain dedicated to an anti-Russian policy. The Ukrainian Orthodox Church in Ukraine wanted to mend fences with the Ukrainian Orthodox in America, and had to walk a narrow tightrope between appeasing their Russian neighbors to the north and appealing to the American-born, anti-Soviet and anti-Russian faithful in the West.

Before that would happen, however, Archbishop Hryhorij died: in 1985, at his church's headquarters in Chicago.[8] Only a year after the death of his own father, Andrew Prazsky was suddenly without a protector.

Archbishop Hryhorij had (impossibly) named Bishop Andrew Prazsky his official successor, something that caused a little consternation in the UAOC. In the first place, Prazsky was not Ukrainian. In the second place, his original consecration by Propheta had been "normalized" by Archbishop Hryhorij in 1969 during Prazsky's reconsecration, so in addition Prazsky was also an alumnus of that famous bishops' mill, the American Orthodox Catholic Church, and thus a distant colleague of suspected Kennedy assassination co-conspirators and AOCC bishops David Ferrie and Jack Martin, among many others. His background was suspect. His administrative skills nonexistent. His agenda—like his true age—secret.

Photographs on the Web of Prazsky attending the funeral of his mentor Hryhorij show a man who looks like he's been kicked in the stomach. His father had committed suicide the previous year, his protector was dead as well, and the Soviet Union was in danger of falling apart and throwing a monkey wrench into the works. As long as the

---

[8] Kenan Heise, "Prelate Hryhorij Osijchuk, 87: Head of Ukrainian Church Here," *Chicago Tribune,* February 16, 1985, 7

Soviet Union remained intact, the Orthodox churches "in exile" could remain aloof and conduct their own affairs without undue interference from the homeland. With the impending collapse of the Russian government, it would be very little time before the Orthodox churches in Russia, Ukraine, and elsewhere behind the Iron Curtain would be running back to the States to reclaim that which was not particularly rightfully theirs. That meant the UAOC would be in the middle of a kind of religious custody battle. Loyalty to Moscow? Loyalty to Kiev? Full independence? Partial autonomy? Prazsky was in no position to make any decisions of that nature, and besides, he had already alienated most of the Orthodox world by his constant scheming and backbiting.

There is another photograph, showing Andrew Prazsky in Cairo with the Coptic Pope Shenuda in 1989, attended by his faithful Bishop Raphael: Michael Hubak of the stolen books. Hubak had managed to get a job in Egypt, teaching English (although he would say that he was teaching theology at the Coptic seminary there), and was the go-between for Prazsky and Shenuda. Andrew was evidently looking for ways to outmaneuver the Ukrainians by forming other alliances, like a High Mass version of *Survivor.* Andrew, however, would have only one more year to live.

In 1990 the Patriarch of the Ukrainian Orthodox Church, Archbishop Mystyslav, flew to the United States after his installment as Primate of the church that November in Kiev. Like Hryhorij, Mystyslav had been consecrated in Poland during the war and was now, almost fifty years later, taking charge of the UAOC after the fall of the Soviet Union. At a splendid homecoming in Bound Brook, New Jersey— attended by many of Prazsky's colleagues and several men he had ordained and/or consecrated—Mystyslav proclaimed

the rebirth of the Ukrainian Orthodox Church. Archbishop
Metropolitan Andrew "Andrei" Prazsky was not in attendance; oddly enough, considering his close relationship with
Mystyslav's old colleague, Hryhorij, and Prazsky's own status as Hryhorih's successor.

That evening, as the festivities were underway in Bound
Brook only steps away from the graves of SS General Pavlo
Shandruk and his faithful men, Archbishop Metropolitan
Andrew "Andrei" Prazsky, son of William Anthony Prazsky,
mixed a lethal combination of poisons in his metal-plating
shop and died, on December 16, 1990, alone except for his
aged mother and his cat. He was forty years old, and had
been a bishop since he was nineteen. The story put out by the
church, informally, was that he had died of a tragic accident
in the shop.

Yet, only days earlier, Archbishop Andrew had destroyed
all his church's archives and records, burning them in one of
his antique coal stoves.

The same way he had burned his stolen books.

According to people close to the investigation and questioned by Peter Levenda, Mrs. Prazsky knew that her son did
not die by accident. She reportedly blamed former colleagues of her son—priests and bishops—for pushing him to
suicide. Mrs. Prazsky—Petronella—died almost thirteen
years later, on April 7, 2003, at the age of ninety-two.

But was Andrew's death a suicide?

Rumors that Andrew had been the victim of foul play flew
around the gossip mills and bishop mills with reckless abandon in the days and weeks after his death. These were Eastern Europeans, after all, and they played hardball. Some of
these men had suffered under the Soviet commissars and

had been beaten and imprisoned in the gulag by Russian goons. Some of them had worked side by side with the Nazis in their race to the East. These were not ecclesiastical dilettantes, covering themselves with glory and fancy titles, lusting after new consecrations and parchment dignities. These were people who had opposed vicious and lawless regimes in their homeland, and bore the scars to prove it.

Could they possibly let this effete, scheming youngster from the Bronx—a young man who had so easily hoodwinked old Archbishop Hryhorij—stay and participate in the newly energized, newly empowered church in America?

The Cathedral of St. Andrew no longer stands on Hunter Avenue. The property has been sold off, and the church itself is in disarray. There is, in truth, nothing much left of the religious operation two teenage boys from the Bronx, fueled with strange dreams no one else can truly understand—and with individual dreams that one could not even share with the other—set up in 1968 in the shadow of Co-Op City. The Prazsky family is dead; two men by their own hand, and two women of old age and despair.

As if the Testimony of the Mad Arab quoted above was a prophecy rather than a history, seven years after I left the church, the family were all dead by their own hands.

The next one to fall was Herman Slater.

As we have seen, Slater was a prime mover in the *Necronomicon* affair. It was his advice that led to the translation and publication of the book; it was in his store that Larry Barnes wandered one day and discovered the manuscript behind the counter. It was Herman Slater whose mailing list became the source for selling out the first edition. And it was Herman Slater who tirelessly promoted the book, like a seasoned salesman telling anyone whatever version of the truth about the book they wanted to hear.

Herman Slater's lifestyle would be considered risky today, but it was perfectly natural in the context of the 1970s. He was an initiate of the bathhouse and the leather bar, and was a hilarious drag queen when circumstances—or a party—demanded it. His affair with the younger, slender Wiccan high priest Ed Buczynski lasted all during the formative period of the Warlock Shop and the discovery and publication of the *Necronomicon,* but eventually the two lovers would part ways. Ed would die from the AIDS virus in 1989. As the 1980s became the 1990s, Herman fell in with a rougher, tougher crowd and began wearing leather pants and a biker jacket. It was during the late eighties that we learned that Herman Slater had contracted the AIDS virus and was HIV-positive.

He had struck a deal with me to translate a few medieval grimoires, such as the *Red Dragon* and the *Black Pullet,* from Italian and French copies that we uncovered in various places. I eventually provided him the translation of the *Red Dragon,* as well as a follow-up volume to the *Necronomicon,* entitled *The Gates of the Necronomicon.* Both of these books were set in type and prepared for publication when Herman Slater lost his battle with AIDS and passed away to the Summerland in July 1992. He was only fifty-four years old. I was one of the last people to speak with him by phone, but he was too far gone at that point and in too much pain to be coherent.

The day he died, I was looking up into the heavens and saw a shooting star, a meteorite falling to earth. As corny as it sounds, at that moment I knew Herman—my old friend and colleague—had died. I mourned his loss then, and mourn it now.

The *Red Dragon* and the *Gates of the Necronomicon* were both advertised in his mail order catalogue as available in May and July 1992, respectively. They never made it into print. The whereabouts of the manuscripts and the typeset copies is still a mystery, in the manner of their forebear, the *Necronomicon* itself. One company advertised them briefly and then disappeared. It is assumed that they are intact somewhere and that someone is waiting until everyone concerned has died before they put them into print. I am sorry to have to disappoint them on both counts.

The Gates of the Necronomicon still exists in manuscript, and it has been revised and enlarged. It will be published. If there is still a market for my English translation of the *Red Dragon,* then that too will see print.

Then, nine years later, an even sadder loss.

I remained in contact with Larry Barnes on and off for years. He had moved from the East Coast in the late 1980s and wound up in El Cajon, California, where he and his wife—a telephone psychic—opened an occult bookstore, Inner Journey. Neither the wife nor the bookstore were meant to be: the store burned down, and Larry and his wife were divorced after a nasty fight. The communications I received from him from time to time during that period were always the same as those I'd received in the old days, and I had no reason to believe that Larry had changed at all. His cards and notes always had drawings of alien beings in the margins, and the wording was all Marvel Comics word balloons. My travels abroad meant that it was difficult for us to keep in touch (this was before e-mail, and anyway, the

countries I visited had poor telephone service and even
worse snail mail). When it looked as if Avon Books wanted
to republish what Herman Slater had called the *Necronomicon Report* as the *Necronomicon Spellbook,* Larry eventually
did manage to reach me and was insistent that we sign the
contract. I had second thoughts about the *Spellbook,* if only
because I felt that it would detract from sales of the *Necronomicon* itself. The *Report* had been Herman's idea, since he
felt that a "guide" to the *Necronomicon* was needed by some
of his clientele. While I was satisfied with the work—and
used it as an opportunity to provide more background information about the *Necronomicon*—I thought it could have
been expanded more fully, much like the missing *Gates of
the Necronomicon.* There was, however, no time to do this,
and the publishers were happy with the *Report* as is, so it
was reborn as the *Necronomicon Spellbook*—only after some
legal wrangling with Herman, who wanted to retain the
rights to publish it even though our contractual obligations to
him had long passed. He had not republished or reprinted
the *Report* in years, and had his hands full with *Red Dragon*
and *Gates* anyway.

And, quite frankly, Larry needed the money.

Since Larry had nothing to do with *Red Dragon* or the
other works I had contracted with Herman, the only income he was getting was the biannual check from Avon
Books for the *Necronomicon.* He would pester our agent for
weeks about getting the check or an advance on the check,
since he was always short of funds. The *Necronomicon
Spellbook* would be another money earner, and so I relented.

As it happened, it would be nearly as popular as the
Necronomicon itself. Containing a method for using the
Fifty Names of Marduk the way a simple grimoire of low

magic would—as spells for obtaining various goals—it was slim, easy to read, and easy to understand. Those who considered the original *Necronomicon* a hoax were quick to criticize the *Spellbook* as a dangerous shortcut through the minefield of *Necronomicon* magic. It seemed that there was virtually nothing we could do to satisfy the critics. If the book was a hoax, then there was nothing dangerous about the *Spellbook;* if the *Spellbook* was dangerous, then the *Necronomicon* obviously was not a hoax. However, critics of the book are generally able to keep two mutually opposed ideas in their head at the same time and are probably evidence of some strange new kind of spiritual initiate.

In truth, the *Spellbook* has safeguards built into it, as anyone with any occult training would spot. However, this has apparently slipped the notice of the most vociferous of our critics, as it should.

With the *Spellbook* in print—and available throughout the world, sometimes showing up in the Harry Potter section of chain bookstores!—Larry at least had another source of ongoing income. As for me, I was busy with other matters and lost touch with Larry after the new contract had been signed. I did not know that his battle with drug addiction had been renewed and that he was again—or still—in the grip of its unrelenting fury.

I was deep in the Southeast Asian rain forest when I got the news, months later. Larry Barnes had died in the hospital from cardiac arrest as a result of complications due to an untreated leg infection, made worse by his heroin addiction. The date was December 18, 2001. He was forty-nine years old.

It was eleven years—almost to the day—after the suicide of Andrew Prazsky on December 16, 1990, himself the son of a suicide.

* * *

Larry Barnes and his brother Wayne had both died prematurely and tragically. Wayne's death occurred at precisely the time I was completing the final work on the *Necronomicon,* on October 12, 1975. Larry's death occurred on the anniversary of the suicide of Andrew Prazsky. Larry and Wayne were brothers who died from the same addiction. Anthony and Andrew Prazsky were father and son, who both killed themselves. Herman Slater and Ed Buczynski both died from AIDS. I don't want to fuel gossip about a "curse of the *Necronomicon*" since I don't believe in it; instead, I see the connections that exist between these groups of individuals—connections whose common denominator is the *Necronomicon*—as a framework, a matrix for the action of some mysterious power that has used us to midwife itself into consciousness.

Larry was perhaps the most sensitive of all of us to this phenomenon. He was able to express in art—and even in his entire personality—the feelings we were experiencing as a result of our proximity to the "black book." His perception that the forces of the *Necronomicon* were somehow alien forces would be echoed later by Kenneth Grant, but Larry was not an occultist *per se.* He saw the world as infested with signs and symbols of the influence of these cosmic forces, everything from suggestive license plate numbers, invoice numbers, and addresses, to the names of individuals with whom he came into contact on a daily basis, plus UFO reports, Egyptian deities, random figures and designs on sidewalks, street corners, and storefront bodegas. His desperate search for meaning in the ordinary things of life may have reflected a deeper unease over the death of his brother and its eerie connection to the *Necronomicon,* a fact that cannot be denied but just as certainly cannot be explained. One thing is certain: shortly before his death, Larry's art had changed.

While he still concentrated on alien landscapes and weird, hydrocephalic-looking creatures with stern and staring eyes, he began to insert *himself* into the paintings. More and more we see *Larry* as the alien, Larry as "Kosmo," actively taking part in the otherworldly scenarios that so obsessed him. As Larry intruded more and more into his art, he receded more and more from the rest of us.

As I look at his art now, I see him—in spacesuit and helmet, flying saucer and tractor beam—looking back at me from the depths of outer space with that weird expression of one who has seen more than you have, an expression that is at once challenging and humorous, superior . . . but waiting to see if you get the punch line. Kosmo, I can't help thinking, you've gone home.

There were others who made an impact on the occult renaissance who left this world prematurely. LSD and expanded-consciousness advocate Timothy Leary and *Illuminatus!* author Robert Anton Wilson both lost family members to suicide or violence. Bonnie Claremont, the former wife of Marvel Comics author Chris Claremont and a fixture in the StarGroup One organization, lost a long-running battle with cancer and died all too young. Ed Buczynski died from AIDS three years before Herman Slater. Martin Mensch, one of my students and an accomplished flamenco guitarist, as well as a natural occultist, died from a bullet ricochet during a shootout in the Lower East Side. Richard Guernon, an OTO member and bishop of the Gnostic Catholic Church, died by means of a drug overdose in March 1988, a possible suicide. (He had been very interested in obtaining valid lines of apostolic succession for the Gnostic Church.) This list goes on and on.

I am tempted to look upon these tragic victims as a kind of late twentieth-century version of Gurdjieff's *Meetings with Remarkable Men*. Andrew Prazsky, Herman Slater, Larry Barnes . . . these were all men involved in a spiritual quest but one that they at times resisted. They were Americans, rather than Gurdjieff's assorted Russians and Central Asians, and they lived in the heart of technological Western society and not in the Steppes or the Caucasus or the Himalayas or the desert places of the world. As such, they distrusted the mainstream religion and homespun spirituality of their parents and ancestors, and sought instead a deeper, more profound experience in the forbidden, the forgotten, the outré. In the case of Herman Slater and Andrew Prazsky, their sexuality made them automatic and unwilling outcasts in a society that prizes machismo above all else; in the case of Larry Barnes, it was his artistic sensitivity mixed with an unspoken sense of doom related to his older brother's death that caused him to seek affirmation in alternate realities. They were all forced to look beneath the fabric of our common, human experience to find and identify the spiritual conspiracies that take place below the range of our physical senses. Andrew Prazsky sought this affirmation in an orgy of self-glorification, costumed in the rich robes and jeweled mitres of the Church . . . all the while, in a paranoid frenzy, studying the books of the sorcerers that had been stolen by his monks from the libraries of the world; a throwback to the cardinals of the Renaissance. Herman Slater sought it in the pagan rites of witchcraft, in the embrace of an ithyphallic God and a maternal, forgiving Goddess. Larry Barnes sought it in the deep reaches of space and in the cryptic messages delivered by mysterious beings from other dimensions, other continuums . . . and in the temporary solace of heroin, a refined form of the drug cultivated as poppies in the fields of Iraq: that is, of ancient Sumer and Babylon.

As I look at their photographs tonight, however, I seem to remember only the positive things about these men. I remember laughing with each of them, feeling the energy of a fierce creativity and intelligence, of *engagement* with the world. I can only remember Larry Barnes in a good light; I honestly can't think of a time when we fought or argued, even though he gave me many good reasons over the years. The same with Herman Slater. In the case of Andrew Prazsky, I remember a tormented soul with no means of escaping the prison of his own childhood. He went from adolescent to archbishop with no time left for growth or experience of the world. He bore a burden of unbelievable guilt, and I cannot help but think that he had been incapable of choosing any other path. His death, and that of his father, still saddens me immensely . . . but I can only remember them both in better, sunnier days. The intense precocity of those two teenagers, Andrew Prazsky and Peter Levenda, that flared to sudden brightness in 1968 is still astounding, especially in this age of the slacker and the cynic.

Not everyone involved with the *Necronomicon* died prematurely, however. Jim Wasserman is alive and well at the time of this writing, and is an author in his own right specializing in ancient Egyptian religion, the Cult of the Assassins, and related topics. Peter Levenda—after years of traveling abroad in Europe, Asia, Australia, and Latin America—still found time to write *Unholy Alliance,* a study of Nazi occultism that bears a foreword by Norman Mailer. Having learned the fine art of gate-crashing at the funeral Mass for Senator Kennedy, he practiced it once again at the mysterious Nazi colony, Colonia Dignidad in Chile, which forms the framework of that book, and nearly paid the ultimate price. "Brass it out, my son." His next work, *Sinister Forces,* a massive and heavily documented study of the interface between religion, occultism, and politics and the "sinister forces" that link them all in coincidence and conspiracy, is due out in several volumes in 2005 and 2006. Allyn Brodsky, another member of StarGroup One, now resides peacefully on the West Coast, if that is indeed possible. My old martial arts instructor and sometime student, Bokar, still seeks the ultimate initiation . . . or was that "inebriation"? An enthusiastic exemplar of the Drunken Monk technique, he is probably the only one who teaches the method with a bottle of Rolling Rock in one hand. Larry Kirwan is successful as a musician, novelist, and playwright . . . and husband and father, to the shock of us all. Then there was Pierce Turner, Copernicus, Alan Cabal . . . so many others. With the exception of Larry Barnes and Herman Slater, everyone else mentioned in the Acknowledgments to the *Necronomicon* is, to the best of my knowledge, still alive and well. Thus, along with the "curse" there have also been blessings.

These were my "remarkable men," these and a few others whose names are not recorded here but who nonetheless make my personal list of those who sought an honest, alternative reality in a world where sin is forgiven, where differences are accepted without judgment, where the "negative emotions" of fear, anger, and rage have a venue of their own: a place where they are not denied, but allowed expression in ways that are not harmful to other men but only to the *jinn* that haunt our dreams, every day, in this dangerous and unfeeling world where the gods have forgotten us. The pictures their portraits here painted are not particularly pretty, but they are real. They are genuine. These men lived their passions—no matter how recklessly or selfishly—and many died for it, young and before their time. A slaughter of the not so innocent: men who paved the way for the incarnation of the *Necronomicon*.

10: Summa Necronomica

The *Necronomicon* has been attacked on the Internet by numerous people who feel qualified to pronounce sentence, and also attacked, most especially, in a book entitled *The Necronomicon Files* by Daniel Harms and John Wisdom Gonce III. The attacks are too numerous and too wildly varied to permit me to respond to every one, but I hope that this book generally—and this chapter in particular—will help to correct much of the disinformation that has been peddled under the rubric of informed criticism. I will address the main points of the attacks, and anyone who is motivated or interested can judge the credibility of other criticisms on their own merits. My intention is not to prove anything one way or another, but to refute some of the poor scholarship and biased judgments that have proliferated on the Internet and in print by those who insist they are in a position to analyze the *Necronomicon* and pronounce it a fraud. Once these main points are answered, the reader should be able to better understand and appreciate the importance of the *Necronomicon* from an occult perspective, as well as from an academic one.

One of the critics who have appeared in print is Kalyn Tranquilson, a "queer activist" and historian who has since passed away but whose work, *Babyloniana,* has been excerpted in various places on the Internet, most notably on a site devoted to "chaos magic." Tranquilson (a questionable source cited several times by Gonce), in the guise of stern academic contempt, states—among many other objections—that I "make some extremely untenable historical assertions, such as that the Sumerian language is 'closely allied to that of the Aryan race, having in fact many words identical to that of Sanskrit (and it is said, to Chinese).' "

I respectfully submit that these assertions are not untenable at all. At the time the Introduction was being written, this was being seriously discussed among scholars of Sumer, and it is still discussed today. I direct the reader to a wide variety of academic authors and Web sites for more detailed analysis of this assertion: Michael Witzel of Harvard; Dr. Jahanshah Derakhshani of Teheran, especially "Some Earliest Traces of the Aryan: Evidence from the Fourth and Third Millennium B.C."; I.M. Diakanoff, especially "External Connections of the Sumerian Language," in *Mother Tongue,* III, 1997, 54–62; a Web site devoted to Sumerian and Indo-European equivalence, www.lexiline.com/lexiline/lexi37.htm, dated October 22, 2004; the ongoing work of Professor Gordon Whittaker of the University of Goettingen; and the works of Paul Kekai Manansala, which are devoted to showing a relationship between Sumerian and the Austric language group and a refutation of the Aryan Invasion Theory.

Tranquilson then goes on to complain that my interpretation of Cthulhu as a variant of the Sumerian KUTHA-LU, man of Kutha or the Underworld, is utterly wrong. He insists that the correct rendering would be LU-KUTHA and that therefore my interpretation is incorrect. This itself has been corrected by other commentators on the Sumerian language who admit that either rendering—KUTHA-LU or LU-KUTHA—would be grammatically correct.[1]

Tranquilson goes on to say that my identification of the ancient city of Kutha with the Underworld is in error; this has been addressed already in Chapter Six, and demonstrates that Tranquilson himself is in error here.

He then attacks some of the language of the incantations, stating, "The language of his given translations is hardly accurate and the ABRACADABRA phrases at the end of the invocations are garbage." In the first place, how could Tranquilson know that the language of my translations is hardly accurate unless he had the original Greek manuscript in front of him, which is perhaps possible but hardly likely since he never mentions it? In the second place, the phrases at the end of the invocations are what Crowley and numerous other experts have described as "barbarous names of power." These can be found in many Gnostic texts, such as those from Nag Hammadi, and have a long and respected pedigree. That they are "garbage" depends on your point of view, but their function is acknowledged among Gnostic scholars as well as ceremonial magicians (such as Crowley).

A Reverend Xul has commented on this essay by Tranquilson, and also points out that it "would've been nice if you pointed out the inaccuracies [in the Urilia Text of the *Necronomicon*] . . . such as Humwawa not being the lord of decay but actually being the guardian of the Cedar Tree which is a gate to the heavens." While Reverend Xul has taken a moderate stand on the usefulness or veracity of the

---

[1] These commentators include Ryan Parker on the alt.discordia newsgroup, Christopher B. Siren at http://home.comcast.net/~chris.s/ (dowloaded on October 23, 2004), and others.

Necronomicon, I must hasten to correct this common misconception of Humwawa.

Reverend Xul is not alone in his criticism. Gonce has said that the description of Humwawa's face as a "mass of entrails" is wrong, that it was used as some kind of divinatory apparatus, and that Humwawa was a beneficent being. A close reading of the Epic of Gilgamesh tells a somewhat different story, for therein we read that Humwawa was a monster who had to be defeated—and beheaded—by Gilgamesh, and that his breath was loathesome and stank of decay. His face *was* depicted as a mass of entrails, specifically the small intestines.[2] I believe that the glyph of Humwawa in the *Necronomicon* showing his face as a mass of entrails is probably how he was perceived in later Sumerian and Babylonian mythology, and further, that only his head is shown in this glyph may be an allusion to the fact that the monster was beheaded. Occult literature is full of stories of "talking heads" of one kind or another, and I believe that this tale of Humwawa was a prototype for these later ideations and may have given rise to the use of the head of Humwawa for a divinatory apparatus, as entrails have been used in divination since time immemorial. The face of Humwawa is thus clearly a "mass of entrails," for the entrails—in this case, the intestines—were believed to be representative of the labyrinth: the crooked and twisted path to enlightenment. This has been noted many times, in many places, such as in *Hamlet's Mill* and on Web sites such as Biblica Arcana.

---

[2] See, for instance, Carel J. Du Ry, *Art of the Ancient Near and Middle East* (New York: Abrams, 1969), 115, for a depiction of the head of Humwawa and a description of it as a mass of entrails used for divination, the most commonly accepted interpretation.

* * *

When we discuss published attacks on the *Necronomicon*, however, we must address the writings and interviews of the team of Daniel Harms and John Gonce.

While Harms attempts to deconstruct the *Necronomicon* in a scholarly fashion, and exercises some restraint, Gonce attacks it from the point of view of a self-described pagan and ceremonial magician. He claims that since he is both, his views have authority and carry some weight. Of course, anyone can describe themselves as a ceremonial magician; there is no board of commissioners for magic, no pedigree that is universally recognized. So we must disregard Gonce's claims to some special insight or eminent background and, rather, take his objections (and those of Harms) at face value.

Both Harms and Gonce—who wrote separate chapters in *The Necronomicon Files*—first of all assume that the *Necronomicon* is a hoax. Insisting that the book is a deliberate fraud is quite different from claiming that it is simply not the *Necronomicon* of the Lovecraft oeuvre, and this is where their competing attempts to "disprove" the *Necronomicon* fall on dangerously thin ice. This is especially true in the field of ceremonial magic, in which virtually every famous grimoire is, in fact, fraudulent to some extent. *The Greater and Lesser Keys of Solomon*, for instance, are patently not the work of Solomon the biblical king. There is even some debate over whether Solomon actually existed as a historical figure.

The *Grimoire of Pope Honorious* was not written by Pope Honorious.

The *Fourth Book of Cornelius Agrippa* has no relation to his previous three books and was clearly not penned by the same person.

The list goes on and on.

There is a tradition among the medieval and Renaissance authors of grimoires to ascribe their authorship to someone else, someone with more "weight." It also probably helped to sell books. One wonders if Gonce is comfortable with the grimoires of that period; if not, why does he not attack them all as being "hoaxes"? Perhaps because it would automatically devalue the entire field of ceremonial magic, which is based almost completely on the rituals appearing in such "hoaxes"? I submit that the reason he does not attack the supposed medieval hoaxes is that it has become a moot point by now: regardless of whether or not Solomon actually wrote the *Keys* attributed to his name, the grimoires are popular because so many eminent magicians—Mathers and Crowley, to name but two—have translated them, published them, added introductory material, even corrected errors in previous editions, and in general promoted their use. Crowley went so far as to append translations of some of the incantations found in the *Lesser Key of Solomon* into the Enochian (or Angelic) tongue. Clearly, he intended people to use them as he used them himself. The fact that Solomon was not the author did not deter Crowley in the slightest. The magic worked.

We can also cite the Gardnerian *Book of Shadows* as a forgery, or a hoax, as well as the infamous Cypher Manuscript, which led to the formation of the Golden Dawn. Indeed, as Peter Levenda has pointed out, even the Church of Jesus Christ of Latter Day Saints (more popularly known as the Mormons) was founded on something called the *Book of Mormon,* which Joseph Smith Jr. claimed he received from an angel during the performance of a ritual of ceremonial magic.[3] Smith went on to misidentify an ancient scroll as the

---

[3] *Sinister Forces, Book One: The Nine* (Eugene, OR: Trine Day, 2005)

original of the *Book of Mormon* . . . until it was identified many years later as part of the *Egyptian Book of the Dead*. If we go back even further, the New Testament itself is a cut-and-paste job of various gospels that were considered "politically correct" at the time and worthy of inclusion in the Scripture; a Scripture designed by a committee with a political agenda.

So, where do we begin? Why is the *Necronomicon* singled out for such vitriol by some magicians? (Obviously, not *all* magicians . . . for there are groups of occultists around the world that use the *Necronomicon* as a grimoire and record substantial progress with it.) Why does Gonce, for example, feel that he is qualified to judge—and dismiss—the practices of other occultists? Perhaps because he had a publisher?

One of the problems both Harms and Gonce seem to have with the *Necronomicon* is that it has been successful as a literary property. Not many hard-core occult works can make that claim. In fact, only Anton LaVey's *Satanic Bible* comes to mind as a work that has probably sold as many—or probably many more—copies as the *Necronomicon*. If not for the book's commercial success, it would have never attracted as much attention from the cranks on both sides of the issue (Christian fundamentalist, New Age pagan) as it does now.

Another reason for their distaste is the fact that the book is available virtually everywhere on Earth. It is the first book of its kind to reach out to the masses of people, and ceremonial magicians—or people who claim to be ceremonial magicians—are desperate to consider themselves elite and above the vulgar herd. If anyone can go into a bookstore and lift the *Necronomicon* off the rack for a few dollars, go home, and begin to practice magic, then what is the value in being a "real" ceremonial magician? (In other words, a person who has waded through Waite and Crowley and Francis

Barrett and wrestled with the Latin, Greek, and Hebrew words—many of them already hopelessly mangled—in the thankful privacy of their own basements.) When an acned seventeen-year-old, replete in his goth attire, chants spells from the *Necronomicon* . . . it aggravates the self-anointed, self-appointed elders of the Western occult tradition.

Another claim made in *The Necronomicon Files* is that the *Necronomicon* bears some culpability for crimes committed by persons who have read the *Necronomicon* or had the book in their possession, a charge already addressed in the previous chapter. It is hard to know where to begin to discuss this allegation. In the first place, how many crimes have been committed—and are committed every day—by persons who have read the Bible or had a copy in their possession? Evil is evil, and will find its way out regardless of book or cult. There are something like one million copies of the *Necronomicon* in existence on the planet. Harms and Gonce can only come up with two instances in which a crime has been committed in the *vicinity* of the book . . . notwithstanding other books that were also involved, such as the *Satanic Bible*, the novels of Anne Rice, and even some Disney videotapes. Their insistence that the publishers and I remain somehow callously aloof of all of this and ignore the tragedies being perpetrated by our publication in order to reap material reward—like drug dealers in the schoolyard— is idiotic. In fact, as I write these lines, I have just learned of a man who, after watching the environmental disaster film *The Day After Tomorrow,* was moved to set fire to his couch. Are the producers of that film now to be held liable for destruction of private property?

Gonce in particular insists that the *Necronomicon* speaks approvingly of human sacrifice. (So does the Bible, in the story of Abraham and Isaac for example, but that is beside the point.) Nowhere in the *Necronomicon* does the narrator, the Mad Arab, speak approvingly of human sacrifice. Nowhere. Yet mention *is* made of ancient cults that did. This is perfectly consistent with Sumerian history. As Woolley points out in his groundbreaking study of ancient Sumerian civilization:

> The burial of the kings was accompanied by human sacrifice on a lavish scale, the bottom of the grave pit being crowded with the bodies of men and women who seemed to have been brought down here and butchered where they stood.[4]

Much more interesting, though, are the many instances in which Gonce attacks the credibility of the book on various seemingly academic grounds. Therefore, I believe it is useful to answer some of the more outrageous of these claims in this place.

(The page numbers used here refer to the Samuel Weiser edition of *The Necronomicon Files*.)

Page 133: He ridicules the idea that Michael Hubak and Steven Chapo actually stole any occult books since these books are not mentioned in the news stories! That issue has been addressed throughout this book. Obviously, the news reports—which even got the name of the church wrong, for instance—were incomplete; they did not pretend to give a full inventory of all the books that were stolen. In addition, the occult books went to their bishop and protector, Prazsky. They were not likely to implicate him in their crimes, for then there would be no one around to bail them out or take care of them when they left prison.

---

[4] *The Sumerians* (New York: W. W. Norton and Company, 1965), 39

~⊙ Page 133–34: He then questions the fact that the original manuscript is not available for public inspection, citing that as evidence that it never existed. However, he then goes on to state that even if a manuscript were produced, "it would be no guarantee of authenticity, since the history of literary antiquities is rife with spectacular fakes." In other words, there would be no way to satisfy Gonce that such a manuscript ever existed, even if he was handed the original.

~⊙ Page 134: A notorious claim by Khem Caigan that he was allowed to "change and re-create" the drawings of the *Necronomicon* from the typescript is taken at face value. This is, of course, entirely false. No such permission was given to change or re-create anything. Khem Caigan was hired to *redraw* the sigils and seals of the *Necronomicon*, to prepare them for printing, and nothing else. Any claims he may make to the contrary are fictitious. Gonce goes on to state:

> The illustrations, sigils, and diagrams—including the beautiful quasi-pentagramic "Elder Sign" on the front cover—were all created or developed by Khem himself, not taken from an ancient text.

This last is an infamous charge, and patently untrue. Khem Caigan worked from the typescript, which contained every single sign and symbol which appears in the *Necronomicon,* and which he was hired to redraw for the printers so they would be clearer and easier to reproduce. The only design that Khem Caigan *possibly* created himself is the design that the author claims is "quasi-pentagramic": it is a combination of three signs appearing in the *Necronomicon*, found on page 10, and they are the ARRA, the AGGA, and the BANDAR. The first is the Pentagram, the second is the Elder Sign, and the third is the Sigil of the Watcher (as fully described on page 11 of the *Necronomicon*). These three signs appear in their natural form on the covers of the hard-bound editions. The combination sigil that appears on the cover of the *Necronomicon* is most assuredly *not* the Elder Sign as claimed by Gonce, nor is it "quasi-pentagramic." In fact, I was told at the time by Larry Barnes that *he* designed the combination drawing, and that Khem Caigan had simply executed Larry's original design, which was then expanded to include the "eye in the triangle" motif (so beloved by Larry) in later editions. It was a bone of some contention between us, because I felt that every sign and illustration used in the book should be original. Larry eventually won the day on that issue, however, when the cover of the book was shown to me, with the three original signs placed there beneath the composite. The effect was stunning—although a little overblown for my taste!—and it was decided to let it ride since there was no "cover art" in the original manuscript anyway.

According to Gonce, Khem Caigan complained that "Avon Books used his art from the Magickal Childe edition without giving him any credit." In the first place, there was no Magickal Childe edition. Herman Slater did not publish the *Necronomicon*, nor did his company, Magickal Childe. In the second place, Khem Caigan had been hired as a contractor to do some simple work on the book to prepare it for publication. The art—aside from *possibly* the composite sigil—was not his own; it was there in the typescript. In addition, all the copies I have of the Avon paperback credit Khem for his contribution. In any event, I can personally refute his charge that he redesigned or created the seals and other illustrations from the *Necronomicon*.

Gonce goes on to state, in reference to the episode mentioned in the Preface to the Second Edition—in which Jim Wasserman discovered that a locked room he used for occult work had been opened from the inside, and that the typesetters on the floor below his in the same building had been subjected to a plague of rats until a lost Hindu idol was found and the rats disappeared:

> Nor does Khem remember any plagues of rats or poltergeist activity accompanying the "translation" of the book . . .

Of course he doesn't. He wasn't there. He came in as a contractor to Jim Wasserman and Larry Barnes long after the translation was complete. He was not there earlier, nor did he spend much time at the premises of Barnes Graphics or Magickal Childe during this period. In fact, I don't recall ever meeting him myself! But according to Gonce, whose gullibility has now become a problem, "All of this casts considerable doubt on the Simon *Necronomicon* being an ancient work." It would, if only any of it were true.

⌒ Page 134–36: In this section, Gonce attacks the entire idea that there is a "Sumerian Tradition" in modern magic, a patently untenable position that flies in the face of the (documented) facts. In the Introduction to the *Necronomicon*, I quote Aleister Crowley, who said, "Our work is therefore historically authentic; the rediscovery of the Sumerian Tradition." According to Gonce, he and Daniel Harms "searched diligently" for the citation among Crowley's published works and "sifted painstakingly" through their "considerable libraries" and "enlisted the help of mages on the alt.magick. newsgroup on the Internet," many of whom claimed to have a "knowledge of Crowley's writing that exceeds our own."

They claim that if the quote exists, then it is obscure and that I am "deliberately exaggerating its importance."

Although they claim to be familiar with the works of Kenneth Grant, Gonce and Harms fail to note in their tirade against the *Necronomicon* that Grant refers to the Sumerian Tradition himself many times over the course of his body of work. In fact, the citation by Crowley mentioned above comes from Grant's early work, *The Magickal Revival*, where it is found on page 52. Grant assigns to the Sumerian Tradition the importance it deserves, and has done so consistently both before and after the publication of the *Necronomicon*. Jack Parsons, one of the members of the OTO's Pasadena lodge in the 1940s, refers to the Sumerian Tradition several times in his own writings, thus demonstrating that it was not unknown to the "mages" of that time and that Order. I cannot imagine what sort of occult experts Harms and Gonce had contacted, or of what books their considerable libraries consist, but these references to Sumer are in Parsons, Crowley, and Grant. Grant in particular explores the Sumerian Tradition at length, and in addition one can find perhaps a hundred references to the *Necronomicon* in his work.

Gonce claims that my attempt to link Lovecraft with Crowley "is just one of the more recent (and moronic) attempts to develop a 'Lovecraft/Crowley Axis.'" This despite the fact that Kenneth Grant—a man whom Gonce himself describes with the words "there is no greater living scholar on the subject of Aleister Crowley than Kenneth Grant"— also sees the connection quite clearly and repeatedly; for instance, in his book *The Outer Gateways*, which is a study of how the works of Lovecraft and Crowley reinforce each other, a book to which Gonce actually refers. How did Gonce miss all of this? He has taken so many liberties with published documentation, and has shown so much (willful?) ignorance of his subject matter on this and other aspects of the occult, Lovecraft, Crowley, and Sumer, that I am afraid he cannot be considered a reliable source for any of it.

What he is a good source for, however, is gossip, and there is plenty of that in *The Necronomicon Files*.

➤ Page 138–46: The beat goes on. One of the issues that bothers Gonce considerably is the connection between the *Necronomicon* and Beat author and philosopher William S. Burroughs. It is one aspect of this case that rankles him, and he goes to great lengths to somehow "deconstruct" it. His source? The ever-helpful Khem Caigan.

The story of how Burroughs came to discover the *Necronomicon* as it was being set in type is well-known to all of us who were there at the time, Khem Caigan's version notwithstanding. Jim Wasserman, at that time a member of the OTO and the book's designer (not Barnes or Caigan), was there and reported the incident with a great deal of awe. Burroughs did not sit down and read a few pages, as reported by Caigan, but read the entire book in galleys in one sitting. At that time, he was living in his "bunker" in Manhattan, and would later attend the 1978 Nova Conference in New York. Larry Barnes was equally in awe of the man, and would visit him in the bunker from time to time, where the two heroin addicts would vibrate off each other like mismatched tuning forks, Larry showing Burroughs some of his alien art while Burroughs showed Larry pictures of naked men.

Burroughs eventually agreed to write us a letter about his reactions to the *Necronomicon*, and these have been unfairly represented in the Gonce version of the story as something coerced out of Burroughs by Larry, which is far from the truth. That Burroughs was deeply impressed by the *Necronomicon* is obvious from his own work, such as the often cited *Cities of the Red Night*, whose "Invocation" is a paean to the *Necronomicon* forces. I feel that, had Burroughs written something similar for the Harms and Gonce volume, they would have been loath to characterise it this cavalierly; but since they must attack absolutely everything about the *Necronomicon* that they can find, regardless of the veracity of their claims, the Burroughs relationship becomes fair game.

He then goes on to give a precis of other reviews of the *Necronomicon*, including that of the Bob Larson, Christian fundamentalist version. Larson states that the Sumerian language "resembles Hindu Sanskrit," and Gonce attacks this by saying, "Sumerian has no known linguistic descendants, and has no known relationship to Sanskrit," something we already have shown to be untrue and which Gonce would have known had he tried to research his thesis just a little harder.

～ Page 146–56. This is the only section that addresses anything of value, and that is the Sumerian roots of the *Necronomicon*. One only wishes that it had benefited from the scholarship of a genuine Sumeriologist and not from the biased agenda of Mr. Gonce, who claims, "I am in an especially good position to assess how well (or poorly) the Simon book depicts Mesopotamian magick, since, as a Neopagan, I am a worshiper of the great Goddess Inanna/Ishtar, and practice authentic elements of a Sumerian/Mesopotamian magick and religion based on years of careful research from academic sources."

My goodness! The fact that I, or anyone else, could claim the same thing has not occurred to Mr. Gonce, who has set himself up as an expert and authority in this field based simply on his own reading, undertaken—one assumes—in his "considerable library." A search through the Endnotes to *The Necronomicon Files* is an indication of the academic sources he consulted, and it is a rather thin list. But let's give him the benefit of a doubt. He states, on page 147:

> Since the Simon *Necronomicon* claims to be a Sumerian grimoire, the first question we should ask is: Who were the Sumerians?

The first answer we should give is: the Simon *Necronomicon* does not claim to be a "Sumerian grimoire" in the sense that Gonce represents it. It claims to be a grimoire written in Greek, presumably translated from an earlier Arabic work, which contains rituals that include Sumerian deities, chants in Sumerian, and a basic Mesopotamian framework of seven Gates, an Underworld, the Descent of a Goddess to the Underworld, etc. We state that it was a Greek translation of an Arab manuscript. We admit quite openly in the Introduction that some of the hymns and legends that appear in the *Necronomicon* are "bastardized," and that many of the seals and symbols appear to be of later, Arab or other Middle Eastern, origin. This is a grimoire, written over a thousand years ago, that is a repository of ancient Sumerian—*and Babylonian*—lore. We said that clearly in the Introduction. We emphasize the Sumerian aspects of the grimoire simply because they appear to outnumber the Arab and Babylonian aspects, but nowhere do we state that this is a grimoire, word for word as it would have been used by a Sumerian magician. Much of the hostility directed against the *Necronomicon* is based on a false assumption that we present this material as a pure Sumerian text, when it is obviously not so

by the very nature of the Testimony chapters, as well as the
various prefaces to the individual chapters by the narrator,
the Mad Arab, who was obviously not a Sumerian! It would
appear that none of our critics can get their heads around
this very basic, very simple concept. What we do insist is that
this is a *pagan* grimoire, and so far no one has attempted to
refute that.

He then goes on to give a (dated) exposition of Sumerian
history, and I will leave that for now, since a discussion as to
where I differ from his version would take too long and
leave too many readers bored with the footnotes, and at any
rate is not material to this case. Instead, let's proceed to his
criticism of KUTULU.

We have already demonstrated that KUTULU is a perfectly valid Sumerian form for "Man of Kutu." In fact, it
would seem from the index to *The Necronomicon Files* that
Gonce was aware of this, as well, for it contains a reference
to Parker Ryan, a gentleman who explored this theme in
some detail in several postings on occult Web sites,[5] and is a
source we referenced ourselves earlier in this book. However, although the index contains Parker Ryan's name, and a
reference to Ryan's work in connection with another book,
mysteriously, Gonce does not refer to Ryan's lengthy exposition of the Sumerian and Arab themes in Lovecraft's tales
as well as the KUTULU/*qhadhulu* relationship. Perhaps Mr.
Ryan's exploration of these themes did not sit too well with
Mr. Gonce since they tend to reinforce our own theories.

In addition, Gonce claims that Kutu's "only association
with the underworld was that its patron deities were Nergal
and Ereshkigal, Lord and Lady of the underworld." That
would seem enough for most people, but even then he has

---

[5] Such as the alt.discordia newsgroup in a posting dated June 6, 1994

missed the mark. As we have shown in Chapter Six, Kutu was the site of a vast necropolis. Disregarding all of this, Gonce goes on to suggest that I got the name Kutu or Cutha from *The Sixth and Seventh Books of Moses*! He then goes on to describe that grimoire and its origins extensively, without showing its relevance to this case. As we have seen earlier, there is a long tradition of associating Cutha or Kutu with magic and sorcery and even, as we now know, with the Quraysh tribe—of which the Prophet Mohammed was a member—who guarded the sacred Black Stone of Mecca for centuries before it was a Muslim shrine.

Gonce attacks the planetary structure of the Walking chapters, claiming that I modeled it "after Western planetary magick," which is nonsense, of course. He and Harms cite a work by Jeremy Black and Anthony Green (*Gods, Demons and Symbols of Ancient Mesopotamia*), which states "the idea that Mesopotamian religion was astral in origin is untenable." The fact that many scholars disagree with this does not bother Gonce, who selects his sources very carefully in order to support his thesis. (Had Gonce bothered to honestly represent the work by Black and Green, he might also have noticed the illustrations of Humwawa and asked himself if perhaps the "mass of entrails" description is more accurate than he would care to admit.) I refer the interested reader once again to Michael Baigent's *From the Omens of Babylon: Astrology and Ancient Mesopotamia*, for a contradictory view, as well as the other sources mentioned in previous chapters. Gonce then claims that the associations between planets and metals, etc., comes from later Qabalistic sources, such as *777* or other Golden Dawn literature, a claim that can easily be refuted by studying the ziggurat discovered by Rawlinson, mentioned above in Chapter Six, for instance, and its close resemblance to the Walking system of the *Necronomicon*. Once again I have to insist that this book was written long after Sumer disappeared and represents a survival of that culture and its occult system. The original Sumerian content will have suffered from being handed down through the centuries, and will have attracted accretions from other systems current in the Middle East when it was finally set down as the *Necronomicon*, but it is still unique among grimoires.

One of his other concerns is that of Humwawa. We have covered that objection already, and Gonce himself struggles with it, admitting that the face of Humwawa was used as an amulet during the Old Babylonian period, but dismisses this as "only because of his association with Enlil," as if that explains everything. But he goes on to insist that once again I have it wrong—in the face of evidence to the contrary—and that therefore the *Necronomicon* is a clumsy hoax.

Finally, on page 156, he begins to admit that it is possible that the *Necronomicon* is simply a garbled version of an ancient occult system; but he then just as quickly changes his mind and denounces this concept since it was not spelled out in the Introduction and was not mentioned to him personally until Peter Levenda discussed it in an e-mail with Daniel Harms. The fact that it was self-evident never occurs to Gonce; that every grimoire represents a garbling of more ancient lore, as Gonce himself admits on the same page; that nowhere in the Introduction do we state that the *Necronomicon* is a pristine system of magic handed down intact over five thousand years, and in fact state otherwise: that its hymns are bastardized from the Sumerian originals. Gonce insists on setting up straw men and knocking them down with glee, and this does no service to his readers or to the cause of occult scholarship in general.

Then, of course, he goes on to attack my pronunciation of

"chthonic," an item that has already been discussed. (In this chapter, Gonce repeatedly spells the word "cthonic," for some reason.) In modern American English, the pronunciation is indeed "thawnik" or "thonik," as he describes; however, the *Oxford English Dictionary* gives it as "ka-tonic," which would also be the way most Europeans would pronounce it. He further states that Leviathan was a sea monster and not a god, and that sea monsters are not chthonic anyway, a fact that is not true, as any good reference work will show.[6] He even stretches his point to assert that Cthulhu "is not a sea monster, he is an extraterrestrial creature trapped under the ocean"! I stand (somehow) corrected!

Page 159: The Gates. Gonce goes to all kinds of lengths to identify sources that "influenced" me in my alleged creation of the *Necronomicon*, from Meric Causabon's *True and Faithful Relation* to the Gnostic texts found in G.R.S. Mead, to the writings of Aleister Crowley. Since his basic assumption is that I created the book, these charges are not unusual. Had he taken the opposite approach—that the *Necronomicon*, no matter what else you say about it, is a genuine grimoire—he would have come to the realization that it is consistent with elements of Gnosticism (such as the aforementioned "barbarous names") and other practices of the ancient Middle East that would have been known to the Mad Arab at the time.

Gonce then criticizes the fact that there is no casting of a magic circle in the *Necronomicon* . . . while at the same time admitting that the lack of a circle is familiar to anyone who

---

[6] For instance, in W.R. Smith, *Lectures on the Religion of the Semites,* 198, "As regards the northern Semites, the chthonic associations of the Baalim as gods of the subterranean waters are unquestionable . . ."

has read *The Book of the Sacred Magic of Abramelin the Mage*, a favorite of Crowley's, and the more recent phenomenon of Maat magick, which was developed by a Kenneth Grant initiate. While stating this, he then appears to reject all of it by quoting a "Wiccan friend" of his who claims that performing magic without a circle is "suicidal."

They can't all be right, but Gonce's bias is showing. He obviously feels that his Wiccan friend is a better source than *Abramelin* or the initiates of Kenneth Grant.

He then claims that "the closest ancient Mesopotamian parallel to the Gate Walking procedure is found in the myth of Etana," which he then goes on to describe at length. He apparently forgot completely (for a while) the Sumerian legend of the Descent of Inanna to the Underworld, which is accomplished by means of passing through seven gates. He uses the myth of Etana—which is *not* mentioned in the *Necronomicon* and has no relation to anything in the *Necronomicon*—as proof that the *Necronomicon* has incorporated it incorrectly! This kind of circular logic and tortured reasoning is untenable and does nothing to advance his thesis.

Finally, on page 163, Gonce states that "it appears [Simon] based his Gate Walking initiation on a bastardized version of *The Descent of Inanna*." While disregarding for the moment the fact that I did not "base" anything in the *Necronomicon*, I am led to wonder why Gonce devoted so much space to the irrelevant Etana legend if the Descent of Inanna appears in the *Necronomicon* virtually alongside the Walking and the Gates? It should have been obvious to him that this was the case. But he was so dedicated to setting up another straw man to knock down that he could not help himself, I suppose.

He then goes on to state, once again, that "Herman Slater, who definitely played a role in the publication of the Simon book, used *The Descent of Inanna* as a model for a Wiccan initiation ritual in one of his books on witchcraft." Once again, we are in fantasy land, with Herman Slater writing the *Necronomicon*. Or was it Simon? Or was it Larry Barnes? Or was it Ed Buczynski?

~○ This leads us to the next chapter in the Harms-Gonce book, the one devoted to the "True Origins of the *Necronomicon*." This chapter is a compilation of gossip, rumor, and innuendo, none of it verified or confirmed by anyone else. Gonce has no problem in presenting all sorts of wild stories and is perfectly capable of believing in all of them at once. The first such tale comes from someone he identifies only as "Nestor," who has this tale to tell: the *Necronomicon* was created as a result of a beer bash held above the old Warlock Shop in the early 1970s.

I have no idea who Nestor is, and he obviously does not know me either, since his references to me are full of errors. In the first place, he refers to me as a member of the OTO (I never was), and says that I talked about the Lovecraft tales concerning the *Necronomicon* (I could not have, as I didn't know anything about Lovecraft before becoming involved with the *Necronomicon*), and then we all—Herman Slater, Ed Buczynski, Leo Martello (!), myself, and many others all evidently got drunk one night and came up with things to incorporate into a bogus *Necronomicon*, with Ed Buczynski as the stenographer.

The Necronomicon *and "Nestor"*

In the first place, Gonce speaks of a "Simon Peter" who was a member of the OTO. Neither Simon nor Peter Levenda (the only Peter who was around in those early days) were ever members of the OTO, as the OTO itself will readily and heartily agree, and as Harms and Gonce could have discovered for themselves had they only asked.

In the second place, the genesis of the *Necronomicon*—according to Nestor—was a beer bash held at the Warlock Shop. Again, this is virtually impossible. There was simply no room to hold any kind of party at the Warlock Shop, either downstairs in the claustrophobic surroundings of the overcrowded storefront or in the minuscule apartment upstairs. It is simply not true.

It is also not true that I ever attended such a beer bash or other drinking party or any party of any kind at the Warlock Shop.

I never mentioned the *Necronomicon* and how absurd it was that people were taking the stories to be true, quite simply because I had never heard of the *Necronomicon* at that time.

Ed Buczynski had never suggested creating a *Necronomicon*, had never spoken to me about such a project, and neither he nor Herman Slater—as much as I liked them both—had the capability to come up with the type of hoax Nestor claims the *Necronomicon* to be. It just wasn't in the cards: not the Tarot cards, and not a poker deck either.

The idea that Ed was taking notes on what the "others" contributed as ideas for the hoax is also beyond belief for anyone who knew Ed, Herman, or myself. It doesn't make sense. A look at the book itself will tell you that. No matter what others may say about the book's "true" origins, it is obviously internally consistent and of one piece, and not something cobbled together by a committee.

The entire story is false from start to finish, and I can only wonder at Nestor's reason for inventing it. I have no idea who Nestor could be, since the authors of *The Necronomi-*

con Files do not identify him beyond the pseudonym, but it does not matter. The story related by Nestor is as fictional as his name.

It gets worse.

Nestor's delusion is compounded by the idea that the *Necronomicon* was somehow created to be a training tool for neophytes! What neophytes? I wonder. Ed Buczynski had no "neophytes" beyond some Outer Court pagans and witch wannabees. Ed did not train anyone in ceremonial magic, since he had no background in it whatsoever. Further, he had all the Wiccan training materials he needed in the form of the Book of Shadows and other pagan literature available at the time.

Based on Nestor's e-mails to Harms and Gonce, the authors conclude that the *Necronomicon* was designed with booby traps and other intentional errors, booby traps designed by Ed and his beer bash hoaxers. Of course, these booby traps are never identified; it is one of those charges that is so easy to make and virtually impossible to prove, but Gonce makes those charges again and again, both in his book and in an interview published in *Paranoia* magazine.[7] In any event, since the basis of the story is false, so is everything else that Nestor claims is true about the book, its origins, and the intentions of its "creators." Harms and Gonce claim that Nestor's statement must be true, since Peter Levenda's communication with them spoke of a "*Necronomicon* group." Obviously, there was such a group; the Acknowledgments section of the book names a number of people who made contributions of one kind or another. To claim, however, that these people were part of some drunken party that

---

[7] This can be found on http://www.paranoiamagazine.com/necronomicon. html.

came up with the idea of the *Necronomicon*—that they were parties to a hoax—is ridiculous. In fact, Harms and Gonce also state that Nestor himself made contributions to this project. Since we have no way of knowing who Nestor might be, there is no way to directly challenge him in this regard. However, as someone who was involved with this project from the very beginning through its publication, I can categorically state that Nestor's tale has no relation to reality. How Harms and Gonce fell for this story is beyond me. Why they did not double check the story with those who know better is further evidence of the poor journalistic practice that permeates their book.

However, I believe what Nestor may be referring to is the creation not of the *Necronomicon,* but of the Minoan Tradition of Wicca that Ed Buczynski *did* create upstairs at the Warlock Shop, but not during a beer bash and not with a dozen people sitting on the floor. Ed was totally upfront about creating this "tradition," feeling that the spirits had guided him to this stage, and he enlisted the help of others to draw up some basic rituals for it (patterned largely on the existing Wiccan rites). I was never a part of that, and neither was anyone else involved with the *Necronomicon.*

Nestor's parting shot implies that Herman was behind the "hoax" and that his motivation was, naturally, money. Nestor claims—without saying how he knows—that Herman "made a bundle off it." That is a common and easily disproven misconception. Herman was the bookseller, the retailer, of the *Necronomicon.* He did not share in the book's profits in any other way. He did not finance its publication. His function was to simply sell the book once it was in print, and he received the standard retailer's discount, forty percent off retail price. Gonce then goes on to gleefully state that Herman's motivating factor was money, "more M-O-N-E-Y than Magickal Childe Publishing had ever made before."

Except that Magickal Childe Publishing—Herman's publishing subsidiary of the Magickal Childe bookstore in its Manhattan location on West Nineteenth Street—did not publish the *Necronomicon*. The first, hardcover editions were published by Schlangekraft Publishing Company, a New York corporation that had nothing to do with Herman Slater, and Barnes Graphics, which was Larry Barnes's company. Each company owned fifty percent of the *Necronomicon*. The paperback editions, of course, were published by Avon. The Gonce and Nestor contention that Magickal Childe Publishing was making money off of the *Necronomicon* is therefore without any merit. There is no mention of Magickal Childe Publishing in the original hardcover editions, nor in the paperback editions. (In fact, the earliest mention of the *Necronomicon* is in an edition of *Earth Religion News*—published by Herman Slater—in 1974, long before he moved to Manhattan and created the Magickal Childe bookstore. It clearly states that there is as yet no publisher for the *Necronomicon*.) Again, Herman Slater's income from the *Necronomicon* was limited to his standard retailer's discount. The remainder of the income went first to pay any costs Barnes Graphics had incurred in the design, printing, binding, and advertising of the book; after those costs were covered, the remaining profit—if any—was divided equally between Barnes Graphics and Schlangekraft.

Magickal Childe Publishing had a list of other credits, everything from *Pagan Rituals* to expensive reprints of famous occult works, all done during or after the *Necronomicon* was published by Schlangekraft and Barnes. In fact, the only time Herman Slater made any money on the *Necronomicon* was at the time he published the *Necronomicon Spellbook* (entitled, at the time, *Report on the Necronomicon*). Eventually, the rights to that slim volume were also picked up by Avon for wider distribution, after Magickal Childe Publishing let their ownership of the rights lapse after several years of nonpublication. Thus, to insist that Herman Slater was making enormous amounts of money from the book is not consistent with the fact that he couldn't even keep the *Spellbook* in print for any length of time. Further, the claim by Gonce that Herman Slater's famous *Magickal Formulary* is "*Necronomicon*-related" is equally absurd. How this very popular compendium of oil and incense recipes can be considered related to the *Necronomicon*—beyond a single recipe called "Starry Wisdom" oil, which is a reference to the Lovecraft *oeuvre*—is beyond me. Certainly the pagans and witches who use the *Formulary* would be horrified to learn that it is "*Necronomicon*-related." It was never a factor in the book's production, sale, or distribution. It was never marketed as a supplemental volume to the *Necronomicon*. But Gonce is so eager to connect everything to the *Necronomicon* in a neopagan version of the Jewish libel or the "satanic cult survivor syndrome" that he pulls at every possible thread to show the insidious nature of this "black book."

Nestor then goes on to state that he didn't know "Simon Peter all that well" and thought that perhaps I was the same person involved with the "Brooklyn OTO chapter at the time." Of course, I knew all the OTO chapters in New York, as well as Jim Wasserman, Grady McMurtry, and others prominent in one faction or another of the OTO in the 1970s and 1980s. The claim that he didn't know me "all that well"—besides being obvious by his imaginary tale of the *Necronomicon*—leads one to further question his story, since the editor of the *Necronomicon* is clearly me. He then goes on to state that I was part of the Warlock Shop crowd—which is true, I suppose—and that I claimed to be a bishop in "a Ukrainian Orthodox Rite church," whatever that is, which is *not* true. This is again a case of confabulation. That I was a priest of an Eastern Orthodox church is true; that I was a "bishop in a Ukrainian Orthodox" church is most assuredly not true, and I never claimed to be. In any event, I do not speak Ukrainian, am not Ukrainian, and my Russian is pretty rusty too.

Gonce goes on to speculate on the reasons behind the "rush to print" that was mentioned by Khem Caigan, another confabulator. The reason for that was simple: the occult calendar. We wanted the book out for the thirtieth anniversary of Crowley's death on December 1, 1947. That same year— 1977—also marked the fortieth anniversary of Lovecraft's death. Thus, the "rush to print." There is no other, more arcane or sinister, motivation behind it, despite of the stupid speculation on this point, except for the fact already mentioned that Herman had taken advance orders for the book that he had to fill. As anyone who was present at the elaborate book party that took place on December 1, 1977, will tell you, it was a deliberate and carefully planned gesture in honor of Crowley and of the resurgent Thelemic movement in the United States, which owed at least some of its power to the publication of the *Illuminatus!* trilogy and the resurrection of the OTO. That Khem Caigan was not aware of this is only further proof of how far removed he was from the scene.

Gonce then goes on to state that the seals and sigils that appear in the *Necronomicon* were invented, "made up by brainstorming to look scary and magickal and, of course, to make a quick buck," not like those to be found in the medieval grimoires that were obtained by "scrying and gematria" (page 180). Where is the evidence for *any* of this?

Again, this claim only makes sense if you believe that (a) the book is a hoax, and that (b) during the execution of this hoax no one took the time or the trouble to "scry" or to use gematria to create "genuine" seals. The authors of *The Necronomicon Files* cannot maintain any degree of honest consistency in their attacks on the book and switch stories to match whatever agenda they are trying to promote. How, for instance, do the authors know for a certainty that the seals and sigils in these unnamed grimoires were derived from "scrying and gematria"? Except for those planetary intelligences for which planetary squares are given in the same grimoire, it is very difficult to prove "gematria" as a source for the seals; it is even more difficult, if not completely impossible, to prove that "scrying" was the cause of the seals' designs, since in none of the classical grimoires is this claim ever made. Yet, they accept this explanation for ancient grimoires without hesitation, simply because this idea supports their own version of events. Gonce then states, unequivocally, that the seals in the *Necronomicon* were invented to "look scary" and to "make a quick buck," whereas he has absolutely no proof of this whatsoever. It is a bit like using "spectral evidence" in the Salem witch trials: someone "sees" an invisible being tormenting them when no one else can, and this "evidence" is introduced at trial as being reliable. The Harms and Gonce book is full of such "spectral evidence."

On pages 185 to 196 of *The Necronomicon Files,* Gonce reviews what he claims are tapes of "Simon" discussing the *Necronomicon* during a series of lectures at Magickal Childe in 1981. At the same time, he does not believe that the "Simon" on the tapes is the real Simon, but only the "public face" of Simon, who—he states—is a "composite pseudonym

of two or more individuals." Of course, he must believe this
because he has presented so many different Simons based on
conflicting stories from so many ill-informed individuals
that he can no longer state with any certainty that there exists one, single Simon. The easy way out of this problem is
to claim that Simon is a "composite," and then attack the
composite!

While I did give many lectures over the course of my time
with Magickal Childe, I don't remember any being taped.
That is not to say they weren't; it's just that we are talking
about many lectures (sometimes two or three a week) given
over the period 1972–82, in Brooklyn, Manhattan, and elsewhere. So, let's accept that the tapes they have are genuine. I
still can't respond adequately to their content since they are
quoted out of context and transcripts are not given in full. Of
course, I don't believe that Gonce ever expected I would be
responding to them, since I am obviously a composite character, and we all know how difficult it is to collect all your
composites in one place.

Many of the criticisms Gonce levels at me personally in
this section are gratuitous sarcasms not worthy of him or the
book. I will not address them, of course. Many of the
charges on the tapes have been dealt with already in this
book. He uses some outdated references to support his accusations, and in others he simply laughs without providing evidence that my alleged statements are wrong, a problem with
his approach from the start. In other areas, he makes sweep-
ing statements of his own without basis in fact. For instance,
on page 191 he claims that "no study of the history and literature of the Golden Dawn has ever yielded any hints of a
'secret Arab manuscript.'" I imagine that his considerable
library does not have a copy of Francis King's *Modern Ritual Magic*, where such a manuscript—the "Veils of Negative

Existence"—is mentioned on page 136 of the 1989 edition, and which "purports to be an English translation of an Arab work of the sixth, seventh or eighth centuries" that was cited by Golden Dawn initiate and Mathers protégé R.W. Felkin in a lecture he gave before the occult society Societas Rosicruciana in Anglia in 1915. (An eighth century Arab occult work is certainly suggestive, though by no means a confirmation that the Golden Dawn knew of the existence of the *Necronomicon* in 1915, long before Lovecraft published any stories with that name and placed in that era.)

Evidently, according to Gonce, one of my "biggest problems is [my] utter failure (or willful refusal) to grasp either the solid historical facts or the spiritual essence of ancient Mesopotamian magick and religion" (page 196). It is thankful that we have such an expert in these matters as the sadly misnomered John Wisdom Gonce III to set us all aright!

Later, Gonce goes on to claim that he and Daniel Harms were subject to all kinds of "magickal attack" while working on their book (page 212). He claims that the *Necronomicon* is protected by an *egregore*, which is funny, considering that the translation of that Greek word is "watcher." Who knows? He may be right.

Indeed, it sometimes feels as if I am at a trial and summoning my own expert witnesses to refute someone else's expert witnesses. In the end, the whole thing is a waste of time. The Gonce allegations are baseless, both the competing and inconsistent tales of the "true origins" of the *Necronomicon*, the attacks on what he perceives to be a travesty of Sumeriology in the text or the Introduction (he is never quite clear which part of the book he is attacking, my Introduction or the actual text itself), and his pointless charges of complicity in ritual murder and the approval of human sacrifice. If anyone is out to make a buck on the *Necronomicon*, I submit it is the tag team of Harms and Gonce.

To be fair to them, they state at the outset of their book that they went on the assumption that the *Necronomicon* was a fake, a hoax. They did not intend to write an unbiased study of the book to determine if it was, indeed, a hoax. They had already made up their minds before they even began. Harms tries to soften this in his interview in *Paranoia*, saying that they "decided to sit down and examine the arguments of both sides closely." That does not come through in *The Necronomicon Files*, however, and is largely due to the rants of Gonce on Sumer, multiple Simons (like the multiple Oswalds in the Kennedy assassination?), and so on.

Fair enough, but just as Gonce complains that there should be some kind of consumer affairs group to vet grimoires, I submit that the lack of journalistic objectivity shown by him in his hatchet job on the *Necronomicon* and its editor, its publishers, and everyone else connected with the book is deserving of just such a consumer affairs inquiry. It is vitriol masquerading as scholarship, rumor-mongering as journalism. It has not advanced Gonce's professed beliefs and ideals one iota. In fact, it is difficult to discern just exactly what these may be, since he seems eager to appear to be scientific and logical and says he subjects "occult works to a kind of textual criticism, and a skeptical, scholarly analysis." As we have seen, his remarks are anything but scholarly, and he is not skeptical when he accepts what he hears from "Nestor," Khem Caigan, and assorted "Wiccan friends" and "mages" as proof or evidence of anything.

Gonce cannot help himself in the referenced interview from saying, "Our research has shown that the *Necronomicon* hoax had added significantly to all that strife and violence," another unsubstantiated statement with no "skeptical, scholarly" evidence to support it. Harms, on the other hand, seems to wish to put a restraining arm on Gonce when he says, "We raise those issues quietly, but we leave them for the reader to sort out." Hardly. Gonce leaves nothing to the reader, but makes his bias clear on every page.

What is fascinating about Gonce and his attacks is that he unwittingly falls prey to the very sort of thing he seems so desperate to disprove. The *Necronomicon* must be the only book of its kind in the world whose detractors and supporters *both* believe is a book of power. Nowhere does the same reputation exist for other occult works. The *Satanic Bible* is not singled out for this concentrated fury. Neither are any of the ceremonial magic grimoires. Gonce is saying that the *Necronomicon* is dangerous, that it encourages people to violence, that it contains mysterious traps for the unwary or uninitiated, that even Gonce and Harms themselves have been victimized by magical attacks from users of the book. Not since James Joyce's *Ulysses* was banned by the U.S. government has there been such pseudomoral outrage over a book. In fact, it is probably the only volume of modern times that has been characterized as a book that is itself intrinsically powerful. This is certainly a phenomenon of immense interest and importance: a mere book whose reading of it causes all sorts of extreme events to occur. Certainly every writer's dream!

In other words, what else can this be but the *Necronomicon*, the real *Necronomicon* itself, *exactly as Lovecraft described it*?

Gonce then goes on to state "I hope [*The Necronomicon Files*] will have some positive influence on both the Pagan world and the occult community at large. I hope it will have some influence on Pagan scholarship, which is conspicuous by its absence. (laughs)." I wonder at the laughter. Was it nervous laughter at the realization that his own attempt at "Pagan scholarship" is riddled with inaccuracies, unsupported allegations, selective omissions, and outright lies?

That Gonce may be suffering from some form of guilt over his role in *The Necronomicon Files* is implied by the very last page of the book, which contains an invocation to Ganesha and other deities of various lands and traditions in an effort to protect Harms and Gonce from magickal attack by people who disagree with them. It is a sad and neurotic end to a badly executed attack itself, and Gonce apparently wishes to defend himself against the consequences of his own actions.

I did a great deal of research on Sumerian, Akkadian, and Babylonian mythology, culture, and religion when I was editing the book and writing the introduction. In addition to the archaeology students who formed part of the "*Necronomicon* group," I did not restrict myself to popular works in the field but cast a wider net that covered academic journals and other, out-of-print scholarly works. I respectfully request that Harms, Gonce, and any concerned or interested reader consult these and other works before passing judgment on the quality of my assertions concerning the Sumerian nature of much of the *Necronomicon*. There are now many such works available on the Internet, as well as papers written by specialists in these fields, men and women who have university affiliation and peer review and have published articles and books on these subjects. As discussed at great length already, my sources for everything I assert are excellent, and there has been even more published in the last thirty years that corroborates my position: on KUTULU, on "chthonic," on Humwawa, on the Underworld, on the planetary magic of the Sumerians and later Babylonians, etc., even including a growing body of literature on the Sanskrit and Indo-European connections with the Sumerian language. None of that has changed; in fact, it has been substantiated in many forums by many academics and scholars over the years. The attacks by Harms, Gonce, and others are without academic qualification and are based on very selective readings of popular books on Sumer, on gossip picked up over the Internet, and on consultations with other, self-appointed "mages" and magicians.

Caveat lector.

But what about the danger of using the *Necronomicon*?

For me, the medieval grimoires were always weighted down with assumptions. Foremost among them was the conceit that the practice of ceremonial magic was actually a good thing, with the support of the angels and of God herself. This, in the face of enormous hostility from the Church, which condemned any form of magic or, indeed, any effort by the individual believer to contact God directly and not through the agency of the Church. Thus, the idea that one could safely call upon the angels when performing, for instance, rituals out of the *Greater Key of Solomon* was patently false or, at least, hypocritical. Also, it seemed to relegate the practice of ceremonial magic to those who were believers; that is, baptized Christians in a state of grace or pious Jews. That seemed to me absurd.

As I have said before, ceremonial magic—like all ritual magic—is a technology. That does not mean it can be performed without reference to spiritual forces. Far from it. Ceremonial magic is the technology of manipulating those very forces. As a youth, I longed for a system that would strip the grimoires of their religious facade and go directly to the heart of the matter: treating spiritual forces as forces, pure and simple.

Also, the mental attitude required of the magician in the grimoires seems somewhat craven. One commands spirits, but begs God for assistance in doing so. It is a strange place to stand. Further, although it is politically correct these days to speak of ceremonial magic as a kind of New Age, Western form of yoga, the spiritual forces evoked by the grimoires seem to be concerned with wholly mundane goals, such as wealth and power. As anyone who has studied Hindu mysticism and any other form of occultism will tell you, lusting after these goals is not encouraged. How, then, to reconcile all of these apparently contradictory messages?

In the first place, there is an element of human nature missing from most schools of thought on ceremonial magic and religion generally: the negative emotions. Anger, rage, lust, hatred . . . how to contend with these in a constructive manner when we are told that these emotions must be neutralized? From a strictly Taoist perspective, shouldn't the positive emotions be neutralized as well: love, reverence, joy? Ceremonial magic is not the technology of sainthood; we leave that for the eremites, the mystics, the navel gazers. Magic is a proactive type of spirituality, a kind of "short path" to enlightenment which seeks to balance our human nature by evoking each of the demons that lurk within our hearts and confronting it. We must find a place to stand, a sturdy foundation, and that means we must begin with ourselves and our own natures. Our natures are frought with conflicting emotions and desires, and sublimating them or repressing them is not a function of magic. All those incantations designed to summon demonic forces can be understood as a means of evoking dangerous passions that seethe beneath the surface of our own consciousness in order to control them, to command them, to manipulate them.

The medieval grimoires do not address this problem directly. They hide behind an icon screen of false piety. They contain Biblical references and surround themselves with crosses and stars of David. They know they are suggesting doing something dangerous, but they dress it up in sermons like priests and rabbis. All of the grimoires are dangerous, because they conceal the truth. All the grimoires are dangerous, because they do not contain the complete instructions for summoning spiritual forces.

They are cookbooks, whose writers have assumed that their readers know how to boil water or measure flour; whose writers have assumed that their readers want to taste the kind of dishes that can turn their stomachs.

They are dangerous, because they give power back to the people and take it away from the priests.

None of the grimoires addresses our anger, our "rage against the machine." Instead, they provide instructions for becoming our own priests, our own rabbis, our own CEOs. In this age of the "small business" and the entrepreneur, the grimoires are tailor-made. Seek God directly. Start your own church. Become a boss. Idolize the corporate leaders as you seek to become one of them. Ignore the dangers they represent: to the economy, the environment, the soul.

And they work. And those who have pursued the practice of ceremonial magic diligently and intelligently will agree that they work.

To a point.

The *Necronomicon*, to me, represents something more than what the critics argue over. The phenomenon of its publication and the influence it has had over our culture and counterculture can only be understood if we realize that it is a grimoire of the people and not of the intellectual elite or the self-appointed experts in this wide-open field. It is a grimoire that addresses some of the fundamental issues ignored by the medieval grimoires: anger, rage, even fear and the negative emotions generally. It does not pretend to be holy or saintly; it does not give a recipe for clean living or obedience to God or slavelike invocation of the saints and angels of a morally bankrupt Church. The issue that critics hold against the *Necronomicon*—its availability to a wide range of people in a cheap paperback form—is what gives it its power and, in a sense, its nobility. It brings power—occult power, spiritual power—to the people, to those who have been disenfranchised by the Church, the government, all the institutions of society that have abandoned them or that no longer know how to talk to them. It is no wonder that the book has been adopted by heavy metal musicians and rock groups, among others. It speaks to the same basic instinct, that the society we know is a travesty; it's dishonest, phony, and trite. Those who regard the *Necronomicon* with admiration are those who simultaneously regard organized religion with contempt.

The *Necronomicon* is a work of shamanism, a work of sorcery. It is evil if we believe that our negative emotions are evil. It comes from deep within a well of suspicion and disgust, and these emotions—anger, rage, hatred—are what we use to *survive* the forces of nature and the unwanted violent attentions of our fellow human beings. It is a grimoire of war; and yet, it contains instructions for walking a path through the stars. It is a grimoire of the magician as samurai, of magic as bushido.

Gonce speaks of my alleged "moral ambiguity." On page 196 of *The Necronomicon Files* he says:

> If the sacred duty of the Simonian initiate is to guard the
> dreaded Gate of the Ancient Ones, why does the book give
> tantalizing instructions for opening that Gate? . . . He is like
> a politician who will not commit to either side in a war, but
> sells guns to both, while telling each that they have his ex-
> clusive support. His double loyalty to both the Light and the
> Dark actually amounts to a double betrayal.

I suppose Gonce is now back believing that Simon is no
longer a composite individual but a single individual? Anyway, he misses (perhaps willfully) the point of the *Necronomicon,* which everyone else seems to get except him. The
book was set down at a tumultuous time in Middle Eastern
history. It was a time of war, of invasion, of the setting up of
one religion against all others by fire and sword. The *Necronomicon* makes it clear that it is a wartime grimoire: that
forces are waiting to be unleashed against the world. In the
context of the eighth century Middle East, it would have
seemed as if the Last Days were upon them, and that terms
like "religion" and "armies" were synonymous. As they
seem to be today.

The *Necronomicon* magician is a warrior-priest. In order
to understand the enemy, he or she requires information
about their weapons, their schedules, and their designs on the
planet. They must understand how the Gate can be opened,
and by whom, and when, so that they recognize the signs.
Navy SEALs are trained in the operation of foreign weaponry
for the same reason. American intelligence pays top dollar
for captured enemy technology for the same reason.

That the *Necronomicon* became available to a wide audience was an accident; a literary agent we did not know came
to us with an offer. Thus, when we were approached to sell
the rights to a mass-market paperback version, it seemed as

if the *Necronomicon* itself was deciding its own destiny. Perhaps the prophecies are right; perhaps the world is coming to an impasse, a spiritual conflagration if not an actual, physical Armageddon sometime in the next fifty years. Perhaps there is a need for someone to monitor the Gate, for a talented person or persons in every country to guard the planet against forces coming upon us from some other reality . . . or from deep within our own sick and saddened souls. Either way, it's an Underworld; and it's no coincidence that the ancient city of Cutha or KUTU is in the hotly contested deserts of Iraq.

Our leaders are pushing us into a worldwide conflagration over which we can exert no other form of control. Our environment is being destroyed by these same leaders, choking and poisoning us at home. We are running out of time. We are running out of space. If we cannot seize the reins of our own physical security, we can—and must—seize power over our own souls, our own spiritual destiny.

Perhaps there is a *Necronomicon egregore* and this is its mission: to ensure that the technology for watching the Gate is in the hands of as many people as possible because we can no longer trust our priests, our bishops, our politicians, our scientists, or our cultural heroes to do that for us.

We can no longer trust the self-annointed, self-described magicians and guardians of humanity to have our best interests at heart. We have already been betrayed, over and over, by our spiritual and political leaders. If we cannot take back the reins of government, we can at least take back control over our own souls. It's not easy. It *is* dangerous.

And it's necessary.

The Necronomicon *is real paganism, real flesh-and-blood paganism. It is the paganism of the sacrifice, of howling at the Moon, of demonic forces unleashed in the Mesopotamian*

night. It is the magic of the Outsider, rituals of distress, incantations of anger and rage: the part of paganism—of real
human life and experience—left out of most New Age circles.
It represents spiritual, even existential, desperation. It acknowledges that the world is a very dangerous place, indeed,
and that the Gods have forgotten us.

The Necronomicon is a red flare lit at the top of a desert
ziggurat. The Necronomicon magician is a man or a woman
who has popped smoke to remind the Gods we are here, and
to let them know the Earth is a hot LZ.

The Dark World of
the Occult Illuminated

THE NECRONOMICON

0-380-75192-5/$7.99 US/$10.99 Can

The most feared, fascinating, and dangerous book in the history of humankind, it was written in Damascus in the Eighth Century by the "Mad Arab" Abdul Alhazred and is filled with myths and rituals that have survived the darkest days of magic and occultism.

THE NECRONOMICON SPELLBOOK

0-380-73112-6/$7.99 US/$10.99 Can

A guide that enables anyone to pick up the book and use its ineluctable power—though great care must always be taken when harnessing the primal forces of nature, the heavens, and the kingdom of beasts.

DEAD NAMES
The Dark History of the Necronomicon
0-06-078704-X/$7.99 US/$10.99 Can

The startling true account of the dark and violent history of this most fearsome of books: from its Middle Eastern origins to its reemergence centuries later.